3-
2007

Lost Lands, Forgotten Realms

Sunken Continents, Vanished Cities, and the Kingdoms That History Misplaced

By Dr. Bob Curran
Illustrated by Ian Daniels

New Page Books
A Division of Career Press
Franklin Lakes, NJ

LOST LANDS, FORGOTTEN REALMS
EDITED AND TYPESET BY GINA TALUCCI
Cover design and interior illustrations by Ian Daniels
Printed in the U.S.A. by Book-mart Press

To order this title, please call toll-free 1-800-CAREER-1 (NJ and Canada: 201-848-0310) to order using VISA or MasterCard, or for further information on books from Career Press.

The Career Press, Inc., 3 Tice Road, PO Box 687,
Franklin Lakes, NJ 07417
www.careerpress.com
www.newpagebooks.com

Library of Congress Cataloging-in-Publication Data

Curran, Bob.
Lost lands, forgotten realms : sunken continents, vanished cities, and the
   kingdoms that history misplaced / by Bob Curran.
      p. cm.
   ISBN-13: 978-1-56414-958-9
   ISBN-10: 1-56414-958-7
      1. Geographical myths. 2. Lost continents. I. Title.

GR940.C87 2007
398.23'4--dc22

                                                          2007018168

Dedication

To my wife, Mary, and my children, Jennifer and Michael, for their help and support throughout the writing of this book.

Contents

Introduction:

Somewhere Beyond the Horizon

From earliest times, Man has been both intrigued and fascinated with what lies in the distance, beyond his field of vision. From where he stood, perhaps on a flat and rolling plain, he could see as far as the distant horizon; but what lay beyond that? Lost lands? Forgotten realms? Curiosity, of course, is a human trait, but then so is imagination. Although he could not actually see what lay out there, Early Man was curious about what might lie on the other side of the distant horizon, and it was here that his imagination took over. It populated unseen regions with all sorts of fabulous places, inhabited by fantastic creatures and beings—creatures and beings similar to (or maybe even very different from) himself.

Perhaps an interesting experiment would be to stand on a beach or shore and look out to sea. Try to imagine what lies on the other side of the observed horizon. Is it land? Is it more sea? What kinds of creatures live there? Giants, ocean monsters, ghosts? People like ourselves? Are there islands, shoals of rocks, a lost continent just beyond our vision? Such ideas would not have been dispelled by the cloud formations that sometimes hung low on the horizon, suggesting land masses beyond them. Now look at the sea in front. What lies under it? Wrecks of lost ships or perhaps something that has slipped from the land and down under the waves? These were the problems that confronted early sailors as they voyaged toward the horizon. What lay before them, and what lay under them?

Then and Now

In a sense, such an experiment is already flawed because, here in the 21st century, and thanks to modern technology and increased information, we already know what lies there. And even if we didn't, there are devices using GPS (Global Positioning System) that will actually tell us. Thus, we can stand on our imagined beach and look at a handheld screen that will tell us if there are sandbanks, islands, reefs, shoals, or anything else far beyond our line of vision. Indeed, such devices can often, to some extent, tell us what lies underneath the waves, whether the land slips away and the water deepens, or whether there are hidden rocks. Such technology has, in effect, taken away much of the mystery and fantasy that imagination can sometimes lend to distance or depth.

Today, we think nothing of travel. In these modern times we can jump in our car and journey hundreds of miles without giving the distance a second thought. Or we can board a ship or a plane and be in a foreign country in no time. This was, of course, not always the case. In previous times, traveling, even relatively short distances, was often a hazardous undertaking, and not one to be taken lightly. The roads swarmed with wild animals and robbers, all of which awaited the traveler, and made his or her journey a rather hazardous one. Therefore, people tended not to travel very far, but kept close to their own communities. This was an understandable reaction in a world that was often viewed as hostile and dangerous. Even in relatively modern times, in some parts of rural Europe, people did not journey far, and those who came in from outside were considered to be strange and sinister.

The peasant novelist Emile Guillaumin, writing in 1904 about the world that his grandparents had known (the mid-1800s), tells of a little swineherd who was confronted by a monstrous figure on some remote heathland in

La Châtre, France. This was not a person who came from the three farms that the boy knew, and he spoke a strange and unfamiliar language. The child was greatly afraid and fled. The figure was no more than an itinerant tree-feller looking for a spring at which to fill his flask. He spoke to the boy in a dialect with which the child was not familiar, and to the swineherd he seemed a fantastic creature—tall and dark (weather-beaten from an outdoor life)—from some far-away land. Beyond the edge of the village lay an unknown world, populated with strange creatures, more terrifying than any 1950s science-fiction movie.

Today, we can sit in our living rooms, turn on our televisions, and see things and events on the other side of the world. The miracles of television, DVD, and video can bring the sights of distant countries right into our homes. Moreover, documentaries and films can bring images of the deepest ocean or beneath the Earth's crust directly to us for our entertainment and enlightenment. The global communications system has taken away part of the eerie glamour of distant lands and far-away places. The world has now been largely explored and explained, and while it can, from time to time, hold surprises, these seem to be getting fewer and fewer in number.

Tales From the Other Worlds

The world was not always so familiar though; even in the 19th century, traveling long distances across the ocean was similar to traveling to either the Moon or Mars today. Few journeyed very far, and they relied on those few brave souls who did to provide them with information about distant countries. And of course, those who had traveled such distances were regarded as local heroes or as something special within their various communities. In order to embellish and explain their exploits in distant places, they regaled their audiences back in their own towns with amazing stories, full of fantastic (and improbable) encounters. They gave descriptions of strange and bizarre lands that provided a backdrop for their own wonderful adventures. These stories became known as "Old Travelers' Tales," and were gathered together in a corpus of wild adventures to delight receptive (some would say gullible) audiences. Seafarers especially, those who had visited locations that were far beyond the imaginations of most of their land-based contemporaries, were especially skilled at such stories, which were recorded as fact. And indeed, who was there among their land-dwelling audiences to contradict them? Many of those listening had never been beyond the confines of their own village. The more fantastic the story, it seems, the more readily it was believed. Thus, there were stories concerning tribes of dog-headed men who lived in the deserts of North Africa (probably derived from representations of ancient Egyptian jackal-headed gods) and of islands of men with long ears who slept on one and used the other as a blanket (perhaps based on some of the Polynesian peoples of Easter Island who seemed to have distended ears, which some of their statues there would appear to suggest). In a world in which factual knowledge about other cultures was extremely limited (but not to say nonexistent) such tales passed into the stream of geographical tradition and became part of accepted local knowledge concerning foreign countries and their inhabitants. While many of these early storytellers may not have intended to deliberately mislead their listeners—in fact, some of the tales may have been an attempt to explain what they saw to themselves— they certainly built up fabulous and disturbing pictures of far-off lands and vanished civilizations.

Modern Legends

Throughout the late 19th and early 20th centuries, distant, inaccessible places continued to hold a fascination for the human mind and exercise the imagination. These were places where adventure was set and where strange things happened. They were a convenient backdrop for heroic figures fighting against unimaginable odds—savage tribes, monsters, and inhuman creatures that time had forgotten. The steaming jungles of Africa and South America, for instance, were a haven for dangerous, flesh-eating tribes and monstrous creatures, but they were also the location of lost valleys or plateaus, which had somehow escaped the passage of time and were teeming with giant, prehistoric reptiles, and flora and fauna. Old Travelers' Tales, all but forgotten, suddenly gained a new lease on life as they were adapted to fit in with modern adventure stories. Thus, Africa became the location for the legendary story of King Solomon's Mines (where the biblical King Solomon had mined his vast wealth); South America became the site of the fabled El Dorado which the Spanish conquistadores had sought in the 16th century. However, this is not to say that some of these fabulous lost places did not actually exist.

In 1860, a French botanist, Henri Mouhot, stepped out of the Cambodian jungle to find himself in an overgrown street, amid towering buildings that were wreathed in creeper and vines. He was standing in the main complex of Angkor Wat, a great temple city of the ancient Khmer civilization, which had flourished in Asia between 802 and 1431. It had lain undisturbed and mouldering in the jungle for centuries. Mouhot and his expedition from the Royal Geographic Society had been following old tales told to local French missionaries concerning "a city built by giants" deep in the Cambodian jungle. And, as he discovered, there was a basis of truth in these old legends, fanciful though they initially seemed. Mouhot's discovery intrigued the popular imagination; if Angkor Wat (and the later discovered temple-city of Angkor Thom) had lain undetected in the Cambodian jungle for so many years, might not other legends be true as well?

In the late 1860s/early 1870s, this excitement became more intense as the controversial archaeologist Heinrich Schliemann unearthed foundations on the Anatolian (Turkish) coast, which were identified as the ruins of the fabled city of Troy. Prior to Schliemann's excavations, Troy had been little more than a Greek fable. Schliemann's discovery meant that the tale had been based on fact.

These discoveries excited the popular imagination—if the legendary Khmer and Trojan civilizations had existed, might not others have existed, too? And indeed, might there not be a core of truth in at least some of the other old fables? Many of the old stories that had been summarily dismissed as nothing more than legend—Atlantis, Mu, Shambhala, and so on— suddenly took on a new vibrancy and freshness.

Not only this, but if ancient cities existed on land or deep in the jungle, might they also exist under the sea or even under the Earth, where deep and unexplored caverns stretched for miles underground? Stories of lost lands, deep below the Earth's crust, had existed since medieval times, but now they received a new lease on life. Novels such as Jules Verne's *Journey to the Center of the Earth* emerged in 1864, fueling speculation about subterranean kingdoms and forgotten lands deep in the Earth. There was also a reinvigorated interest in kingdoms such as Lyonesse, a sunken realm that was once said to lie between the southern tip of Cornwall, England, and the French coast. Stories of such a country, overwhelmed by the sea during a great natural catastrophe, appear both in Cornish and Breton, and may indeed have some basis in fact. Geographers have determined that the Scilly Isles, lying off the southern coast of England, are in fact the tips of high undersea mountains—mountains that were once said to dominate Lyonesse. Many prominent and well-established Cornish families claim descendency from survivors of the watery cataclysm. Perhaps, argued some, this was actually proof of some ancient realm swallowed up by the ocean in some former time.

Interest in vanished kingdoms was even further fuelled in the 1920s as archaeologists began to unearth some of the long-lost treasures of the Egyptian pharaohs in the Valley of the Kings. Images of strange and almost forgotten gods were brought back to England and America, and fabulous treasures unearthed in remote areas hinted at opulent civilizations now vanished under the desert sands.

The fascination with fabled realms hidden away in inaccessible areas of the world has remained with us through the years. As late as the 1930s/1940s, the distant land of Tibet exercised its spell on the modern mind. It became a place of magic and mystery where ancient ways were long forgotten, the people knew ancient secrets, and holy men displayed amazing powers of mind and body unmatched anywhere else on the planet. Although that view has gradually changed, there are still those today who cling to notions of a Shangri-La or mysterious kingdom lost somewhere in the Himalayas.

Recently, accounts from remote and relatively inaccessible valleys in Northern India, where remarkable flora, fauna, and insect life (much of it from prehistoric periods) have been noted, suggest that there might be some small kernel of truth in such speculation.

Why has the idea of lost civilizations gripped our ideas and imaginations so strongly? Well, perhaps in our own rather brutal and competitive world, it gives us a sense of hope and perspective. It is always tempting to look back to a former, golden, more innocent, and peaceful world than that which we often see around us. If Mankind can achieve such glories once, the argument runs, it just might be able to achieve it again. So while we battle with each other and destroy our planet, it is perhaps comforting to look back at the peace and prosperity of some former time—whether that period is real or imagined. Advanced technologies and social development may not have brought us the happiness or contentment that we had hoped they would, but perhaps there is still some knowledge or wisdom from a former, forgotten time, still waiting to be discovered, which can aid us and bring us the peace of mind that we crave. The ultimate happiness may lie in the vanished past! At least that's what we fondly imagine. Thus, we seek well-being and mysticism among ancient peoples such as the Celts, the Chinese, and the ancient peoples of India, but maybe there are even older civilizations that can meet our deepest needs. The search, then, continues.

The purpose of this book is to examine the stories and beliefs concerning some of these ancient worlds. Might they indeed have existed? And, if not, why would people wish to believe that they did? What was the effect of that belief on later years? And is such a belief in these places still relevant today? So come with us now as we journey back through time; to remote and almost inaccessible places; under the sea and deep into the bowels of the Earth itself; in search of vanished civilizations and disappeared cities and countries. It is a journey not only into the unknown, but also into our beliefs and perceptions. It is a glimpse into the very way in which we view the world—deep into ourselves and our relationship to the world around us. Perhaps for many of us, that might be the most frightening journey of all!

Section I:
Mythological
Places

Mythological Places

Even in today's society, many people share the view that there may well be some form of existence beyond the material world that we can see and touch. Indeed, this has formed the basis for a number of the world's religions—from a simple idea of a realm of spirits, coexisting alongside our own, to a more sophisticated view of an Afterlife, existing after death. Such places are said to lie well outside our realm of consciousness, and although they are all around us and their inhabitants may be "aware" of us in our day-to-day living, we are totally unaware of them. For example, many Christians believe that God and/or angels or saints see and hear everything we do in our own world, though we are not directly aware of them. Nor are we even dimly aware of the place in which they exist, although it is said to be "everywhere around us," impinging on our own sphere of existence. We cannot see it, touch it, or even taste it, yet the Christians declare with certainty that it is there.

This Life and Beyond

Modern Christians are not the only ones to believe in such realms. Nor are they the first to do so. From very early days, men have believed in places that they could not see, or the location of which they could not exactly specify. Such places did not appear on any maps, nor were there any guide-posts to them, but it was believed that they existed somewhere just beyond the realm of the human senses. Some of them were extremely close at hand—the mystical world of fairies and goblins was all around us, but actually outside our sphere of vision (there really might be "fairies at the bottom of the garden"); the location of others was more problematical and perhaps further away. They existed in a sphere outside our human sensibilities but they were there either in foreign lands or where we could not see them.

The Garden of Eden, for example, was supposed to lie either in the Middle East or in North Africa, but even if we were able to travel there, we would still not be able to find it. Similarly, Shangri-La, a mythical kingdom "somewhere" among the Himalayan Mountains, was frequently talked about, but the location was never specified. Others, such as the legendary village of Brigadoon was always there, lying invisible among the Scottish mists (its location is given as a number of sites across the Scottish Highlands) although it reappeared for mortal viewing every hundred years on the anniversary of its alleged initial disappearance in 1754. The "spell" that was cast over Brigadoon was put in place to protect it from advancing English Redcoats during the Jacobite Rebellion, and it is said that the village goes on about its business (invisible to the human eye and stuck in some sort of time warp that is always in the year 1754) before briefly reappearing each century. So famous has the legend become that it is the subject of both music and film. Curiously, the original tale concerning the vanishing village is not Scottish at all (although the Highland mists do add a sense of romance and mystery), but German. The dark and disturbing legend of the cursed village of Germelshausen, the bells of which can be heard ringing out across the Bavarian Mountains, is recorded in a collection of ghostly folktales by the Brothers Grimm. Those who follow the sound of the bells and enter the village are never seen again, and though they try to return to the mortal world (of which they are apparently fully aware), they never succeed. Germelshausen is allegedly inhabited by dark and evil forces that only seek to harm Mankind—a totally different scenario from the Scottish romance and jollity of Brigadoon. Yet, Germelshausen is still there, tucked away in the Bavarian hills, unseen by the human eye and ready to draw the unwary traveler into its curse.

Germelshausen is not the only such village like this, for there are tales of invisible villages and towns that occasionally appear and disappear from many

different places including France and Cornwall. Most of these places coexist alongside us, but for some reason we cannot see them; and yet they may exert a beneficial or malign influence on our own world with people crossing and recrossing from them on various nights of the year when the veil between their world and ours is at its thinnest.

From Ireland, too, come tales of mysterious houses, into which people have inadvertently wandered during the course of a night's (often drunken) traveling. These are always grand places, hung with great finery, where all manner of jollity goes on—usually amongst the fairies who seem to dwell in it. In the morning, of course, the protagonist finds him or herself in the middle of some field, moor, or other lonely place with no sign of the building anywhere around; yet, he or she is certain that it was there. Of course, it is easy to say that it was all a dream or the result of strong drink, but if it was, its source must lie in the belief that such fairy houses existed invisibly all around the Irish countryside. In both Irish and Scottish folktales, fairies sometimes give mortals a magic ointment, which, if they rub it into their eyes, they can see the fairy world that coexists with them. Unfortunately in many tales, this turns out to be a curse; once the mortal is given the "sight," it can never be taken away and the knowledge of such another world is sometimes too much for the mortal mind to bear. However, these stories are said to provide evidence of the unseen world that is everywhere around us.

The names and nature of this other existence varied depending on the culture, time period, or even religious outlook. For some they were the Otherworld, for others, the Fairy Realm, and for others yet, Eden or (in Arthurian myth) the Isle of Avalon. In some cases they were a distant and nearly unattainable Paradise—the home of heroes and saintly people. In others, they were a dreaded land from which those who accidentally wandered into them could not escape. Latterly, however, they were the epitome of the heart's desire, some wonderful place in which both contentment and perfection reigned supreme—a Paradise that lay just out of reach.

The idea continued into the 20th century, arguably achieving its acme in the 1939 film *The Wizard of Oz* (based on the book *The Wonderful Wizard of Oz* by L. Frank Baum) with a magical, mystical land "somewhere over the rainbow." The themes of the film serve to show the strength of the idea of a mystical world close at hand within the modern mind—an idea that has continued down through the centuries to the present day. This is the idea that we shall now explore.

1

The Otherworld

Almost all cultures have at least some concept, no matter how vague, of the Otherworld—a nebulous realm that usually lies beyond death, but to which, nonetheless, certain individuals such as heroes, prophets, kings, or Shamans, have journeyed, and from which some of them at least have returned. Indeed, all that we know about the Otherworld comes from visions and descriptions given by these people either through dreams or upon their "return" to the mortal world.

A substantial number of ancient cultures viewed death in a slightly different way than we do today. Nowadays, we tend to think that whatever lies beyond the grave is a separate reality, and those who journey there are traveling to their just reward. Their involvement in our day-to-day world ceases, and they take no further interest in our affairs, nor can we contact them and establish where they are. However, this was not always the case. Death was simply viewed as an act of transition from one sphere of existence to another. It was also believed that this "other existence" could sometimes be seen, or even visited, by certain gifted individuals, either in dreams or in actuality. Furthermore, those who had gone before could sometimes return from this realm, going back and forth when they pleased, or else at certain appropriate times.

Visions of the Underworld

Given the number of people who claimed to have journeyed to the Otherworld, it is not surprising that many descriptions of it are either confusing or contradictory; nor is it surprising that some descriptions remain vague and nebulous. Cultural differences also played a part in how visions of another world, lying beyond death, were interpreted. Among some people—for example, the ancient Egyptians—the Otherworld was simply akin to a continuation of the mortal sphere, which it closely resembled. Thus, if a Pharaoh died in this world, he would reasonably expect to be a Pharaoh in the next, and enjoy the same lifestyle. Therefore, his retinue of servants would be entombed with him, in order to serve him in the Otherworld along with his favorite pets, so that he could continue to enjoy their company when his transition was complete. Not only this, but gold and ornaments were also left with him in the grave in order to pay his way in the Otherworld, and to denote that he was a man of status and wealth. This belief that the Otherworld was a continuation of the mortal existence came from the earliest times and was not unique to the Egyptian culture. Prehistoric graves have been found in the Middle East and elsewhere, which, in addition to the body, contained enough food for a journey, including grains from cereal crops to help the dead person start a living when they got to the Otherworld.

For the early Hebrews, however, the Otherworld was a somewhat different place. Known as Sheol, it was simply a misty realm where the shades of the departed simply congregated to wander aimlessly and eternally. There appears to have been nothing in this realm, save rocks and a perpetual mist. The dead were not even aware of a world close at hand where their descendants might still be living, or, if they were, they had little interest in it. The inhabitants of this place seemed torpid and stupefied, barely aware of each other as they wandered through the mist and stone, talking softly and endlessly to themselves.

Among the Nordic peoples—especially the Viking races—the notion of the Otherworld was very different. For them it was an endless hall, known as Valhalla, in which feasting, drunkenness, and fighting abounded. In a sense, this too was a continuation of the life that at least some of them followed—a roistering, barbaric, drunken orgy of excess. This was a warrior's world (in order to gain admission to it one had to die in battle) and reflected the views and aspirations of Viking society. Moreover, great warriors might return from

Valhalla in order to fulfil some task (usually to deal with former enemies) that had been left uncompleted in life. They would then return to the Otherworld.

It was through all this back-and-forth transitioning, and the dreams of those who may have had direct contact with ancestors, that we know these things about the Otherworld. Of course, no location as to its physical whereabouts was given—it might be close at hand or far away. However, it was inaccessible to most mortals. The general opinion suggested that it might be close at hand, because those who had gone there were able to keep an eye on their descendants or on the affairs of the mortal world and could intervene when they chose. Therefore, the Otherworld, it was reasoned, was relatively close at hand.

What Was It Like?

Possibly for many ancient peoples, as we have seen, it may not have been all that much different from the existence they already knew, although for some, such as the Semites and Hebrews, it was a little different. For the Greeks, it might be a place of judgement where major wrongdoers suffered the consequences of their actions in life. Therefore, it could, for the evil person, be a place of intense torment. The Celts, on the other hand, were extremely vague about what the Otherworld might be like. Some described it as an "earthly Paradise," filled with rolling hills and pleasant meadows, populated by the shades of those who had gone before and by kindly spirits, while others described it as a bleak, freezing place where only terrors and dark forces dwelt. Even its function was unclear. Was it a land to which the dead went when they left the mortal world, or was it a realm inhabited by spirits and forces that sometimes interacted with Humankind? In a sense, it was. Indeed, some Celtic descriptions detailed it as a world of poetry and art, where the Muses that inspired the great singers, musicians, and poets of the mortal world dwelt. Those who visited it in their dreams were often inspired, and composed great poetry or music as a result of their visitation. All the same, descriptions of it remained unclear, and there was no real indication as to where this wondrous land might lie. Some accounts said that it was everywhere, but it couldn't be seen by mortal eyes; others said that it was somewhere on the other side of the horizon, just beyond the furthest point that the mortal eye could see. Presumably, this tied in with cloud formations, which were often seen along the horizon. This, of course, was suggestive of another land with mountains, valleys, and promontories.

Encounters of the Otherworld

Odd mirages and reflected images also added to the confusion; for example, in 1837, Irish people in the seaside town of Portstewart, County Derry, found themselves gazing at a large castle that had suddenly appeared in the middle of the bay. Flags and turrets on the structure could quite clearly be seen, as could a road flanked by a number of houses, leading up to the main gate. Dimly, through this vision, the hills of Donegal on the other side of the bay could just be seen. The mirage (for that's what it most probably was) hovered there for most of the morning and created a great stir in the locality. A number of prominent local men arrived in their carriages to marvel at the phenomenon, while a number of fishermen set out for the apparition in their boats, but were unable to reach it. Even as they watched, people appeared to come and go from some of the houses, and a wagon made its way up the road to the castle. Around midday, the vision faded and then vanished, and the coasts of Donegal were quite visible again. It was, of course, an optical illusion, albeit a rather spectacular one. Some sort of atmospheric phenomenon had reflected a scene from another part of the world and imprinted it on the landscape around Portstewart Bay. However, to many of the people who came to see it, it was akin to having a glimpse into another world—one that laid beyond their normal field of vision. Such "visions" would strengthen the idea of a phantom world, lying somewhere all around us, unseen by mortal eyes. It also furthered the notion of sunken lands that might briefly return to the ocean surface from time to time. Nor was the mirage at Portstewart the only one to be recorded in Ireland.

In his book *Irish Wonders*, D.R. McNally recounts another such incident in County Cork about 40 years later. On the afternoon of Sunday, July 7th, 1878, he states that there was great excitement in the general area around Ballycotton Bay because of a sudden appearance of a mysterious landmass far out at sea where none was known to exist. The day before, many fishermen from the village had been out in their boats, and they had seen no trace of any such country where one now seemed to appear; but there was now no denying the evidence of their eyes.

On the distant landmass, they could make out hills and woods. The watchers could also make out what appeared to be deep glens with buildings along their sides, which sloped down through a series of fields to the water's

edge. There was no doubt in their minds that it was another country, the very edge of the Otherworld. Upon seeing the vision, several local fishermen climbed into their boats and set sail for the distant shoreline. However, as they neared it, the landmass became fainter and dimmer in outline, less vivid in color, and eventually faded away altogether.

Stories concerning the miraculous appearance were soon circulating. With each telling or retelling of the tale, the landmass grew more wonderful and more exotic. Fishermen claimed to have seen castles and palaces along the coast as well as cathedrals, towers, steeples, extensive plains, and distant cities as they drew near. Much of this was, of course, simply exaggeration, and had to be limited by the skepticism of the listener.

Other such appearances were experienced off Ballydonegan Bay, also in County Cork. In County Kerry, the population of Ballyheige saw a strange landmass appear in Tralee Bay between Kerry Head and Brandon Head, which was complete with cottages and tilled fields. A few days before, the villagers of Lisneakeabree, just across the bay from Ballyheige, had witnessed another such landmass between their own village and Kerry Head, while the local fishermen had also seen it appear in St. Finan's Bay.

Even in the North, similar images appeared around Gweebara Bay in Donegal and near Rathlin Island in North Antrim. There was little doubt in the minds of many that this was the Otherworld manifesting itself to mortals, and that the hills and fields they saw were those of the land of the dead or of Fairyland. Whatever the visions, they were indisputable evidence of another world that lay all around them, but which was generally invisible.

What, then, was this land? What was the name of this mysterious country? And how and why did it impinge upon our own world? The Celts, of course, would give it a name: Flath-Innis, the Noble Isle, or Tir-na-Nog, the Land of Eternal Youth. It was to this country that mighty, kings, warriors, and poets went when they died. It was also the realm of the old gods and fairies who came and went between this world and Earth. From this world, great strength and inspiration continually radiated into our own mortal sphere, inspiring human heroes, musicians, and writers. From this land, the inhabitants bestowed the gifts of valor, strength, music, and poetry upon those whom they favored, but they might also carry away certain individuals whom they especially cherished, perhaps never returning from the Otherworld.

Abduction

The most famous tale of such abduction is, of course, the ancient Irish story of Oisin, greatest of all Irish poets. Oisin, the son of Fion mac Cumhail (Finn McCool) was one of the great heroes of the Irish kingdom of Ulster. One of the fabled Knights of the Red Branch, he was also skilled both as a musician and as a poet. He was also strikingly handsome, and this was to be his downfall, for he attracted the attention of the Queen of the Otherworld. There is little clue as to what this being might have been; some accounts say that she was a fairy, others that she was a spirit. However, she fell madly in love with Oisin and resolved that he should be her husband and jointly rule the Otherworld with her. Using a fairy horse, which he chased and tried to capture, she lured him away from the mortal world into her realm, and he found that he could not return to his own country. In the Otherworld, he had everything that his heart desired; in fact, he was a ruler there, but he was neither content nor happy. He pleaded with the Queen to let him return to the mortal world—a gift that only she could give—and in the end she agreed. But he was only to return for one day, and then he would live in the Otherworld forever at her side. Giving him a magic steed, she opened the gates of the Otherworld and allowed him to ride into the mortal sphere. There was a condition, however, that he was not to dismount or set foot on the ground, or it would be the worse for him. When he had ridden through, Oisin gradually realized an important truth: Time passed much more slowly in the Otherworld than it did in the mortal realm. Although he'd only spent a few days away, more than a hundred years had passed in his own country, and nothing he saw was familiar to him. The Pagan time of heroes was long gone and Christianity now abounded in the Irish countryside. Men were smaller and punier than they had been. While riding along, Oisin came upon a group of men trying to move a stone from a ditch and stopped to help them. He was able to move the heavy stone with one hand, and he leaned down from his saddle to do so. However, the saddle girth around the horse's belly snapped and Oisin fell from the horse onto the ground. Instantly, before the eyes of the astonished workmen, he aged a hundred years and turned to dust, which blew away in the wind. In other variants of the same story, Oisin, realizing that there was no place for his kind in the world, sadly and reluctantly returned to the Otherworld forever. It is a fitting end for a hero and poet— almost the equivalent of ascending into Heaven—and it symbolically ensures that his genius, poetry, and strength live on forever, albeit in another sphere.

Time

The notion of the time differential is a common feature in tales concerning the Otherworld. Those who have accidentally strayed there, or who have been carried away by supernatural beings and returned from it, have usually found that great periods of time elapsed since they left. While the Otherworld has stayed pretty much the same as when they entered it, their own world has changed immeasurably. All that they knew has been swept away, and those that they knew are either dead or incredibly ancient. In most cases, those who return opt to go back to the Otherworld.

During the rise of Christianity, the Otherworld took on rather different proportions, reflecting its many supposed attributes. In the first instance, it became a Paradise where none grew old, suggestive of the wonderful Fairyland or Tir-na-Nog, which some believed it to be. This was where God Himself might live, and where souls ascend after death. It was believed to be located somewhere in the sky among the clouds. Alternately, it might be a place of eternal torment, located somewhere in the bowels of the Earth in which the unworthy were punished for their sins and offenses. It was where the Devil, the enemy of Mankind, dwelt and was the complete antithesis of the wonderful Paradise. This brought into play the developing medieval notions of personal morality, and of reward and punishment. Some largely Celtic notions (although a number of other races held them as well) considered it a place of rest and/or judgement between the worlds. This would become Purgatory, a kind of intermediate stage that appears frequently in the Christian canon. Indeed, Purgatory had many characteristics in common with the Otherworld. Both were rather vaguely described and located, and from this vantage point, those who had "passed beyond" could watch their descendants, urging them to say prayers for them so that they might ascend into Heaven. Again, parts of the Church taught that some of these souls might briefly reappear from Purgatory (just as they had done from the Otherworld), though only by a special dispensation from God, in order to urge religious observance.

The basic idea of an Otherworld was to form many other beliefs concerning lost lands and mystical realms. Out of the vague and nebulous concept— whether it be splendid Paradise or terrifying Hell, or simply some other ill-defined form of reality—many other concepts grew and it is to some of these that we now turn.

2

The Garden of Eden

Now The Lord God had planted a garden in the east, in Eden, and there He put the man that He had formed. And the Lord God made all kinds of trees to grow out of the ground—trees that were pleasing to the eye and good for food.

—The book of Genesis

No mysterious realm symbolizes the concept of an earthly Paradise more aptly than the biblical legend of the Garden of Eden. The story, which is found in the book of Genesis, not only speaks of a wonderful realm in which all is perfection, but also provides an explanation for the origins of Mankind. It also explains the reason for Mankind's current inability to enjoy this realm through our ancestors' disobedience of God's edicts, and through what has become known as the doctrine of original sin.

Creation

The creation story of the Garden of Eden is a common theme in the Abrahamic religions that emerged out of the early Semitic tradition, taking their name from the patriarch Abraham, the first post-Flood leader to reject idolatry in favor of a single God. It is used to explain not only the creation of Mankind, but also the entrance of sin into the world, as characterized in the Fall from Paradise.

In essence, the story states that Man (usually known in the legend by the name Adam), and his companion Woman (usually known in the legend by the name Eve) were created out of the dust of the Earth, and were placed in an earthly Paradise, which lay somewhere in the East. Here they acted as gardeners and attendants, and were given free run of the entire Paradise with one notable exception. They were not to eat the fruit that grew on the Tree of Conscience (rendered as the Tree of Knowledge in the Christian version of the tale). The Paradise, however, also harbors an evil spirit that takes the form of a serpent, and this tempts Woman to eat the fruit of the forbidden tree, and for Man to do likewise. God discovers their disobedience, and casts them out of the Paradise into the wilderness beyond, and forbids them or their descendants—that is, humanity—ever to return.

Theories About Eden

Although Eden is referred to as a "garden," it is suggested that it is a much larger territory than a simple plot of land or enclosed orchard. Indeed, the name is thought to have derived from a very ancient proto-Persian language meaning "hunting ground or estate." This was thought to have been a specially designated area where ancient kings carried on their hunting, tended to by stewards. This may give the impression that God was equivalent to a monarch, with the Garden as his estate. Adam and Eve are therefore to be counted as stewards or wardens of the land, reflecting ancient Persian custom. However, in some of the early Semitic literature, it might appear as something else. In the biblical work *The Song of Solomon* for example, it appears to be a garden, a walled enclosure in which plants of various kinds are grown, but in some other texts it is described as a park or orchard, an enclosure where fruit tress are grown.

The idea of a beautiful garden, where all is perfection and bliss, probably comes in part from Greek tradition. Taking the Otherworld as their example, the Greeks spoke of a realm inhabited by nymphs and other aerial spirits known as the Garden of the Hesperides. This was a place of utter tranquility where there was only beauty and goodness. The Hesperides were benevolent,

winged spirits who bore more than a passing resemblance to Christian angels. Similar to Eden, their Garden was allegedly located in various places. Some tales located it in the Arcadian Mountains in northern Greece, while others suggested that it might lie somewhere amid the Atlas Mountains in Libya. There were even those who asserted that it lay on a blessed island somewhere in the Mediterranean close to "the edge of the world."

The Greek writer Hesiod suggested that an old name for Cadiz in the Iberian Peninsula (Spain) was Erythea, which signified the land in which the Garden of the Hesperides lay. The Greek geographer Strabo placed it in an area that he called Tartessos, which roughly corresponds to the area of modern-day Andalusia, also in Spain. There seems to be little doubt that the Greek idea of the Garden of the Hesperides probably served as a template for the concept of the Garden of Eden, and that these two ideas may have fused into the biblical story that we know today. In the ancient mind, the Garden became equated with some form of terrestrial Paradise, evidenced by the emerging Semitic word *Eden*, which is taken to mean "delight" or "extreme or intense satisfaction." Although now referred to as a "garden," there is little doubt that Eden was not simply confined to an enclosed space, but was perhaps envisaged almost as a kingdom in its own right.

Inside the Garden

There appear to have been two major trees within this realm: the Tree of Life (from which, it is assumed, both Adam and Eve could eat) and the Tree of Conscience (from which they were forbidden to eat). It was their eating from the latter that led directly to their expulsion from the Garden, which in some Christian belief systems counts as the original sin, and which doomed their descendants to a permanent exclusion from Paradise. According to the tale, they appear to have been exiled into the wider world, implying that there were other lands somewhere beyond the Garden, where their children grew up. One of their sons, Cain, killed his brother Abel and was exiled into "the Land of Nod," which seems to have been another realm lying to the east of Eden. The word "Nod" is simply an ancient Hebrew root word meaning "wandering" (the passage is usually recognized as a simple mistranslation— Cain was cursed "to wander forever," rather than going to an actual land), and it is possible that his descendants were simply a nomadic people.

Locating Eden

So, if the Garden of Eden truly existed (as some claim that it did) where was it located? A general consensus is that it lay "somewhere in the East" (the book of Genesis simply states: "God planted a garden eastward in Eden"), and so various locations have been suggested, such as Sri Lanka, Japan, Java, and the Indian Ocean. There have also been some more bizarre suggestions, such as Florida or Jackson County, Missouri. Some more reasoned speculations have suggested Ethiopia, but one of the favored locations is ancient Mesopotamia. This is based on fragmentary ancient texts that mention the Garden, many of which also appear in the book of Genesis. It is stated that a river flowing through the Garden separated into four branches within its confines. The four rivers that flowed out of the Garden were the Hiddekel (an ancient name for the Tigris), the Euphrates, and two other more obscure torrents, the Pishon (or Pison) and the Gihon. This would place the Garden directly in the northwest corner of ancient Mesopotamia, and would correspond to the location of another fabled land—the realm of Havilah. Havilah, it is said, had a thriving civilization of Mesopotamian origin, and was an agricultural Paradise, irrigated by a number of rivers. The modern-day Egyptologist David Rohl has identified the Pishon with the Uizhun River in Iran, which may well have been one of the main tributaries of Havilah. Therefore, this fabled realm and the Garden of Eden would seem to correspond to each other in many ways. Rohl has identified the site of the Garden as a lush valley that lies about 10 miles east of the Iranian city of Tabriz. He points out that Uizhun is known locally as the Golden River, and is mentioned in works of great antiquity. Also of note, the Golden River merges with another river, the Araxes, which he suggests may be the Gihon.

Other historians, however, disagree, and place the Garden at the site of the development of the Sumerian civilization, now modern-day southern Iraq. The Mesopotamian and the later Sumerian civilizations flourished from roughly 9000 B.C., with the first major city states appearing around 4000–3000 B.C. From around 10000 B.C. however, there is evidence that many of the hunter-gatherer groupings in the Iran-Iraq area were coming together to form permanent settlements, particularly around rivers, and were domesticating wild animals and beginning to till and manage the land. This continued down the years so that, at the height of its power and influence, the Sumerian civilization had a solid agricultural base that depended largely on the Tigris and Euphrates Rivers. This, argue some historians, provides the basis for the Garden of Eden story and moves the location of the Paradise into Iraq (ancient Persia). They argue that the two mysterious rivers mentioned in Genesis— the Pishon and the Gihon—were in fact not rivers at all, but were artificial irrigation canals constructed by the ancient Sumerians using the waters from the Tigris and the Euphrates. Apparently, such canals were extremely successful in fertilizing and refreshing such a dry and arid area, and were used to produce wonderful fields and gardens; hence, perhaps, the basis for an idea of Eden. It also fits in well with the idea of ancient Havilah, which was fabled as an agricultural Paradise.

There is, of course, another connection with the Sumerian civilization. Parts of the book of Genesis closely resemble the Enuma Elish, a Sumerian creation tale; in fact, there are so many similarities that some have argued that Genesis has borrowed from the Sumerian text. The Enuma is a Sumerian creation story written around the 12th century B.C. in cuneiform on at least seven clay tablets that were discovered by archaeologists in the middle of the 19th century in the ruins of the palace library of Asurbanipal (now Mosul, Iraq). These tablets are written in Akkadian (a Semitic language spoken in Mesopotamia), and detail an extremely ancient Sumerian creation story. There are such striking parallels between this and the book of Genesis that scholars have suggested that the two texts (including the Garden of Eden story) may come from an earlier single source, which might be Sumerian; however, this is merely speculation and nothing has actually been proved.

Another line of thought sites the Garden in modern Turkey. Such theorists argue that because the Tigris and Euphrates flowed out of the Garden, it may lie far to the north of the Sumerian civilization, which was centered around the confluence of these rivers. This, they argue, places it in a mysterious Armenian region of eastern Turkey. The idea of the rivers of Gihon and Pishon may simply have been idealized far-away lands rather than actual rivers in that region.

And of course, some historians have argued that the Garden of Eden must be situated somewhere in Egypt. They argue that the characteristics of the great river flowing through the Garden roughly correspond to the Nile.

Ancient texts speak of parts of the Garden being shrouded in a mist, which came from the river and aided the growth in the Garden. Those who put forward Egypt as a possible location state this could only have been because the Nile, which flows underground at certain points and releases vapors into the upper air. They dismiss the Tigris and Euphrates simply as distractions or mistranslations.

Others have also tried to make a particularly strong case for the land of Israel as a site for the Garden. The argument runs that God's Chosen People (the Jews) could only have emerged from Eden, and, to prove this, a number of Jewish scholars have interpreted the river that ran through the Garden as the Jordan, which, they assert, was much longer in those days. The Gihon, they interpret as the Nile. Therefore, this theory states that Ancient Havilah would lie on the Arabian Peninsula, and would form a part of the Garden itself. They largely discount the Mesopotamian or Sumerian theories for the Garden's location.

A few theorists have even put forward East Africa or the island of Java as the site of Eden. This, they argue, is where human life started, pointing toward anthropological evidence (skulls and hominid bones that have been found in these locations) as their evidence.

These are the more "reasoned" theories but there are a number of fanciful ones as well. Some accounts seem to state that Eden lay on some primordial supercontinent that has long since been destroyed. A prime contender for this continental landmass is said to be a massive area known as Lemuria, which was swallowed by the sea in some prehistoric cataclysm. This would mean that Eden may lie somewhere beneath the waters of the Indian Ocean. The idea of Lemuria (named after the lemur animal) has been used to explain the distribution and connections between land animals on the continents of Asia (particularly in India) and Africa. Many of those who believe say that Lemuria was probably also the birthplace of the human race, and therefore may have been the site of the Garden of Eden. Unfortunately, it is impossible to know if the supercontinent even existed, let alone the Garden within its confines. Much of the belief, however, would simply appear to be an amalgam of speculation and legend.

And there have been even more amazing claims, two of which relate to locating the Garden in America. In 1886, the Reverend D.O. Van Slyke

published a small pamphlet, based on biblical and scientific research, which stated that the Garden of Eden had been somewhere in an area between the Allegheny and Rocky Mountains. Van Slyke's theory was that it actually lay on the east bank of the Mississippi (which was the great river mentioned), and that it existed somewhere between La Crosse, Wisconsin, and Winona, Missouri. When he was put out of the Garden, Adam had not strayed too far, and in fact his descendants had continued to live in a land close to it, which would later become Wisconsin. Noah had, in fact, been living in Wisconsin at the time of the Flood, and had been carried to Mountain Ararat in the Middle East in his Ark as the deluge overwhelmed the planet. Therefore, the pamphlet claimed that the true origin of Mankind was in Wisconsin. Many contested this thesis, but until his dying day, Van Slyke maintained that it was an accurate one, although he never produced any evidence—either scientific or biblical.

The second Eden-American connection is held by some branches of the Church of Jesus Christ Latter-day Saints. This suggests that the Garden may have been situated in what is now Jackson County, Missouri. While passing through Davies County, Missouri, the founder of the Mormon Church, Joseph Smith, came upon an odd stone, which he claimed was all that remained of an altar that had been built by Adam soon after he'd been cast out of the Garden. Therefore, the original site of the Garden must have been extremely close by. Smith determined that it was about 40 miles away, near what is today the city of Independence, Missouri. At the altar, Adam had blessed his children and rededicated them to God. Smith planned to build a Mormon city there to celebrate the "discovery" of both the altar and of Eden, which he hoped to name Adam-ondi-Ahram, but the suggestion met with such resistance from locals that he was forced to abandon it. Nevertheless, several Mormon groupings still hold that Missouri is the original site of the Garden and a place where Adam and his children will one day be reunited under God.

Some even more fanciful suggestions have located the Garden not on Earth at all, but on another planet. Following a theory that human life may not have originated on Earth, but somewhere out in space, the prominent UFOlogist William Francis Brinsley Le Poer Trench, the eighth Earl of Clancarty (1911–1995), claimed that the Garden lay on the surface of Mars.

The "canals" on the surface of the Red Planet, he claimed, had originally been irrigation channels used by the ancients to water the Garden. In his book *The Sky People*, the Earl claimed that Adam and Eve were in fact the creations of interstellar beings known as the Sky People who were conducting an experiment on the surface of Mars. This experiment was remarkably successful, and many generations of the "created" beings emerged—even Noah dwelt on Mars—until the Martian environment was accidentally destroyed by a climatic catastrophe brought about by the Sky People tinkering with the planet's atmosphere. The survivors were then obliged to seek shelter on Earth, to which they were transported by the Sky People. These are the origins of life on our planet. Although there is literally no scientific or mythological evidence to support such a theory, it did gain some ground, and some UFOlogists still give it credence to this day. Variations of the speculation have placed Eden on one of Saturn's moons or on the planet Venus, which God later turned into the boiling and poisonous cauldron that we know this world is today.

For a number of people, however, particularly fundamentalist Christians, the Garden of Eden did not have an earthly (or interplanetary) location. Even today, many Christians claim it to be a spiritual place, not of this world at all, and a kind of annex to Heaven where God sits, which therefore cannot be accessed by mortals. This was probably some sort of resurrection of the ancient idea of the Otherworld, which has already been discussed. It also served to explain why no trace of the Garden had ever been found: it had never existed in this realm of space and time. It also opened up the idea of Eden as a psychological concept.

Eden was not an actual place, but rather an aspiration—the achievement of perfection, the rediscovery of lost innocence, the ultimate embodiment of purity. Rather than simply being thought of as an actual place, the Garden of Eden now became something of an icon.

This notion has been developed into the doctrine of original sin as held by certain Christian groupings. By disobeying God in the Garden, and eating of the Tree of Conscience, Mankind brought sin into the world, and it was to atone for this original sin, committed in the Garden, that Christ died on the cross. This idea fits in well with what has become known as "Born Again Theology." All Mankind shares in Adam's sin, and so each individual must

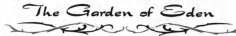

accept Christ and be "reborn" through Him into a more perfect state—only in that way can Paradise be achieved, and only after death. Many such people elevate the notion of the Garden of Eden as an ideal of the life to come, and, as such, forms the core of their theology.

So is the Garden of Eden an actual place, hidden away from human eyes, or is it no more than an ideal, hope, or inspiration? In many respects it doesn't matter. The idea of Eden has provided the template for religion, poetry, and art. (For example, the 16th century German religious painter Lucas Cranach in his beautiful representation of the Fall of Man.) Perhaps the true perfection lies not in the reality of the Garden, but in the inspiration that it can bring us.

Avalon

The idea of an Otherworld—a country or land that lies unseen just beyond mortal gaze—has been a central element in the definition of many mystical realms, particularly in Celtic perception. One such land may be Avalon, an unseen kingdom of perpetual tranquillity and beauty, which bears more than a passing resemblance to Fairyland, the Spirit World, or Paradise. According to most thinking, Avalon was an island, located somewhere in one of the world's western oceans, invisible to all but a few sea travelers.

The name Avalon itself has two possible sources: One is the Celtic word *annwyn* or *annwn*, which was an ancient name for the Otherworld itself, and, until recently, was still used in Wales to denote a subterranean kingdom ruled by elves and demons. The other root may be the Celtic word *abal*, which means "an apple." This is because in some mythologies, Avalon was supposedly covered in apple trees, which gave the sweetest fruit imaginable. It was in many respects a garden island, not unlike Eden or the Garden of the Hesperides.

Avalon's Origins

Although Avalon is generally considered to be Celtic in theme, some have argued that the roots of the belief lie in Greek tradition. It is thought that the island itself may well have been one of the Isles of the Blessed or

Fortunate Isles, which appear in Greek folklore. These were a number of Paradise-like islands that were inhabited by gods and spirits who welcomed the souls of worshippers to their beautiful domain after death. They were said to be located somewhere in the western ocean, lying toward Britain or the Strait of Gibraltar. The ancient writer Flavius Philostratus (c. 172) located them somewhere near the Libyan coast, but others equated them with Madeira or the Canary Isles. Still others asserted that the main island in the group, Avalon, lay somewhere close to the coast of Britain. Some thinkers seem to have equated it with the island of Anglesey in Wales, which, at one time, was a stronghold of the Druids during the Roman occupation. This would give the island a sort of mystical, magical connection that would continue right down through the ages. Gradually, the tradition arose that Avalon was an extension or annex of the Otherworld, and it was a place populated by great bards and heroes who went there when they died. It was, in effect, another expression of Paradise. The ideas of perfection and ancient wisdom also began to coalesce in the thinking—if Avalon had indeed been a Druid Isle, then it might also be a repository of strange knowledge, sacred to magicians and witches. This idea seemed most prominent in the Celtic world—particularly amongst British Celts. What may have started out as a Greek ideal was now becoming a largely Celtic one.

Arthurian Concept

It was as part of the Arthurian Cycle (the legends and stories surrounding the figure of King Arthur of Britain) that the concept of Avalon came to major prominence. The Arthurian concept, which flourished in the Middle Ages, rose out of the more ancient Celtic beliefs, probably giving them greater definition and shape. Avalon had been a mystical and enchanted isle, which had existed either on or off the coast of Britain during the Dark Ages, following the collapse of the Roman occupation there. It was the abode of Arthur's half-sister Morgan (or Morgana) le Fay (a woman whose surname betrays her fairy origins) who was widely regarded as a powerful enchantress or witch. Using her great magic, she could shut her island off from mortal gaze; therefore, it was spared the numerous invasions that wracked Britain at the time.

Morgan le Fey

The name Morgan le Fay may have been a variant of the Irish Celtic name of Morrigane or Morrigu, who was an ancient goddess. Therefore, the concept of Avalon may have referred to an island on which she was worshipped, and on which she may have had a shrine. Such an island could have been spared in the various waves of invasions of Britain during the fifth and sixth centuries.

However, in a series of works containing French and British myths relating to Arthur, and known by scholars as the Post-Vulgate Cycle, Morgan le Fay takes on greater depth and color. Although Arthur's half-sister, she becomes the implacable enemy of the king and Queen Guinevere, constantly trying to do them harm. It is from her island stronghold in Avalon that she plots and contrives to overthrow Arthur's reign. And yet, at some point, both she and her half-brother seem to have become reconciled for, following Arthur's death at a battle against his son Mordred in the Vale of Camlan, it is Morgan le Fay who heads the sibyls (wise women) to carry the dying king away to the resting place for heroes in distant Avalon. This has led to the idea that Arthur is not actually dead, but is merely sleeping in Avalon, waiting until England is in grave danger and needs him again. In this he is the once and future king, and Avalon is his royal seat.

Arthur's Resting Place

So persistent was the idea that Arthur had been buried in Avalon that, during the 11th century, a rumor emerged linking the enchanted isle with Glastonbury Tor, located in Somerset, England, where his grave was reputed to lie. The legend was probably spread by the monks of Glastonbury Abbey in order to raise the profile of and revenue for their foundation, but it had the effect of bringing a Pagan concept right into the Christian tradition. Although today, the ruined monastery at Glastonbury stands on the top of a steep hill, there is no doubt that in former times the surrounding flatlands were once fen and bog, and the tor itself resembled an island in the middle of it. This, said the legends, was indeed the fabled Isle of Avalon which lay, not off the coast of Britain, but actually in Britain. It was to Avalon, they said, that Joseph of Aramethea, the wealthy Jew who had donated his tomb to the body of Jesus, had come after becoming a Christian and shortly after the Crucifixion. It was here that he reputedly brought some of Jesus' relics (some legends even say that Jesus himself visited the island) and founded a church there—reputedly the oldest Christian church in Britain. Because of the sanctity of the place, it was considered an eminently fitting site for the great Arthur to be laid to rest.

The idea of Avalon as Arthur's final resting place may well have come from the writings of Geoffrey of Monmouth, who compiled a work known as *A History of the Kings of Britain* around 1136. Slightly later, Geoffrey would write another work titled *The Life of Merill* (Merlin), which stated that Arthur had not been killed, but had been mystically transported to Avalon where he had been revived by the sorceries of Morgan le Fay and two other ancient queens. It claimed that he lay sleeping on a golden bed waiting for a time when England would once again need a great hero, and when he would ride into battle once more. Confusingly, there is also mention of a tomb on Avalon above which the following legend has been carved: *Hic iacet Arthurus, Rex quandum Rexque futurus* (Here lies Arthur, the once and future king).

Around 1237, another text appeared linking Arthur and Avalon. This was *La Mort le roi Artu* (the Death of the King Arthur) and it was on this that Sir Thomas Malory is thought to have based his more famous work *La Mort d'Arthur* (written in 1469 and originally printed in 1485 by William Caxton). This work is part of a larger medieval French prose work that scholars have styled the Prose Lancelot or the Post-Vulgate Cycle. The author of this collection is unknown, but it is thought to have been composed by at least three (unknown) writers. Following his fatal injuries at Camlann, according to this text, Arthur is carried off to the Isle of Avalon by three queens: Morgan le Fay, the Queen of the Northlands, and the Queen of the Waste, the latter two possibly very ancient figures. It was in Avalon that he was to be revived and healed. Although French in origin, the legend concerning Avalon was thought to place it somewhere in England; however, the precise location is never specified. Many links were made in the popular mind to Glastonbury—a tradition that still remains alive today. The linkage between Arthur, ancient

king of the Britons, and Avalon, then, seems to have been well established, certainly by the early 11th century.

The legend connecting Arthur, the Isle of Avalon, and Glastonbury Tor seems to have developed and taken shape around the late 10th and 11th centuries, as some of the area around the tor (known as the Somerset Levels) began to be drained for agriculture.

Further Investigations

According to the writer Gerald of Wales (late 11th century), one of the abbots of Glastonbury—Henry de Blois—was so taken with the story that he ordered an investigation to be carried out and certain excavations to be made. This investigation allegedly took place during the reign of King Henry II (1154–1189) and occurred during the writer's (Gerald's) own lifetime. Gerald goes on to state that he was told that the monks had unearthed a massive oaken casket, lying about 16 feet below ground, which bore a curious inscription: *Hic jacet sepultus inclitus Rex Arthurus in insula Avalonia* (Here lies King Arthur in the Isle of Avalon). The Abbot now declared that this was indeed the grave of Arthur, and that Glastonbury Tor had indeed been the mystical Isle of Avalon to which the body was transported following the Battle of Camlann. Further legends grew up around the place—it was specially blessed by Joseph of Aramethea who had also deposited the Staff of Christ there and other such tales—and Glastonbury became one of the principal English places of pilgrimage until the Reformation. Indeed, it was alleged that, during the reign of Edward I (1272–1307) the oaken casket was exhumed and reburied, together with another body that was taken to be Arthur's queen, Guinevere, in front of the high altar of Glastonbury Abbey in the presence of the king. This made the abbey appear even more sacred, and it became more of a focus for religious devotion.

The story of the finding of the casket was almost certainly a fraud, and was probably perpetrated by Henry de Blois and his monks to give their abbey great status and importance in the developing Christian world. The idea that Glastonbury Tor was in fact the mystical Isle of Avalon served to unite both Pagan and Christian mythologies, and made the abbey more appealing to those who were dubious about the Christian faith. Scholars have pointed out that the Latin inscription on the alleged coffin is something of an anachronism in the period known as the Dark Ages, when Celtic would have been the common linguistic form. They also point out that the description of the grave in which the coffin was found appears to be a Romano-Christian site rather than one suited for a Celtic chieftain or king. If the story of Arthur's grave is a fraud, they continue, then so must the association of Glastonbury Tor with the Isle of Avalon. The Tor was certainly a place of Pagan and Celtic (and probably pre-Celtic) significance, but was it in fact Avalon? There have been numerous claims for a number of other sites scattered all throughout England, which are connected with the Arthurian tradition.

The most frequent of these is the village of Burgh (pronounced Bruff rather than Burg) by Sands on the Solway Firth in Cumberland, close to the town of Carlisle. This is said to be extremely close to the site of the Battle of Camlann where Arthur was mortally wounded, and from which he was taken to die. The area around the village may well have been an island, and it is known that a Roman garrison was quartered there at a fortress known as Aballava in the latter days of the Roman occupation of Britain. This was a garrison that was supposed to guard part of Hadrian's Wall from invasion from the Picts and Scots. Many of these soldiers may have come from areas in North Africa and may have been considered as "strange or foreign looking" by locals. These strange-looking soldiers may well have given the impression of "some other place" or "some other country," such as the Isle of Avalon, and may have added to the legend in the North of England.

The Isle of Avalon also appears off the coast of Brittany where it is equated with L'Isle d'Daval. This location is also connected into Arthurian legend because it was widely regarded as the dwelling place for the sorceress Vivian, who was the lover of the wizard Merlin. It was Vivian, or Vivienne, who eventually spurned Merlin's love, and who turned him into an oak tree. Another name for her is the Lady of the Lake. She is the spirit figure who gave Arthur his enchanted sword Excalibur; she claimed it again when the king died at Camlann. Interestingly, she is reputedly one of the three mystical queens who carried the body of the dying monarch off to Avalon. Yet another name for this enchantress is Ninue, or Mneme, which may be a shorted form of Mnemosyne, one of the nine spirit Muses who gave weapons to the Greek hero Perseus prior to the Trojan War. She, too, lived on an island that may have been a Greek prototype for the idea of Avalon. It is also interesting that in the medieval text *La Mort le roi Artu* the name of one of the queens who tends to the wounded Arthur is also given as Ninue; suggesting a tentative link between Celtic/medieval legend and Greek tradition.

The name Vivian, or Vivienne, may, however, denote another more Celtic goddess. The original name may be Vi-vianna, which may also be a version of Ci-vianna, an ancient British goddess also known as Coventina. She was an ancient Celtic water goddess whose cult was rather widespread across parts of Western Europe; she has been equated with the Romano-Greek deity Dianna, and with another Celtic goddess, Rhiannon. She has also been associated with Merlin's actual wife Gwendoline, and it may be that the Isle of Avalon was her stronghold, or at least a site dedicated to her worship.

References to Avalon

There is another connection between Avalon and medieval Arthurian cycles, for the blessed island appears in another romantic work from that period. Reference to it appears in a cycle of works known as *The Lais de Marie de France*, written around 1160–1170. Nothing is known about the author except that she was a woman, and she was, in all probability, a member of the aristocracy—it has even been suggested that she was a half-sister of the English king Henry II. Not even her nationality is known because she wrote in Anglo-Norman, which was certainly spoken in England, but was also spoken in large areas of northern France. So she was, in all probability, either French or English. She wrote a series of 12 lais, or poems, which were widely read in the medieval world, some of which drew upon old stories and beliefs from previous times. One of these—*Lanval*—is Arthurian in tone and concerns the knight Lanval, who has offended Queen Guinevere and, as a result, was thrown into a deep dungeon. There he is visited by a fairy or spirit in the guise of a beautiful woman who is greatly taken with him. She helps him to escape, and together they flee to Avalon—the country of the blessed—which is the home of all good spirits and may well be a part of the Otherworld. Lanval is never heard from again and presumably continues to live there forever. The lais serve to demonstrate the transition between more ancient traditions of the Otherworld (and possibly of ancient Celtic, Greek, and Roman myths concerning a beatific alternative reality) into the medieval and more Christianized era.

And Christian mythology was not slow to claim Avalon for its own. Besides having been the place where Joseph of Aramethea landed in England, and the place where he founded the first Christian church in the country, other references began to also creep in. For example, in parts of Brittany it was imagined that Avalon was the place where the Virgin Mary had gone when she fled from the Middle East following the Crucifixion. She was portrayed as one of the "queens" of that mysterious realm, and was equated with the three magical women who carried off Arthur. Not unconnected to this belief is another tradition that the Isle of Avalon is the repository of the Holy Grail, the mystical cup that Christ used at the Last Supper, which also may have served as a receptacle for His blood. The Grail itself is supposed to rest in a church upon the Isle and can only be discovered and seen by the pure of heart. It was supposedly guarded by three angels (representing the three queens) who can confuse and obfuscate those who try to discover it and are unworthy of doing so. The Isle itself remains invisible to all but the eyes of the blessed.

The Meaning of Avalon

Similar to the Garden of Eden, the Isle of Avalon represents both an extension of the Pagan Otherworld and the representation of an earthly Paradise that was later taken over by the Christian tradition. Its roots may lie in early Celtic (even Greek and Roman) traditions, but these have been amended and molded, especially during the medieval period, in order to fit in with other beliefs and tales—particularly that of King Arthur. And, in a sense, Avalon is real, for if it is the home of the Muses and inspirational spirits (as most traditions hold that it is), then it has certainly inspired much poetry and prose stretching down from early medieval times to the present day. Even today, Avalon is featured in many modern fantasy novels such as the celebrated writer Marion Zimmer Bradley's *Avalon Series*. Perhaps the idea of some mystical island paradise still holds both a timeless fascination and attraction, even for the modern mind. And perhaps, too, the idea of Avalon

still holds that psychological connection for us to some former, less complex and more romantic time—an ideal (whether true or not) which, for some at least, the passage of the years can never erase.

4

Yggdrasil

Trees have always featured heavily in many ancient mythologies; for example, the Tree of the Knowledge of Good and Evil in the Garden of Eden in Semitic folklore; and the apple trees on the Isle of the Blest, in the Garden of the Hesperides (or in Avalon in Greek, Roman, and Celtic legends). It is not surprising, therefore, to find the tree motif once again in both Norse and early Germanic mythology.

In such legends, the tree is known as Yggdrasil and, although no indication is given as to its exact location, both its roots and branches span a multitude of realities. Tradition describes it as a monstrous ash, and often uses the term "world tree" to denote its massive span.

The Making of Yggdrasil

The name Yggdrasil (Old Norse: Yggdrasill) is a curious one, and does not relate to a tree at all. Rather, it translates directly as "terrible steed," referring to a horse. However, Viking mythology provides an explanation for this: It is said that an ancient name for the supreme Norse god Odin was Ygg, and in order to obtain great knowledge (apparently derived from Mimir, an extremely ancient primal god who possessed great wisdom), he hung from the branches of the tree for nine nights. He obtained the wisdom in the form of runes and thereafter the tree became known as Yggdrasil (or Odin's steed). The purpose of the Great Tree, however, spanned its roots and branches, embodying almost every mythological existence known to the early Norse and Germanic peoples. Thus, its branches extended upward into the realm of the gods, somewhere beyond the clouds, while its roots descended deep into the Underworld where the shriveled spirits of the damned and wicked dwelt. The Great Tree connected all these separate realities and presumably provided passage between them. In Norse mythology, three main existences were to be found along its spreading branches. These were: Asgard, which was a general realm of the gods; Vanaheim, which were a specific race or clan of gods ruled by a very ancient god named Njod; and Alfheim, the home of elves and other lesser supernatural figures.

Realms of the Tree

The trunk of Yggdrasil cut straight through the realm of Midgard, or Middengard, which was the home of humans (our world). This was surrounded by the realm of Jotunheimr, which was the kingdom of giants, and by Niovellir, or Dark Fields, the land of the dwarves who often made weapons for the gods. The roots of the Tree stretched into the Underworld and down to the realm of Hel, which took its name from the dark goddess who ruled over it. (She herself dwelt in Eliudnir, a realm or great hall similar to Valhalla.) Also in the Underworld lay the realm of Muspelheim, or the kingdom of fire, ruled over by the fire demon Surtur (sometimes rendered as Surt). The last of the nine existences that bordered on the Tree was Nefelheim, the land of the Frost Giants who were fierce and aggressive, and who blew snow-flecked winds whenever they roared or shouted.

In Scandinavian mythology, Yggdrasil was fed through its roots by three springs or wells. The first and most sacred was in the realm of Asgard, general home of the gods. This was the Well of Urd (Urdarbruner meaning *fate*) and the root was tended by three wise women known as Norns. These three ancient crones were initially regarded as the repositories of all worldly knowledge (something similar to the Sybils of Roman mythology), but later became equated with the span of each mortal's life, as were the Greek Fates.

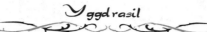

They seem to have been more powerful than even the gods who left them alone to tend the root of the tree—watering it from the ancient fountain at Urd, so that its sap remained green. The root that grew halfway along the trunk lay in Jotunheimr, the land of the giants, and was reputedly guarded by a number of fierce ogres. The Well of Mimir was named after the primal deity, and was said to be the oldest, and perhaps most potent, of all the springs that served the Great Tree.

The last of the three wells from which Yggdrasil's roots drew their nourishment lay deep in the Underworld. This was the Well of Hvergelmir, which means either "roaring cauldron" or "roaring kettle." This well was in the deepest part of the Underworld, and the waters that surrounded the root were so fierce that not even the wasted souls that inhabited the area could approach it. However, as is usual in Norse mythology, there are variants and complications. Yggdrasil is alternately known by a number of other names, perhaps reflecting the myriad of Northern influences on Scandinavian mythology, two of which are Mimameir and Larao. As Mimameir—the Well of Mimir—it was also believed to have a root in Valhalla, which was the final resting place of the heroic dead where they feasted and sported themselves. The shoots from this root fed the sacred goat, the einhejar, which provided milk for the goblets of the dead heroes as they sat around tables in Valhalla. The goat feasted on the green, and in turn supplied the most delectable milk for the warriors to drink.

Legends of the Great Tree

The legends concerning the Great Tree can be partly credited to two medieval texts written in Iceland around the 12th and 13th centuries. These were the Poetic and Prose Eddas, which formed a core for much of early Scandinavian literature. The Poetic Edda, or the Codex Regius, is deemed to be the oldest and, though it has long since vanished (around the 17th century), used as source material by later Norse writers. Written in Old Norse, it was certainly in the hands of Brynjofr Sveinson, Bishop of Skaholt (1605–1675), who sent it to the Norwegian king, hence its Latin name. He had attributed it to an early medieval Icelandic writer Seamunder Froi, or Seamunder the Learned

(1056–1133). However, later scholars have dismissed this and attribute the work to a variety of writers—perhaps to monks writing in the Icelandic monasteries of the early 1100s. The Edda is a collection of poems relating to ancient legends that were probably passed down orally, among which is that of Yggdrasil. Some of the themes in the Poetic Edda formed the basis for the Prose Edda written by the influential Icelandic historian, poet, and politician Snorri Sturluson (1178–1241). As a mythographer, Sturluson investigated many of the old Scandinavian tales, writing them down and seeking to interpret them, and it is through him that stories about Yggdrasil continue to appear. Additions may also have been made to it from a number of other Northern traditions around the time that he was writing.

Protection of the Tree

As a tree, Yggdrasil was often subject to damage from the amount of creatures who lived along its length in the nine probable existences, and who sheltered under its branches. But there were other vandals, too. For example, the trunk of the Great Tree was under almost constant attack from Ratatosk, the great squirrel whose name meant "swift teeth," and who was a notorious gossip and mischief maker. His function was also that of messenger between the various existences along the tree, particularly between the gods in Asgard and the men in Midgard.

And around the deepest roots, far below even the realm of Hel, lay the great serpent Nidhogg, or "tearer of corpses." This serpent had encircled the entire root in the Underworld, and continually gnawed at it, threatening to bring Yggdrasil down. His sustenance was the corpses of the dead, and his mission in life was to destroy the World Tree, which he would eventually do on Ragnarok, the last day of all things. However, Nidhogg was not the only serpent that was trying to destroy Yggdrasil. There was also Vidofnir, whose name simply meant "tree snake"; he lived along the length of the Tree, traveling up and down its trunk. Similar to Ratatosk, he ate the bark of the Tree seeking to destroy it and hasten the day of Ragnarok when all the realms would come to an end—even those of the gods—and existence would be

consumed in fire and ice. A number of other serpents also traveled along the length of the Great Tree, gnawing at its bark, and stripping it away. Among these were Goin and Moin, who were considered to be especially poisonous, and infected Yggdresil with their venom. Such poison would eventually weaken the Tree.

Ragnarok

Indeed, Yggdrasil was central to the myths of Ragnarok, as its falling signaled the end of the Universe, which it supported, and in some myths, opened the way for a new breed of gods to set up their realms along the fallen trunk. Its fall came about when Nidhogg finally succeeded in gnawing completely through the supporting root in the Underworld, and at the same time, a number of the other pests managed to devour the roots in the other spheres of existence. The Great Tree toppled over, destroying everything that existed along its length, causing the realms of the gods, men, elves, and dwarves to pass away.

Shortly before Yggdrasil fell, all realms along its length would experience Fimbulveter—the Winter of Winters. This was a period of intense coldness that wrapped itself around the Great Tree, paralyzing all the existences except the realm of the Frost Giants. Yggdrasil itself started to wither. This made it easier for creatures such as Ratatosk, Goin, and Moin to burrow their way down to Yggdrasil's heart and kill it, the venom from the serpents now poisoning the wood. Yggdrasil started to groan and sway—a signal of the approaching end. Along with this, wars between men, giants, and gods began throughout the existences and into this conflict, elves, dwarves, and other such beings were drawn. Great warfare broke out, and this too threatened the continuance of the Tree. The conflicts reached the realm of Mulpelheim, the region of fire, and infuriated the demon Surtur, who ruled there. As Yggdrasil fell, he arose from his fiery pit and attacked the Tree himself. His great breath consumed the Tree, reducing it to ashes, and so signaling the end of Ragnarok. Nothing was left and yet, out of Yggdrasil's ashes, new life emerged, just as new life arose from shattered and burned trees in the forest. Two humans were said to have survived Surtur's fire by hiding in the ruins of Yggdrasil.

Their names are Lif and Lifthraser, and they formed the nucleus of a new race, which would inhabit the realm of Midgard. They were, in fact, the poetic symbols of life and hope.

Where Is the Great Tree?

Where exactly was Yggdrasil? Could it be placed in some specific location? If not, how did the beliefs come about? The ancient texts, particularly the Eddas, give no exact location for the Great Tree. In a sense, the ancients believed that it had a root in every world and in all of the nine possible existences. And yet, it also seemed to have an existence of its own, which was independent of them all. However, similar to the Otherworld of Celtic myth, no actual geographical location was actually attributed to it, though some traditions claimed that its branches could sometimes be seen, stretching against the sky when viewed from a certain valley in the "dark lands of the North." However, the location of this valley was always as obscure as that of Yggdrasil itself. It has been suggested that the movement of cirrus clouds, when viewed from some of the northern valleys, might be mistaken for the branches of a gigantic tree.

Other Tree Legends

However, there may have been other origins for the belief in Yggdrasil. Many students of myths and legends have noted that the Norse, Saxon, and Germanic peoples have a widespread tradition of tree worship, and Yggdrasil was not the only mighty growth that was prominent in such belief.

For instance, in the sacred temple grounds at Uppsala in Sweden, a tree known as "the Sacred Tree of Uppsala" grew. Although accounts of this tree are sparse, it was certainly an actual growth—reputedly an evergreen of unknown type (although it may have been an oak)—and is mentioned by the important German medieval chronicler, Adam of Bremen, who lived in the latter half of the 11th century. Not much is known about the temple near which it stood except that it was very old and had originally been raised for some sort of prehistoric gods, perhaps connected to the growth itself. It was also said that human sacrifice was carried on at this tree, and members of

various Swedish ruling houses may pay homage there. What became of this great tree is unknown, but it is probable that early Christian missionaries to Sweden may have cut it down. Could the idea of this Pagan tree at Uppsala have formed the basis for a belief in Yggdrasil?

There is also reference in early Germanic folklore to a special pillar made of oak that connected both Heaven and Hell. This was known as *Irmimsul* (meaning "great pillar" or "Irmin's pillar" in Old Saxon), and it took its name from an ancient Germanic god named Irmin. It was from Irmin's father, Manus that the Germanic peoples claimed descent, and Irmin himself was reputedly the father of a tribe known as the Irminones who inhabited parts of modern-day northern Germany. According to the Germanic tradition, Irmin himself erected the pillar, which he carved from a massive oak tree, so he could easily communicate with his father who reputedly lived in the clouds. It was said to have been located in an area known as the Teutoburger Wald (or Teutoburger Forest) in northwestern Germany—the area refers to a particularly forested mountain area in Lower Saxony. Interestingly enough, something similar to the pillar appears in 12th-century Middle Eastern Christian art; the form appears to be similar to a tree at the feet of Nicodemus (who hid in a tree so that he could listen to the teachings of Jesus). Perhaps this shows the absorption of some Pagan ideas into the developing Christian tradition.

There were many other instances of tree worship among the Germanic and Nordic peoples. There was a tradition, the origins of which have been lost, of decorating fir trees and leaving offerings beneath it to placate the spirits. In later Christian times, this tradition became known as that of the "Paradise Tree," which reputedly had connections into the Garden of Eden, supposedly representing the Tree of Life that grew there. Nonetheless, old Pagan traditions still persisted beneath the surface. These may form the basis of the traditional idea of the Christmas tree, decorated with lights and baubles, and with presents ("offerings") lying underneath it.

There were many more instances of tree-worship, particularly among the Germanic and Nordic peoples, encountered by the early Christians. Most notable was the famous Thor's Oak, which was dedicated to the Scandinavian/ Germanic god Thor, and at which human sacrifice was reputedly carried out. This was the sacred site of a Germanic tribe known as the Chatti, and was located near the village of Geismer, which would later become part of the modern-day town of Fritzler in Northern Hesse. It is believed that human sacrifice to Pagan gods was carried on there. This so shocked St. Boniface (680–755) that he cut down the oak and challenged Thor to strike him down for doing so. When the gods did not, many of the Chatti converted to Christianity. Later, the story became slightly muddled and, taking the saint's Saxon name of Winfryth, many chroniclers attributed the "miracle" to St. Winfred and changed the location of the tree to England. It is also recounted that various holy men such as Boniface's companion, St. Wigbert (around 734), cut down similar trees in parts of present-day Germany. Could legends surrounding these trees have come together in mythology to form the basis of Yggdrasil?

Christianity and Yggdrasil

The idea of trees and their death (that is, crucifixion) also played a very important part in the transition from Pagan to Christian thinking, particularly in the Nordic/Germanic world. According to the Christian faith, Jesus Christ was crucified on a wooden cross (sometimes referred to as a "tree" in Christian iconography). This had its parallels in Norse mythology when Odin hung on the branches of Yggdrasil for nine nights. This act of self-sacrifice was done in order to gain knowledge of the infinite, which made Odin a chieftain among the gods. Such imagery would, it is assumed, have made the Norse tribes more easily converted to the new Christian gospel. It is possible, of course, that this part of the Yggdrasil legend was added much later by Christian monks, specifically for the purpose of impressing the Pagans and obtaining converts. But the closeness of the early Norse mythology and later Christianity cannot be ignored.

Was Yggdrasil an actual place or was it something more abstract? The suggestion is that it was probably more of an ideal than a specific location. It combined notions of an Otherworld with a kind of connectivity between the various forms of Norse mythology. As such, it may have represented cohesion between various ideas of mythological places and gave them some shape, meaning, and place in the Universe. It may also have provided a link with earlier tree myths and sites of tree worship, as well as with primal gods and beliefs. Whether Yggdrasil existed as a specific geographical location or not, it was still similar to many other mythological places: an important factor in ancient mythology and legend that has served to inspire writers and poets to this day.

5

Hy-Brasil

Although not strictly considered a sunken land (that is, it was never overwhelmed by an ancient catastrophe and subsequently consigned to the depths of the ocean), Hy-Brasil nevertheless has many features that can link it to places such as Atlantis and Lemuria. However, the concept of Hy-Brasil may actually be an amalgam of a number of so-called "phantom isles" or "lost lands," which appear largely in Celtic mythology and folklore.

Initially, the concept of Hy-Brasil may have been little more than an extension to the Celtic Otherworld, perhaps inspired by cloud formations glimpsed far out at sea, which may have suggested the cliffs and headlands of an unknown, supernatural country. Maybe, it was assumed, the gods or the dead lived there. However, with the passage of time, other concepts may have crept in, shaping this idea and giving it substance, but still keeping the supernatural element intact. As seamen voyaged further and further across the world, they encountered other unknown lands—some of which were maybe no more than glimpsed on the horizon during the course of their journey—which they may have later imbued with many strange and wonderful attributes, or may have associated with magical and mysterious notions. Of course, many of these so-called "landmasses" were no more than cloud formations or sea animals that, in often uncertain light, took on the appearance of far-away shorelines. Some voyagers, however, actually did visit relatively unknown lands—islands in remote areas of the oceans, for example—and gradually their stories became tales of wonder and imagination as they were told and retold. All of these elements, impressions glimpsed in the half-light or a part of the mysterious Otherworld, gradually coalesced and formed themselves in the idea of a single land, Hy-Brasil, Brasil, or Brazil, or the Island O'Brasil, which is primarily an Irish version of the idea. Just to add some complexity to the notion, the location is also known under a number of other names (Green Island, Isle of Maam, St. Brendan's Island), and may be sunken or merely obscured from mortal view, depending on the version of the story. In most cases, a direct view of it is believed to be hindered by heavy clouds or mists, which permanently surround it. Although many claim sightings of it (usually of the briefest sort), few seem to have actually been there.

Writing in 1684, however, the Galway historian and geographer Roderick O'Flaherty in his book *A Chronological Description of the West or H-lar Connaught* states: "There is now living Morogh (or Murrough) O'Lay who immagins (sic) he himself was personally on the Island O'Brasil for two days and saw out of it the iles of Aran, Golamhead, Irrosbeghill and other places of the West continent that he was acquainted with."

The Disappearance

However, Morogh O'Lay was one of the very few who claimed to have actually set foot on Hy-Brasil (most sailors claimed that it faded away if approached) and O'Flaherty seems to treat his story with an element of suspicion and disdain. In spite of such scepticism, however, between 1325 and 1865, a number of maps also show the island as an actual place, clearly marked and lying to the southwest of Galway Bay. On some maps it is given the name Brazil Rock. On most maps it is largely circular with a central river or channel running through it, and a number of high hills or small mountains around its edges. In the late 19th century, it disappears from the charts specifically relating to the Galway coast, but can still be found lying slightly to the south of Rathlin Island in County Antrim (between Church Bay and Ballycastle) where it is marked as "Green Island."

The name Hy-Brasil, or Hy-Breasal, probably derives from a clan of that name who inhabited the west of Ireland allegedly during the second and third centuries. There are still families with that name living in parts of Clare

and Galway counties even today. Breasal was also the name, in ancient Irish mythology, of the King of the World, a legendary figure who had made his home on the island. Indeed, the List of High Kings of Ireland mentions a king named Breasal Boidhiobhadh who ruled a large part of the west of Ireland during the third century. His reign was notable for a great plague among cattle, which had wiped out many herds. Nevertheless, he seems to have been elevated to an almost god-like status, and may well have been worshipped long after his death. In fact, many believed that he had not died at all, but had gone to live on the Island O'Brasil, away from human eyes. This, then, became his kingdom, over which he ruled forever, akin to a benign god.

The People

One of the visitors to this realm was reputedly a certain Captain Nesbitt, who brought a ship there in the late 1500s or early 1600s. Nesbitt dropped anchor in the great bay and came ashore with some of his crew. They found thick and almost impenetrable woodlands, in the center of which stood an extremely ancient castle. The men went in, but, although the fortress was splendidly furnished, it seemed to be abandoned, with everything covered in a thick layer of dust. While they were examining the place, according to Nesbitt's account, three very old men appeared, each bowed over and leaning on a staff. Nesbitt hailed them but received no answer. Then one of the old men spoke in some sort of archaic tongue, which neither Nesbitt nor his crew understood. However, there was such a palpable air of menace around these three aged men that the superstitious sailors drew back and fled from the place. They reached their ship and sailed away as the mysterious island seemed to sink behind them into the ocean. This was one of the more descriptive (skeptics might be tempted to say slightly fanciful) accounts of landing on the island. Nesbitt added that within the castle was a large empty throne, which he assumed belonged to Breasal, King of the World.

And So the Legends Begin...

Gradually the legend of Hy-Brasil developed. It was said, for example, that the mystical island only appeared once every seven years (seven being a mystical number) when it either rose from the depths of the ocean or the clouds that circled it. It was also said to be a place where fairies and other supernatural entities dwelt, and at the time when Hy-Brasil appeared, they would come ashore to interact with mortals.

The famous Rathlin Island storyteller of the 1950s and 1960s, Rose McCrudy, for example, frequently told of how the fairies from "the Green Isle" would come ashore to the Hiring Fairs in Ballycastle to hire humans to work at the fairy island on their lands. These contracts would last for seven years until the Green Isle reappeared again off the southern coast of Rathlin. At that time, those who had been hired either had the option of remaining with the fairies for another seven years or going home. Rose spoke of a woman, allegedly still living in Glenshesk in the Glens of Antrim in the 1950s, who had been to the fairy isle to act as a housekeeper for a fairy man. She had come home again, but had tried to return to the Green Isle (once the contract was terminated, mortals were never allowed to return there) and had been struck blind by the fairies. Many of the older people living in the Glens knew this woman very well and believed her story. The Green Island can still be seen, marked on extremely old maps of the region, although some have confused it with the tiny island of Sanda in the Inner Hebrides.

Such mistakes may have been more common among ancient sailors and cartographers than we suspect. For instance, some geographical historians have suggested that Hy-Brasil might have been Helluland (the Land of Flat Stones), discovered by the Viking explorer Lief Erikson around A.D. 1000. Legends say that Erikson encountered giants living there who made mighty axes and powerful spears. This may well have been the Dorset culture that is thought to have occupied the coast of Greenland and some of the smaller off-shore islands around this time. These people were much taller than the incoming Inuit tribes and were renowned for their axe and spearhead making. The Vikings, however, called them *skraeling*, which meant "barbarians" or "coarse forigners." Erikson landed but did not stay, sailing south toward what is now northern Canada (Markland); geographers now think that he had visited present-day Baffin Island in the Labrador Straits.

Maps

Indeed, many maps detailing parts of the northern oceans from a period between the 13th and 17th centuries show a number of islands that since appear to have been "lost," and which might also be referred to as Hy-Brasil. Some of these may be simple mistakes that have been passed from one cartographer to another, and some may be actual frauds, detailing exotic lands which the mapmakers actually knew were not there, but were simply added to make the map seem more interesting, exotic, and appealing. Such a place was Estotiland, far northwest of the Atlantic Ocean. This large island appeared on the celebrated Zeno Map prepared in the 15th century by the Venetian mapmaker Antonio Zeno. During the mid-1400s, Antonio's maps, together with those of his brother Nicolo, were much sought after and trusted by mariners; however, most of them were false, owing more to the imaginations of the cartographers than reality. Many of these locations depended largely on the fanciful stories of mariners who claimed to have visited such places—stories that were then embellished by mapmakers, including the Zenos. By the late 17th century, the island of Estotiland had disappeared from all navigation charts, as had several towns and ports that were also marked.

Other maps dating from the 1500s and mid-1600s show another major island near the coast of Newfoundland named the Isle of Demons. It was said to be a wild and terrible place where ghosts, demons, and devils dwelt amid cold and snow. Those who claimed to have landed there allegedly experienced terrible ordeals usually involving phantoms and monsters; many mariners were advised to shun these far seas and their islands. By the late 1600s and early 1700s, the Isle of Demons had vanished from all maps and now simply remains as a legend. Many of these islands were often confused with the concept of Hy-Brasil, that mysterious island that seemed to avoid contact with the rest of the world.

Other Names

Traveling further south across the Atlantic Ocean, other accounts referred to Hy-Brasil as "St. Brendan's Isle" after the sixth-century Abbot of Clonfert in County Galway, who is also regarded as a famous navigator, explorer, and possible founder of the island. The first account of his landing there comes from the ninth-century manuscript titled *Navigatio Santi Brendani Abatis* (The Voyage of St. Brendan the Abbot), which states that he encountered the island as he sailed across the Atlantic to bring Christianity to northwest Europe. No precise location is given for this island, and some geographical historians had claimed the isle to be "the eighth Canary Isle." Others have suggested that the saint might have visited what is currently called Macronesia—a group of volcanically created islands in the North Atlantic, comprising the Azores, Madeira, the Canaries, the Cape Verdi Islands, and the Savage Islands. Saint Brendan and his company landed there and found the place to be an earthly Paradise with many trees laden with luscious fruit. Some commentators speculate that this was one of the Fortunate Isles referred to by the Roman writer Flavius Philostratos in his *Life of Appolonius of Tyana*, in which he mentioned almost paradisiacal islands, laden with apples. The island of Avalon was said to be one of these locations. Brendan and his companions sailed away and, according to tradition, the island seemed to disappear into a cloud which then sank into the ocean. Writing later in the 11th century, the monk Borino states that he, too, visited the island and found it to be a wonderful place. When he left, the island was once again consumed by clouds and appeared to sink into the ocean.

Both the Spanish and Portuguese of the 16th and 17th centuries fervently believed in the existence of the island and referred to it as San Brandon. In fact, when the Peace of Elvira was signed in June 1519, in which the Portuguese ceded the Canary Islands to Spain, one of those islands was La Isla Non-Trabada o Encubierta—the Inconstant or Mysterious Island, which is taken to refer to St. Brendan's Island or Hy-Brasil. Sensing that this could be a new territory, several Spanish governors of the Canaries tried to locate it. They used old maps prepared by both Spanish and Arab cartographers, the most notable of the latter being Abdullah al-Bakri—the celebrated Spanish-Moorish mapmaker—which showed a number of islands that appeared to have since been "lost." Several ships were dispatched from El Herrio in an attempt to find "San Brandon," but none were successful. Portuguese interest in the island had been intense ever since a sea captain had appeared at the court of King Henry the Navigator (1394–1460) speaking of a strange island that he had encountered in the North Atlantic. The seaman said that he had tried to approach the island to make landfall, but had been driven off by tremendous storms; when he had approached it again, the island had disappeared. Sometime later, another captain from the island of Madeira had turned up at the royal court during the reign of John II of Portugal (1481–1495) begging for a caravel to reach an island that seemed to appear regularly on the

horizon. This piqued Portuguese attention, and they began to take such accounts extremely seriously. In 1556, a combined Spanish and Portuguese investigation under Dr. Hernan Parez de Grado, first regent of the Royal Canaries Court, began using the accounts of both Spanish and Portuguese sailors. Old maps and accounts were reconsulted. With the initial investigation inconclusive, the Spanish now began to enquire themselves, headed by Fernando de Villasboas, military governor of La Palma. This, too, was inconclusive and no trace of the mysterious island was found.

There was another flurry of interest in 1570, when an account was allegedly given to Spanish authorities in Cadiz by a sea captain named Marcos Verde. He had been returning, he said, from the Berber Coast (northern Morocco) to La Palma in the Canaries when he had been blown off course by a sudden storm. Spotting the highest point of an unknown island, he made for shelter and dropped anchor in a large bay. There he waited until the storm had passed. On the edge of nightfall, he went ashore with some men to try to find supplies. The island appeared to be thickly wooded and the landing party split up into groups, each one taking different trails. Verde said that suddenly, he could hear the screams of some of the other parties in the darkness and "sounds so hideous" that he recalled his crew to the landing boats. Some of the crew did not return from the forest and Verde was forced to leave them behind. They had barely returned to the ship when another massive storm blew up, causing the vessel to drag its anchor. Thanks to Verde's captaincy, his craft managed to ride out the tempest, but when they returned to their former location, the island was gone.

The following year another seaman, Pedro Velho, wrote an account of another landing on the mysterious island where he claimed he had seen many "wondrous things." He had seen trees, fruit, and even animals, unlike anywhere else in the world. More significantly, he claimed to have seen ruins, mainly ancient columns covered in strange hieroglyphs, and other evidences of human habitation, but it is not recorded if he saw any actual natives. Velho also stated that he had spoken with the captain of a French ship that had also landed there, dropping anchor in the bay in order to make some repairs. A detail of men had gone ashore and had cut some wood from several trees before being driven off by a sudden storm that threatened to wreck the vessel. Although both Spanish and Portuguese enquiries into the existence of the island were largely abandoned, both countries held a hope for many years that there was another land somewhere out there, waiting to be discovered.

Into the 18th century, accounts of a mysterious island lying somewhere in the North Atlantic continued to be reported. For instance, in 1711, a monk named Sigbert de Gembroux claimed to have seen an uncharted island from a ship on which he was traveling. He may actually have seen no more than a school of fish or even dolphins, but he nevertheless claimed that it was land that disappeared before anyone could substantiate his story. Similarly, in 1772, Viera y Clavijo, a captain of the Royal Canary Fleet, mistook the mountains of an unknown island for the cliffs and hills of La Palma while at sea, only to find that his destination lay elsewhere.

The Island O'Brasil, or Brasil rock, remained a legend through the years and it was said that the Portuguese explorer Pedro Alvares Cabral had named the South American country Brazil after the mythical land when he landed in April 1500. It was claimed that he imagined that the jungles were actually the woodlands of the unknown island, which he then claimed for Portugal. However, there are two defects to that argument. First, it may have been a political trick in order to claim territory. It has been said that Portuguese seafarers knew full well that this land was part of South America, but that the area had been declared as Spanish territory by the Treaty of Toresillas in 1494, and had been ratified by the pope, Alexander VI. By pretending that he had landed on an unknown land, Cabral then felt free to claim a Portuguese dominion. The second drawback to the theory is that Cabral himself did not name Brazil. In fact it was not named until later—with Cabral naming it as Isla de Vera Cruz. It was then later named Terra de Santa Cruz (Land of the Holy Cross) and then Brazil much later. The name is actually said to derive from brasa wood and the brasa tree, which gave a reddish tinged wood ("brasa" or "burning" wood) that was extremely popular in Portugal during the 16th century and was actually a trade item.

A number of other explorers have identified Hy-Brasil as Terceira Island in the Azores. Indeed it was named as such (Brazil) by the explorer and cartographer Andrea Bianco on his map of the area, printed in 1431. It is not clear, however, whether it was ever really known as such by many mariners. It was later named Terceira, meaning "third" (because it is the third biggest

island in the Azores group). A number of other smaller islands in various North Atlantic island chains seem to have been similarly identified, but these appear to have subsequently vanished. Perhaps they were little more than a rocky outcropping or large reef, which have since disappeared beneath the waves.

Even as late as the 21st century, there are still accounts of unknown land-masses from time to time. Many of these have usually been glimpsed from a distance—along the horizon or far out to sea—and of course it is always possible to argue that they are indeed no more than a trick of the light, clouds, or perhaps some small reef or rock distorted by the sun on the water. But who knows; perhaps there truly is something out there. Perhaps it is the mysterious land of Hy-Brasil.

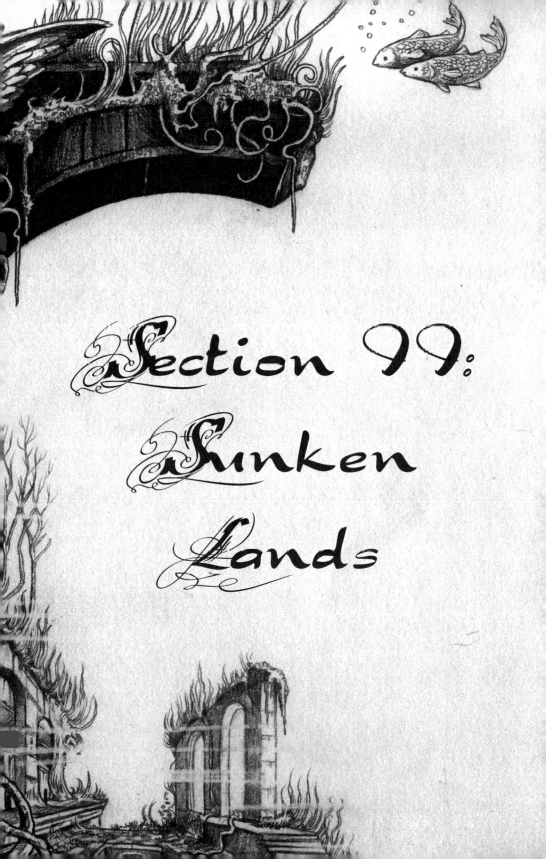

Section 99:
Sunken
Lands

Sunken Lands

Although the ocean can often be awe-inspiring and beautiful, it can also be violent and terrifying; and it can hide many secrets. Sudden storms at sea can often provide a fearsome threat, not only for ships, but for coastal settlements and island communities. Tales of villages, towns, and even cities being overwhelmed by the sea or by severe floods can be found in the folklore of many cultures.

Many such stories have their origins in actual history, for combinations of disasters such as coastal erosion or monstrous seas have ensured the disappearance of many settlements all across history.

One has only to look at, say, medieval maps detailing the coastline of England or Ireland to see ancient coastal towns and villages marked there—settlements that no longer exist. Many have old and evocative names—Ravenspur, Larkscradle, Candleford—probably hinting at their antiquity prior to their disappearance. Some have vanished by coastal slippage, gradually sliding under the waters as the sea-worn coastline fell away; others, possibly more low-lying, were drowned by the waters of the raging ocean at the height of a tempest or hurricane. Even today, many villages around the coast of Britain remain under similar threat.

And in America, we have only to think of the devastation wrought in the low-lying city of New Orleans by Hurricane Katrina in 2005 to realize that such disasters can happen even now. And of course, the Louisiana shore is not the only American coastline to have been affected by such terrific and violent weather. Small communities settled in the South Carolina low country have been swallowed up by the swamps as water levels rose during the era of the rice kings in the early to mid-1800s, and there were similar disappearances all along the Florida and New England coastlines throughout the 18th, 19th, and early 20th centuries.

Forces of Nature

But forces such as coastal erosion and massive seacoast storms are not the only reason why some settlements—towns and cities—and even whole civilizations, might have disappeared. On August 16 and 27, 1883, the volcanic island of Krakatoa, Indonesia, in the Sunda Strait, between Java and Sumatra erupted, creating one of the biggest explosions ever recorded. The force of the explosion was equivalent to a number of atomic bombs, and was heard as far away as Perth in western Australia (more than 1,930 miles away). The island itself was blown to pieces, and the remnants sank to the bottom of the ocean; it is said that this was not the first mighty explosion that had occurred in the area. The *Pustara Raja,* or *Javanese Book of Kings*, a collection of writings dating from somewhere between about 1480 and 1600, detailing the histories and mythologies of the area, makes reference to another explosion (although not as violent) dating from approximately A.D. 416, which caused widespread devastation and loss of life. There are reports of other volcanic activity much later—in the 1500s and 1600s—destroying parts of some smaller islands near Krakatoa.

During the Krakatoa explosion, many parts of Java and Sumatra, as well as towns and cities further afield, were completely overwhelmed and destroyed by massive tidal waves, and some still lie under the ocean today. Thus, volcanoes and earthquakes at sea can cause rising ocean levels that can consign whole towns and cities to the deep. We have only to think of the Asian tsunami on December 26, 2004—caused by a small shifting of the Earth's tectonic plates on the ocean floor—to realize the overwhelming effect of such events.

If volcanic eruptions, hurricanes, and earthquakes are relatively common even now, it is possible that they may have been more common in the ancient world. There are, for example, tales and records of powerful earthquakes in the East and Middle East, and of mighty hurricanes and windstorms striking the coasts of Europe (and later America). This has led to legends of whole civilizations being swept away (and it is extremely possible that a number of them were), and of massive tracts of land being swamped by the sea. Such lost lands and vanished kingdoms are said to lie—still relatively intact—in the ocean's depths, awaiting rediscovery. It is possible that some of the civilizations of the ancient world often faced natural disasters that either threatened to, or actually did, overwhelm them, and may well have consigned them to the deep.

Sunken Lands

Of course through time, fanciful legends began to build up around these vanished places. Even the small coastal towns and villages that slipped under sea level acquired an air of mystery and legend. At Ardfert in County Kerry, Ireland, for example, it was said that the bells of a submerged church rang out on certain nights of the year, tolled by undersea beings who now inhabited the sunken building. Other such places of the coast of England also held legends of sea people dwelling among the ruins of former human settlements— but these were only local tales, and often had a limited effect on the imagination.

It was the tales of lost cities and of sunken civilizations that really inspired speculation. Tales of primal cataclysms often led to stories of whole realms—the lands of prehistoric kings and princes—being submerged in some former time, usually beyond human reckoning. After all, in the mythologies of many cultures there were tales of fearful catastrophes in some historically distant period; for instance, the Biblical story of Noah's Flood that supposedly destroyed all the "sinful" civilizations of the early world (that is, most of the planet). Was it not possible, therefore, that some vast cataclysm had destroyed primordial societies and that this momentous event had been unrecorded, except in folk memory and myth?

As time passed the idea became more and more fanciful. Perhaps inspired by the natural disaster of Krakatoa, the notion of a mighty island civilization engulfed by a powerful volcanic explosion began to gain in popularity in the early part of the 20th century. This, as we shall see when we come to look at the legend of Atlantis, may have had some basis in fact but, through time, additions were made to the basic tale that turned it into something similar to a fantasy. This, it was suggested, might have been some sort of super-civilization, maybe even far in advance of our own, and at the very least, holding secrets and understandings that the world had subsequently lost. It was even suggested that the catastrophe, which had overwhelmed it and caused it to sink below the ocean, was not natural at all, but a misuse of something man-made, created by the civilization itself—something akin to an atomic bomb. Perhaps this was nothing more than an evocation of some imagined Golden Age that had existed somewhere in the past, and a hope that these civilizations could, if discovered, provide at least some remedy for the increasing evils and complications of a modern world. Science-fiction writers were, naturally, quick to develop this notion but so were some anthropologists (albeit in a much more measured way) in order to explain the dispersal of, and similarities in, many ancient peoples.

In the 1960s, fresh impetus was given to these theories as respected geologists began to consider that Earth's continents had been joined into a supercontinent in early prehistoric times. It experienced a number of catastrophes that pushed it apart, allowing oceans to form between them, forming the landmasses we know today. The geologists were following a theory first put forward by Alfred Wagener in 1912, and they dubbed a couple of the mighty continents Gondwanaland (which eventually went on to form some of the countries of the Northern Hemisphere) and Pangaea (which laid the foundations for the Southern Hemisphere), and locating them during the Jurassic and Triassic Periods in Earth's history. This led some to assert that these landmasses had been home to ancient civilizations that had more or less perished by flooding as these supercontinents split up. Many have asserted that evidences of these civilizations still remain deep under the sea, and such evidences simply haven't been found as yet.

So do remnants of strange and sunken lands from an antique time exist somewhere on the ocean floor? Quite possibly, though they may be very different from what we imagine them to be, and may contain few secrets that we don't already know. Their names, however, live on in legend—Atlantis, Mu, Lyonesse—to enthral and intrigue many people even today; for who knows what lies out there beneath the rolling waves—perhaps more than we could possibly imagine!

6

Atlantis

Arguably, no sunken realm has provoked the human imagination so readily or as frequently as the lost land of Atlantis—the island civilization that was allegedly destroyed by some form of natural cataclysm, which is said to have given its name to the Atlantic Ocean. Indeed, during the early-to-mid-20th century, Atlantis was imagined as some kind of advanced culture, intellectually and perhaps even technologically superior to our own, which had dominated prehistoric times. All this, however, was destroyed in either massive volcanic upheavals or earthquakes, which not even the Atlanteans themselves could prevent or control.

Locating Atlantis

But did such a fantastic realm actually exist? Was it as advanced as the writers of the 20th century imagined it to be? And, if so, how did it meet its end?

There is little reference to Atlantis in ancient texts, but the one mention of it in early classic literature is a significant one. The scholar Plato (428/7–348/7 B.C.) makes specific allusion to an island continent of that name lying to the west of Greece, "beyond the Pillars of Hercules" (taken to mean the Strait of Gibraltar). Atlantis appears to have been a significant naval power that established colonies both in Western Europe and in Africa, roughly 8,000 years before Plato was writing. Incredibly aggressive, its naval fleet made war on Athens, but was defeated and driven back beyond the edge of the Mediterranean. Shortly afterward, the entire continent was destroyed in what the writer calls "a single day and night of misfortune." No further mention of it is made, but the implication is that it sank into the sea, according to Plato; all that remained of the once great civilization was a mudbank.

Plato's reference to Atlantis appears in a set of classical literature known as the *Dialogues* (or more properly the *Socratic Dialogues* because they were named after, and sometimes featured, the classical scholar Socrates as a character within the text). These were imagined "conversations" between fictitious or historical characters, usually on philosophical topics and moral problems. The reference to Atlantis appears in what are known as *Conjoined Dialogues* written around 360 B.C. including the characters Timeaus and Crtias. The *Dialogues* consider the structure of the Universe, and how this was mirrored in (or actually determined) ancient civilizations. Parts of it are taken up with musings on the perfect society—a topic that concerned Plato greatly. However, only the character Critias speaks directly of Atlantis, comparing it to Plato's own theories. The structure of Plato's Republic, Critias muses, was possibly as close to a perfect society as men can achieve, whereas that of Atlantis was the very antithesis of that. He claims that his information about the continent comes from a trip to Egypt by the Greek poet and lawmaker Solon (638–558 B.C.) in the sixth century B.C. In the city of Sais in southern Egypt, Solon met a priest who told him a remarkable story. He, the priest, had translated some ancient papyri from early Egyptian hieroglyphics into Greek, which detailed the early histories of Athens and another civilization known as Atlantis.

The gods, according to the priest, had divided up the world between them, and a large portion of land, bigger than Libya and part of Asia Minor combined, had been given to Poseidon, god of the sea, as his own. This was Atlantis. One of Poseidon's sons was the Titan Atlas (who was later envisaged as bearing the world on his shoulders), and it was to him that the god granted this land, making him the first king (the name Atlantis actually translates as "the island of Atlas"). To Atlas's twin brother Gadeius, Poseidon gave the outer limits of the island lying nearest the Pillars of Hercules, as well as some other sections to several other children; for example, Mestor and Azaes ruled there for many years, developing naval strengths with their father.

Land Features

Atlantis was a seafaring nation. Even the interior of the island was inter-cut by a system of waterways and water-dependent defenses. A series of inter-nal defensive moats reputedly encircled the Atlantean heartlands, connected to the coast by a system of locks and carved tunnels. Coastal settlements all boasted complicated docks, all defensively laid out. The Atlanteans were both traders and slavers—indeed it has been suggested that slavery was the back-bone of their civilization—as well as maintaining a powerful ocean-going war fleet. To obtain slaves, it has been suggested that they raided along the coasts of Africa and into Asia, even attacking as far away as Tyrrheania or Eturia in northern Italy. There they attacked cities that had been built by the forerunners of the Etruscan peoples—a civilized society—carrying away booty and scores of slaves.

Past Wars

About 9,000 yeas before the time of Critias (and therefore before the time of Plato) a war broke out between those who dwelt outside the Pillars of Hercules (that is beyond the Mediterranean Sea) and those who dwelt within it. The Atlanteans reputedly used this conflict for their own advan-tage, sending their fleets to pillage and conquer various shores. They con-quered Libya and parts of Egypt, which they occupied, carrying away thousands of people into slavery. Alarmed, a number of Mediterranean coun-tries, under the leadership of Athens, formed an alliance to stand against them and drive them out. The alliance finally crumbled, but Athens now took on the Atlantean navy and defeated it in a series of sea battles. Around this time, Atlantis was destroyed by a mighty internal cataclysm—"the day and night of misfortune"—and sank beneath the waves.

Finding Proof

This is Plato's account of the fabulous continent, but as no other ancient scholars make any mention of the civilization, all subsequent stories concern-ing Atlantis must rely on it. Nor are there any other references in the litera-ture of any other races concerning such a slave-based society that allegedly raided deep into other countries. Indeed, conversely, there is much to suggest that many other Greek philosophers and geographers actually considered Plato's story to be entirely fictitious. The noted philosopher Aristotle (384–322 B.C.), for instance, claimed that Plato had made Atlantis disappear just as quickly as he had made it appear.

Some, however, did take Plato's account seriously. For example, the writer Hellanicus of Lesbos wrote a work that he titled "Atlantis," wrongly attributing the name to a daughter of the Titan Atlas, and mentioning the "Sea of Atlas" (the Atlantic Ocean), which was well known by that name long before he wrote about it. Another disciple, Crantor, allegedly tried to find proof of Atlantis in the mid-fourth century B.C., and is supposed to have set out on a journey to Egypt in order to discover any ruins that might exist. There is no real record of his journey, but another writer, Proclus, anxious to prove Plato's theories about Atlantis and quoting an unnamed source, stated that Crantor actually found pillars in the Egyptian desert, which were covered in hieroglyphs, confirming Plato's account. Proclus also seems to have added to the Atlantis myth by suggesting that it was not a single island at all, but a number of islands, linked by trade and commerce, in the center of which were three major landmasses, one of which was dedicated to the Roman god Pluto. The account is a confusing and contradictory one, and many scholars believe that Proclus simply made it up.

Indeed, throughout the years, Plato's own account has been called into question: A number of subsequent scholars have suggested that, at best, the philosopher was "confused" and mistook some other ancient event for the destruction of Atlantis. Subsequent writers in the classical world have made the same mistake. They sometimes cite the destruction of the Greek city of Helike as a historical event that could be confused with the sinking of Atlantis. The city was a bustling port that was probably destroyed by a major earthquake. Helike was said to "sink beneath the earth, the fissure promptly filled with the sea," dragging many ships docked in port (including 10 warships from the Spartan fleet) after it. Columns of fire (suggesting volcanic activity) spurted up and the sky darkened. This could correspond in many minds with the submersion of the island of Atlantis, and could have been mistaken for it in later texts. Another suggestion is that the destruction of the continent may have become confused with the attempted Athenian invasion of the island of Sicily during the Peloponnesian Wars (about 415 B.C.). During

this conflict, a number of coastal cities were so heavily bombarded by the Athenian fleet that parts of them actually slid into the sea. Could this have sparked the legend of a sunken island civilization?

Some scholars have also argued that the Atlantis legend sprang from another source. Between 360 and 336 B.C., the Greek poet and writer Theopompus of Chios, a Greek island close to the Turkish coast, wrote of an imaginary island somewhere beyond the western limits of Oceanus (the Western or World Sea). This island he named Meropis, and it was inhabited by extremely civilized and erudite people—mainly poets and scholars. Meropians grew to a massive stature (around 8 feet tall) and lived for an incredibly long time (more than 200 years). Although Meropis was supposed to be a Paradise, it did comprise two very different cities: Eusebes (or "Pious Town") in which the inhabitants dwelt in luxury and splendour, passing their days composing works of beautiful poetry; and Machimos (or "Fighting Town") in which the inhabitants were born with weapons in their hands and continually fought with each other. The general work, which Theopompus terms the *Philippica*, was no more than a parody of Plato's work on Atlantis. However, it has been argued that some subsequent writers have confused the two and the writings of Theopompus have been incorporated into the overall Atlantis myth.

By the third century B.C., however, some Greek writers had located Atlantis somewhere within the Mediterranean, citing the Straits of Sicily (between Sicily and Tunisia) as a possible location. They suggested that the so-called Pillars of Hercules lay on the western side of the island, and that this is the spot to which Plato had been referring. Roman writers such as Marcellinus, writing in the fourth century, however, continued to assert that the Straits of Gibraltar were in fact the Pillars. To support this, he citied that certain Gaulish (French) Druids (Celtic holy men) had claimed to come from an island from which they had fled during severe storms, and this was the island to which Plato had referred. However, this may be due to a misunderstanding; the islands mentioned may well have lain in the Rhine, and they were forced to flee when they were submerged by the flooding river. This point was debated among several classical thinkers, but no firm conclusion was reached.

Despite such interest, however, most ancient writers, geographers, and commentators remained extremely skeptical about the existence of such a place, and the myth began to slowly fade in the ancient world.

While there was great interest among scholars in Plato's writings during the medieval period, scant attention was paid to his notions of Atlantis, except where it impinged on his ideas expressed in the *Republic*. Indeed, throughout the late medieval and early modern periods, Atlantis became more of a philosophical ideal than an actual historical place. During the 1600s, when it was mentioned, it referred to the hope of a perfect society, largely based on republican ideals.

Uncovering Discoveries of Atlantis

The name Atlantis came to the fore again in the work of the English thinker, essayist, and statesman Francis Bacon (first Viscount St. Alban). In a work titled *A New Atlantis*, written in 1626, he described a near-perfect island society, based off the coast of America. This was an allegory of a wonderful social order, but the idea would appear again in the works of anthropologists Brasseur de Barbour and Edward H. Thompson, who suggested that the Mayan and Incan civilizations of Central and South America had derived from Atlantis survivors. Allegedly, part of the Atlanta fleet had been at sea at the time of the catastrophe, and supposedly had made landfall in America to found colonies there. Some currency was attached to the idea, and it has remained in vogue in one way or another in certain quarters. Indeed, it received something of a boost around 1940 with the discovery of a bandaged mummy in a remote cave in Nevada. The mummy was originally named Spirit Cave Man, and was attributed to early Indian peoples of the region—possibly mound builders. However, close scientific examination, which included radio-carbon dating, revealed the bandage cloth to date from approximately 9000 B.C., and to have been possibly made on a loom. Tradition stating that many of the Atlantean colonies in Egypt states used mummification to preserve their dead—indeed, it was believed by some that the Atlanteans had taught the Egyptians the art of mummification—and this gave fresh impetus to the idea of a connection between Atlantis and America.

In 1882, there was another burst of interest in the lost realm. This was sparked by the publication of Ignatius Donnelly's book *Atlantis—The Antediluvian World*, which was to become a best-seller in certain circles. Donnelly took Plato's assertions regarding the sunken land very seriously and claimed that Atlantis had been the source of many (if not all) ancient

civilizations. Such theories were keeping with the mood of the times, where people had a growing interest in the ancient world and with "forgotten secrets" that might even pre-date humanity itself. Such ideas lay behind the next major reference to Atlantis, which seemed, at face value, to build upon Donnelly's thinking.

The Grandmother of Occultism

In 1888, the "grandmother of modern occultism" Helena Petrovna Blavatsky (H.P. Blavatsky) published her book *The Secret Doctrine*, a massive work of esoteric lore and teachings complied in two volumes, which she claimed had been revealed to her by Secret Masters, or Mahatmas, who were now living in Tibet. They communicated with her by telepathy and disclosed certain facts about the history and nature of the world, which had been kept secret from common men. One of these was that Atlantis had actually existed, and that the Atlanteans were one of the "Root Races" that had formed modern Mankind (the next would be the Ayrian race, which would shape its future). Madam Blavatsky portrayed the Atlanteans as a race of great thinkers and compassionate beings. This was in fact contrary to Plato, who had portrayed them as an aggressive military naval power who operated a society based on slavery. It was Madam Blavatsky's idea that took hold, however, and the idea of an advanced and philanthropic civilization based in Atlantis was born.

Edgar Cayce

Such a notion gained much credence during the 1920s, particularly due to the intervention of the noted American psychic and occultist Edgar Cayce. In 1923, Cayce made a number of utterances and predictions concerning Atlantis. The Atlanteans, he declared, had been a highly advanced and sophisticated people, who had many technological attributes that have been lost to the world. They had, for example, lightweight building materials, which enabled them to build high and graceful dwellings; they had a road system that incorporated flyovers; and they powered their vehicles by a mysterious energy that they obtained from natural crystals by an obscure means. Some of Cayce's followers (although not Cayce himself) even claimed that the

Atlanteans had space travel and an underground colony on the planet Mars, creating the "canals" that can be seen on the Red Planet. The myth of Atlantis was steadily growing. Cayce also predicted that parts of the submerged continent would reemerge around 1967 or 1968, as evidence of its former existence. This seemed to come true (and was rapidly seized on by his followers) with the discovery in 1968 of the Bimini Road, near Bimini Island in the Bahamas, by archaeologist Dr. J. Manson Valentine. This was an underwater stone structure that resembled part of a collapsed road or wall, suggesting some sort of ancient civilization. It was immediately portrayed as evidence of Atlantis, though this may not be the case. The "road" is still under investigation, and no firm conclusions have been drawn about it.

Minoan Civilizations

Some archaeologists believe that the myth of Atlantis has become confused with the historic Minoan civilization of the late Bronze Age, which flourished in the Aegean Sea roughly between 2700 and 1450 B.C. This civilization was centered on the island of Crete, and takes its name from Minos, the legendary king of Crete (associated in fable with the mythical Minotaur). Little is known about this society except that it was a trading nation, which had colonies in Egypt—traces of Minoan pottery has been found in parts of the Egyptian desert, and it is said that the Minoans maintained an administrative center in the Egyptian city of Knossos until around 1200 B.C. It is also probable that they traded with other cultures for tin, a valuable commodity in the ancient world. Nothing much is known of the Minoan culture—their writings seem to be in a form known as Cretan hieroglyphic, which has so far remained indecipherable.

From about 1400 B.C. the Minoan civilization seems to have collapsed with fragments of it being amalgamated into the emerging Greek culture. During its later period, there seems little doubt that its sphere of influence suffered a series of catastrophes, both natural and man-made. Wars raged through the Aegean, and the area seems to have experienced earthquakes and volcanic eruptions on a large scale. Its last vestiges vanished as a period known as the Greek Dark Ages (1100–750 B.C.) descended, and many of the civilizations around the rim of the Mediterranean collapsed.

Santorini

The main contender for Atlantis is a part of this civilization that lies on what is now the Greek island of Santorini. Between 1645 and 1500 B.C., the island experienced a huge eruption coupled with a massive earthquake, and part of it was submerged. At the time, it is known that the site was inhabited by a culturally advanced people who had built a number of cities there, all of which were lost. Of all the stories of the ancient world, the explosion on Santorini seems to fit closely with the legend of Atlantis.

In his account, derived from Solon, Plato gave the account of the loss of the island civilization as 9,000 years before his (Plato's) time. It has been suggested that Solon mistranslated the story, which was recorded in Egyptian numerals, and that it was only 900 years before the time that Plato wrote about it. This would make it roughly correspond with the explosion on Santorini. Furthermore, evidences of colonization from Santorini, which have been unearthed on other islands, show a highly developed mercantile culture; what records remain tell of a culture that traded all through the Mediterranean based on the island. Plato's description of the end of Atlantis—columns of fire and smoke and ash—are indicative of a volcanic explosion of epic proportions (probably bigger than the one that destroyed Pompeii in A.D. 73). The "mudbanks" and "small islands," which are alleged to have appeared after the submersion of the island, might, in fact, be pumice stone, thrown out by a volcano. Nevertheless, not enough is known about the culture of Santorini, or indeed of the end of the Minoan civilization, to positively identify the island as the site of vanished Atlantis. The sunken island continent still remains an intriguing mystery.

Nazi Philosophy

In the period leading up to and during World War II, Madame Blavatsky's 19th century theories about the coming Ayrian race as the successors to the Atlanteans attracted the attention of the Nazi movement. The idea of the Atlanteans being a super-race, who had mastered much of their known world, and of the Aryan people becoming the dominating race fit in well with Nazi philosophy, and many of the Nazi leaders fervently believed in the truth of

Atlantis. If there were survivors from the sunken continent, it was suggested, they might have wisdom and even technical knowledge, which would be of use to the Nazi movement. In 1938, therefore, following some of the suggestions contained in Madame Blavatsky's books, Heinrich Himmler organized a scientific trip to Tibet in order to find the mysterious Mahatmas (whom Himmler imagined to be the forerunners of the Ayrian race) or any white survivors from the lost civilization. The expedition apparently found nothing of any consequence.

During the 1950s and early-to-mid-1960s, the idea of Atlantis blossomed together with interest in many other "lost lands" and other mysteries. Perhaps the idea of a lost technologically advanced culture appealed to the austere post-War period. Various attempts were made to link the lost realm with many parts of the world. "Atlantis hunters" placed its location in areas such as the Azores in the Atlantic, Antarctica, Indonesia, Malaysia, Cyprus, Turkey, and Ireland, with some even asserting that Atlantis runs all the way beneath the ocean from Spain to Central America. Two of the most favored sites tend to be Cuba and the island of Bermuda, suggesting that still-operating sunken high-level technological equipment, far beyond our comprehension, is creating the celebrated "Bermuda Triangle," which is a mysterious phenomenon in its own right.

The concept of drowned Atlantis, destroyed at the dawn of time, gave fantasy and science-fiction writers a field day, allowing them to combine futuristic civilizations with prehistoric monsters, reptiles, and dinosaurs. But across the years, interest in Atlantis began to wane slightly in the popular imagination and only resurfaced from time to time. It has reemerged of late with the cult television series *Stargate: Atlantis* derived from the hit *Stargate SG-1*. This postulates the lost city of Atlantis somewhere in Antarctica, built by space-travelers called the Ancients and linked to the Pegasus Galaxy—a dwarf galaxy located far out in space.

So, did Atlantis truly exist? And, if so, what was it like? Was it a futuristic, compassionate culture from which many other civilizations sprang? Or was it a militarily aggressive, slave-holding society that preyed on its neighbors and sought to colonize them? We will perhaps never actually know, for we only have Plato's admittedly rather dubious account of it, and little actual evidence to support it. If Atlantis did exist, there is precious little trace of it.

And yet, it is reasonable to assume that many ancient civilizations about which we know either very little or nothing at all, did exist across the world, and Atlantis might well be one of them. Certainly few of these have gripped the popular imagination as the sunken continent has done. Who knows what may be lying out there beneath the ocean?

7

Lemuria and Mu

While the idea of the sunken island-continent of Atlantis derived from a Platonic account of a supposed vanished civilization, the origins of the lost continent of Lemuria, supposedly lying somewhere beneath the Indian and Pacific Oceans, are slightly more complex. In many ways, too, its story is much more imaginative and fantastic. The myth of Lemuria does not take its origins from the writings of the ancient Greeks, rather its main thrust stems from around the mid-19th century.

This is not to say that no ancient accounts of a vanished land exist in the area. Legends among the Tamil people of Southern India speak of a submerged landmass lying between the most southerly part of India and Ceylon (Sri Lanka). Furthermore, a Tamil text, known as the *Cilappatikaram*, which is probably based on earlier Sangam works (the term Sangam refers to a corpus of Tamil literature and poetry probably compiled between 200 B.C. and A.D. 300, detailing many of the ancient legends and stories), which speaks of a country lying off the coast of Southern India that was overwhelmed by at least two inundations of the sea. The name it gives to this lost realm is Kumari Kandam, stating that it was once the home of a powerful trading civilization. It also speaks of the partial destruction of the ancient city of

Puhar (now the town of Poompuhar in Tamil Nadu, India), capital of the Chola Empire between 1,500 and 2,000 years ago (the Chola dynasty reigned in Southern India until the 13th century). Historians now think that this event may have been the result of an ancient tsunami, which destroyed part of the South India coast, and may have laid the foundations for a belief in a lost land in the area.

Further, some old Southern Indian legends speak of a group of strange people who lived on the southern tip of the country, and who spoke a strange language. They were darker skinned than the rest of the country, and have been classified as a race known as Davidian. They were supposed to be survivors from a sunken land, perhaps from Kumari Kandam. Interestingly enough, linguists have noticed certain distinctive traits among groups in the southwest sectors of India that are slightly different from the rest of the country. However, there is nothing to suggest that these are descended from the survivors of an ancient cataclysm.

Lemuria's Beginnings

But it was in the mid-1800s that the notion of lost Lemuria really came to prominence. The continent takes its name from a lemur, which was supposedly native to the land. Lemurs are largely nocturnal animals, today only found on the island of Madagascar and several surrounding islands, taking their name from the Latin *lemures*, meaning "spirits of the night." This may have referred to their night-time appearances and large reflective eyes. They are a species of primate known as protosimians, and are generally considered to have been the forerunners of simians, giving them an extremely long genetic pedigree. Fossils dating back to long ago have been found from Madagascar to India.

In 1864, the English lawyer and zoologist Philip Sclater became puzzled by the fact that although such fossils were found in Madagascar and certain parts of India, none were found in Africa or in the Middle East. He formed the theory that a continent had existed stretching from India to Madagascar, but not connecting with Africa. This continent he named Lemuria after the lemur fossils and, he argued, in some former time, lemurs had been very prolific there. The continent had probably, he continued, been overwhelmed by the sea in very early volcanic upheavals. The theory was greeted with some skepticism in the zoological world, but some naturalists chose to accept it because it seemed to explain the dispersal of some creatures across certain Eastern parts of the world. This was an age when the theories of Charles Darwin (concerning evolution) were increasingly coming to the fore, and an interest in both the survival and spread of species was focusing the academic interest. Sclater and others pointed to the old Tamil legend of an undersea continent as evidence for their assertions; for a long time it was often cited as a fact of prehistoric geography. However, the geologists could not agree on the actual size of the continent, or on the direction in which it lay—some arguing that it lay between India and Madagascar, others suggesting that it might link Asia with the Americas. Today, the theory has been disproved by our understanding of Earth's crust, and our knowledge of tectonic plates and continental drift. Although the theory had been increasingly accepted by a growing number of scientists, it was hastily abandoned in the mid-20th century. Notions of land bridges and sunken continents were discarded as new geological interpretations took hold. However, in 1999, a ship drilling in the Indian Ocean turned up evidence of a sunken land. Core drill samples revealed ancient pollen and traces of wood suggesting that a land, roughly about the third of the size of Australia, had once existed there, but was now beneath the ocean. More research on this ancient landmass needs to be carried out, but many authorities are doubtful that it was a land bridge over which animals crossed.

Key Players

It was during the 1880s that the name of Lemuria became prominent once more, this time in a non-scientific context. It was brought to prominence by alleged communications from an extremely remote part of the world—Tibet. And once more, Madame Blavatsky played a central role; just as she had done with the idea of Atlantis. Thanks to her, Lemuria would become celebrated in occult circles and would assume an air of arcane mystery, which would characterize it even today.

Madame Blavatsky was allegedly in touch with a number of Mahatmas, or "Great Souls"—men of incredible knowledge, who also had an awareness of the supernatural—dwelling in a remote region of Tibet, who communicated with her by telepathy. One of these, Master Koot Hoomi, revealed the true history of the world and the races (or "Root Races") that had dwelt on Earth before the coming of Mankind. Lemuria was home to a third of these races—an 8-foot-tall, hermaphroditic species that had been born from eggs. According to Madame Blavatsky, they had a low mental intellect, and were morally weak. When animals began to evolve on the Lemurian continent, a number of the species tried to mate with them. Outraged by this, the gods destroyed Lemuria by a massive deluge that completely submerged it and obliterated its inhabitants, replacing it with the fourth race of much more knowledgeable and morally upright beings, the Atlanteans. This knowledge, Blavatsky claimed, was to be found in the *Book of Dyzan*, an ancient collection of verse that had been passed down from prehistoric times, fragments that had somehow been shown to her by the Mahatmas. The knowledge from the book would form the basis of her work *The Secret Doctrine*. Although Madame Blavatsky's work has been dismissed as a fraud by many scholars, it is worth noting that certain similarities have been found in some of the verses of the *Book of Dyzan* and the *Tibetan Kalachakra*.

Madame Blavatsky's work opened the floodgates for all sorts of occult and "otherworldly" connections to Lemuria. In 1894, for example, an American writer, Frederick Spencer, published a book titled *A Dweller on Two Worlds*, in which he also made reference to the destruction of the continent. There had been, he claimed, survivors of the catastrophe who had made their way to Mount Shasta, a peak in the Cascade Mountain Range in northern California. These survivors, it claimed, were also in contact with beings from another world and were technologically and spiritually advanced—more so than humans. The Lemurians, Spencer went on to assert, lived in a series of underground complexes, connected by a network of tunnels, deep in the heart of the mountain, venturing out onto the surface only occasionally. They could be recognized as tall, graceful people, usually clad in flowing, white robes. There are many people today who claim to have met Lemurians on the slopes of Mount Shasta.

Mu and Other Legends

As occult interest in Lemuria grew, a number of other legends and theories concerning sunken lands became associated and, at times, intertwined

with it. One of these was, naturally, the notion of Atlantis, but there were others, too—the most notable being the legend of Mu.

Mu was another sunken land, supposedly lying somewhere beneath the Pacific. It had first been mentioned by the writer and traveler Augustus Le Plongeon (1826–1908) who had made a journey to the Yucatan Peninsula in Mexico where he had investigated some very ancient Mayan ruins. Le Plongeon, who had been born on the island of Jersey, and who was also considered something of an amateur archaeologist, announced that as a result of these investigations, he had found the Mayan people to be far older than the Greeks or the Egyptians. He had also stated that they had originated on a continent that was now lost, and to which he gave the name Mu. Although no great scientific importance was attached to his "findings," it was taken up by the British occultist James Churchward (1852–1936), who wrote a number of books, attempting to detail the history of the lost continent and attaching an occult significance to it. He had come across the information while traveling in India, where he had befriended an old priest who had shown him ancient parchments written in a dead language, which only a handful of people could understand (in fact, Churchward was to claim, that only three people in the entire Indian continent could translate it). The priest, who was one of these, taught him the language, and Churchward was able to translate the scrolls that revealed the history of Mu. The scrolls that had been copied from tablets composed by the Nacaal people—the forerunners of the Mayans—seemed to bear out Le Plongeon's assertions and hinted at great mysteries known to this ancient civilization. However, the scrolls were an incomplete record, and there was more knowledge to be had from the actual tablets themselves. Although Churchward was to publish his "translations" in approximately three volumes (he may also have privately published some diaries), his work is regarded at best as not being serious archaeological data, and at worst as spurious and fanciful; much of it still remains in print today.

The idea of Mu, however, became strongly entwined with the idea and mythology of Lemuria, and at one time the two imagined sunken lands were almost interchangeable. Lemuria became the center of dark practices that had been carried out by ancient peoples who had fathered races from the Mayans to the ancient Egyptians, and who had passed down "primordial secrets" to certain acolytes.

Such notions excited many science-fiction and horror writers of the 1920s and 1930s. It is said that it is on Lemuria rather than Atlantis that the writer H.P. Lovecraft based his horrendous sunken city of R'yleh where dead Cthulhu lies dreaming. This, too, is said to lie somewhere under the Pacific Ocean. Lovecraft also interestingly mentions Blavatsky's *Book of Dyzan* among the "nightmarish tomes" that were consulted by some of his protagonists. Another fantasy writer of the same period, Clark Ashton Smith, also set some of his stories concerning diabolism and Black Magic in Lemuria before it was "consumed by the seas." The interest in Lemuria by such writers only served to contribute to its reputation as "a dark and shadowed place" and the original home of various dark arts and evil sorceries.

Another strand of mythology that may have influenced Madame Blavatsky was the Hindu legend of the sunken land of Rutas, or Rama, which was said to lie in the depths of the Indian Ocean. This came to prominence in the works of the French lawyer Louis Jacolliot (1837–1890), who claimed to have translated some ancient Hindu fragmentary tablets that spoke of the vanished landmass. Similar to Mu, this was also a place of great mystery and sorcery, and may have been destroyed by cataclysmic forces raised by the experiments of its own wizards. Although Jacolliot was largely discredited, Blavatsky may have fixed on this legend, which is still related in some Hindu folklore; she added a reference to Rutas in her book *Isis Unveiled*.

Madame Blavatsky also added a further layer to the speculation surrounding the sunken continent, which has provoked yet a further line of speculation concerning it. In her book *The Secret Doctrine*, she mentions that Lemuria was once inhabited by a reptilian race that was almost (but not quite) humanoid. These creatures were great sorcerers, and it was their experiments with dark and evil forces that eventually led to the destruction of their civilization on the continent. This has led to a line of thinking known as the reptilian conspiracy, a set of conspiracy theories promulgated by such figures as the UFOlogist and lecturer John Rhodes and the former presenter and Green Party spokesman David Icke. They claim that, according to a confidant of Diana, Princess of Wales, members of the British Royal Family are shapeshifting reptilian beings, and that George W. Bush may be of the same bloodline.

The notion of an ancient reptile race is, however, nothing new. Stories of human-like reptiles with supernatural powers appear in many ancient traditions. In India, they are referred to as the Nagas, and predate human beings on the planet, while a version of the apocryphal *Book of Jasher* speaks of a serpent race dwelling in the Middle East. The legendary founder and first king of the city of Athens, Cecrops I (the name means "tail in the face") was supposedly half man, half lizard, and was allegedly "born out of the earth." And of course in the book of Genesis, it is the serpent creature that tempts Eve. Perhaps significantly, the Mayan god Gurumatz is portrayed as an upright, plumed serpent, and is probably the forerunner of the Aztec god Quetzalcoatl. In the Yucatan Peninsula, he was worshipped as the deity Kulkucan. Some traditions assert that these serpent-like beings, who would later become gods among humans, derived from the lost continent of Lemuria and survived when it sank. Some legends—which fed the conspiracy theorists—stated that these being were malevolent and were continually seeking to overthrow Mankind, which had supplanted them on Earth. However, it is thought that Madame Blavatsky viewed such creatures as highly intelligent, and her references to the "serpent race" or "serpent men" in her work were simply metaphors for skill and wisdom.

The New Age of Lemuria

Madame Blavatsky was not the only person to speak to the Mahatmas about ancient Lemuria. She was the inspiration behind a grouping dedicated to spiritual living and developing esoteric mysteries, known as the Theosophical Society (which at one time included the Irish writer and poet William Butler Yeats), which promoted many of her ideals. One of these, W. Scott-Elliot, also claimed to have spoken to the Mahatmas through a process known as "clairvoyant transmission," and in 1904 published works on both Atlantis and "lost Lemuria." In these, he revealed the end of the mighty continent. It had not, he declared, been destroyed in a single day and night as had Atlantis, but rather had disintegrated over a period of time. This had been caused by great volcanic activity deep underground, which led to eruptions and earthquakes on the surface. Lemuria was therefore "eaten away" by explosions before it finally sank beneath the waves. While Madame Blavatsky's "third root race" had been too slow-witted (and possibly too immoral) to escape, it is possible that some of the surviving serpent species (who still occupied portions of the continent) did, and this led to some serpent legends in the human world. Scott-Elliot's theories and assertions were largely dismissed, even by other Theosophists. However, he had left behind a vision of a great continent, which had been slowly destroyed from within, and had inevitably perished. Such a potent metaphor would sometimes be used by political groups—for example, some right-wing factions—to describe both Britain and the United States during the period leading up to World War II.

From around the 1930s until the 1950s (and even into the 1960s) much of Europe and North America enjoyed something of a boom in fantasy fiction. The austerity of the Great Depression, followed by World War II and the economic hardships of its aftermath, left the public hungering for tales of wonderful and awe-inspiring lands packed with color and adventure. And, of course, Lemuria with its whispers of an advanced civilization, Black Magic, and malignant serpent men fit into this idea admirably. Writers fixed on the idea of the sunken continent as it had been in its prime at the dawn of time. The works of H.P. Lovecraft and Clark Ashton Smith took on a new resonance, but other writers also came to the fore, such as Lyon Sprague de Camp (1907–2000), who sometimes mentioned the sunken land in their stories. Indeed, de Camp (always eager to debunk some of the pseudoscience and speculation of former years) went so far as to publish a book called *Lost Continents* in which he critically examined some of the popular myths and theories regarding places such as Atlantis, Lemuria, and Rutas. The book was updated in 1970 to take account of the geologist Alfred Wegener's theory of continental drift, first set out in 1812, and later published in his book *The Origin of Continents and Oceans* in 1915, which is largely accepted today. Sprague de Camp's book is still regarded as something of a classic of the genre.

But it was the fantasy writer Lin Carter (1930–1988) who firmly put ancient Lemuria on the map with his Thongor of Lemuria series. Written largely as a response to Robert E. Howard's successful Conan the Barbarian stories, Carter made his hero Thongor, a warrior of the House of Valkh in the prehistoric civilization of Lemuria, a powerful, sword-swinging soldier who traveled across the primal continent fighting vicious foes and supernatural evil wherever he found it. Some of his most persistent and formidable enemies were the Dragon Kings that ruled a part of the landmass, and this is perhaps reflective of the idea of a reptilian race who had ruled Lemuria in earliest times. The series, which extended into a number of volumes, was incredibly successful and firmly placed the idea of the sunken continent in the public mind. It also helped to give rise to a genre of fantasy writing known as "sword and sorcery"—set in mythological landscapes filled with battling (often barbarian) heroes who face magic and monsters almost on a daily basis—which encouraged other authors to write in a similar vein. This genre is still popular today in a large number of computer games.

Lemuria, then, has come a long way from a speculation on the dispersal of lemurs in the mid-19th century to a 21st-century computer game theme. Whether or not it actually existed as a historical place is not the point, rather it is the influence on the popular imagination that the idea of a sunken Pacific continent has exerted that is important. And, in this case, the notion of Lemuria is as potent as if the land truly did lie deep under the ocean's surface.

8

Lyonesse

Of all the sunken realms, perhaps the lost land of Lyonesse, submerged between the southwest tip of Cornwall, England, and the Isles of Scilly in the English Channel, has more historical evidence to back up its alleged existence than some others. Not only do we have some geological and emblematic evidence for its existence, but we also have at least a partial list of its kings. According to tradition, Lyonesse sank beneath the waves of what is now the English Channel somewhere around the middle of the 10th or 11th centuries. From all the towns and cities within its confines only one man survived—a gentleman by the name of Trevellyn who, leaping on a fast horse, outdistanced the waters and rode to what is now Cornwall, where he settled. The coat of arms of the Trevellyn family, which dates back to around this time, still depicts a rider on a horse emerging from the waves as a reminder of this event.

The History

The tradition of Lyonesse, however, stretches back before medieval times and quite possibly into Celtic times. Although it is generally now regarded as something of an extension of the Celtic Otherworld (similar to Avalon, with which it is sometimes confused), and has been incorporated into Arthurian mythology, there seems to be at least some historical evidence for a large landmass lying to the south of England.

The Isles of Scilly

That area is currently occupied by the Isles of Scilly—an archipelago of small, inhabited islands, most of which are the property of the British, administered through the Duchy of Cornwall. Though most of them are relatively small, accounts seem to suggest that in early times they may have been much bigger with a number of fairly substantial landmasses among them. The Romans, for example, know the region as Scillonia Insula—the sunny island, reflecting the balmy climate that is to be found there. It is possible, however, that there were one or two rather large islands with a scattering of smaller islets around them. If this is indeed the case, then the area corresponds to the Greek Cassiterides, or Tin Islands, in which Greeks and Phoenicians traded for one of the most valuable metals of the ancient world—tin. Indeed, so valuable was this commodity that Greek seamen and merchants based in the major trading port of Gades (Cadiz) in Northern Spain kept the location of this area a closely guarded secret. All that was disclosed was that they were a number of islands—including one or two major ones—that contained substantial tin mines, one or two large ports, and a number of towns and cities. According to this tradition, the largest of these islands was called Ennor, which had both a substantial settlement and a port from which tin could be shipped. The location of these islands (now the British Isles), which the Romans included as part of the Pretannic Isles, has since been lost. It has been suggested that what these ancient seafarers were referring to was a single, highly developed landmass that had the facilities for both trade and industry, perhaps slightly in advance of other parts of England. This, of course, may have nothing more than tall tales—the main industry on the Isles of Scilly is farming and agriculture, with little evidence of tin mining when compared to, say, neighboring Cornwall.

Other Island Accounts

This seems to be borne out by later Viking accounts of raids in the area—even into the ninth century. Accounts from the Norse oral tradition mention a large landmass with a rugged coastline and a number of small ports with a number of well-appointed farms, large monastic foundations, and possibly several towns. The inhabitants of this coastline were considered to be rather wealthy, and attacks on them yielded substantial amounts of cattle. However, it cannot be said with any certainty that this was a separate ancient kingdom that lay south of, and independent from, England.

Arthurian Legends

What is the legend and mythology surrounding Lyonesse, and how does it figure in the Arthurian tradition? The name of the country gives us little clue—it is generally taken to mean "Island of the Lion" (though who or what "the lion" might have been in an English Celtic culture is unclear). There is another Celtic tradition, however, that ascribes the name to a lady named Lyonesse, a cousin to King Arthur who was married to the knight Gareth of Orkney, one of Arthur's warriors. It is said that Arthur granted her lands in the south of the country to which she gave her name. Other versions of the tale relate how a lady named Lynette came to Arthur's court in order to gain aid for her sister Lyonesse who was queen of a far (or "foreign") country far south of England. In both versions of the story, these lands had been besieged by the Red Knight of the Red Lands (described in certain versions as "Sir Ironside"), and she asked Arthur to send a champion to defeat him. Instead, Arthur gave her a stablehand who had the name Beaumains (it was secretly Gareth of Orkney, but the king had disguised him as a punishment because Lynette would not reveal her sister's name). They set out, and on the way, they were attacked by several knights; during these conflicts Beaumains/Gareth distinguished himself with valour. They arrived at Lyonesse's castle and the champion defeated the Red Knight, but was wounded in the combat. It was Lyonesse who nursed him back to health and with whom he fell in love. They traveled back to Arthur's court to be married along with Lynette who married Gareth's brother, Sir Gaheris. Lyonesse's name, however, lived on in the name of the "southern land," and it was to this kingdom that Arthur is said to have fled, gravely wounded, after the Battle of Camlann in order to await death. This has, of course, led to confusion in Arthurian legend between Lyonesse and Avalon, another location to which he was supposed to be taken in order to be healed. Further confusion is added by the British poet and writer Alfred Lord Tennyson (1809–1892), who states in his Arthurian work *Idylls of the King* (printed in 1885), that Camlann (Arthur's final battle) was itself fought in Lyonesse. He further recounts the tale of Lynette and

Sir Gareth (albeit as an allegory of 19th century thinking), adding strength to this version of the legend.

In the early 12th century, the land of Lyonesse enters Arthurian mythology again. This probably derives from the poet Thomas of Britain, who is said to have composed a set of verses centered on the romantic hero and Knight of the Round Table, Sir Tristan, which were developed into a popular epic around the years 1155–1160. Thomas's epic is, of course, the basis for the Arthurian tragedy of Tristan and Iseult, which had become something of a classic of medieval literature. In some later texts, Tristan is described as a "Cornish knight" who falls in love with the Irish princess Iseult, but in the original work his birthplace is given as the land of Lyonesse. In fact, Tristan is described as the son of Meliodas, the second king of the country and the grandson of St. Felig (Felec or Felix), the saint-king who was Lyonesse's first ruler. It has been suggested that this idea arises not from a Cornish tradition, but rather from a Welsh one, and that much of what we know of Arthurian Lyonesse springs from Welsh legend and poetry. Certainly some of the supposed rulers of Lyonesse and their courtiers would appear to bear Welsh-sounding names.

Just to confuse matters even further, however, there may also be a Breton connection with the concept of Lyonesse. Some scholars have argued that the name has been confused with Leonaisse—a region in Brittany—although others have argued that this was a French name for the Lothian area in Scotland. It has also been suggested that the 140 churches and abbeys that dotted the land paid their tithes to the great Abbey at Cluny in Brittany, although there appears to have been no evidence for this.

Lyonesse appears in both English and Breton folklore, although in slightly different versions and with slightly different details. For example, in English myth, the name of its capital is given as Carlyon, which is presumably taken to mean "City of the Lions" whereas in Breton fable it is given as Ker Ys—"the city of Ys."

The marvelous and beautiful city of Ker Ys was said to lie submerged beneath the Seven Stones Reef off the English coast. In March 1967, the oil-tanker *Torrey Canyon* struck Pollard's Rock, a large outcropping, and was badly holed, creating a biological hazard on the Cornish and French coasts as tons of oil spilled out from her hold. Although divers were sent down of the

Reef to make her safe, no trace of any sunken buildings or ruins relating to Ker Ys were found anywhere in the vicinity. However, at Land's End there may be some stronger evidence of an undersea landmass at Mount St. Michael. The old Cornish name for this island rising out of the sea is Carrack Looz en Cooz, literally "the grey rock in the wood." The Mount was said to be the great hill where the last king of the Cornish giants, Cormoran, had his fortress, and where he was defeated by King Brute of Britain in prehistoric times. The hill was also supposed to have been surrounded by a mighty forest, which stretched all the way into Lyonesse and was, in later times, the hunting lands of the kings there. This forest was said to have been submerged when Lyonesse sank, and, at low tide, the stumps of a petrified woodland can still be seen, stretching out under the water, giving at least some credence to this assertion.

Both Cornish and Breton traditions contain a number of differences, and yet there is a third tradition that may have been invented as a "compromise" between these differing elements. It is said that following the disastrous Battle of Camlann against his illegitimate son Modred, reputed to have been in A.D. 537, a badly wounded Arthur and several of his knights fled to Lyonesse for safety. The country was low-lying and protected by dykes as in the Breton version. However, Arthur was pursued by Maelgwyn, Modred's second-in-command (Modred himself being wounded and dying), who then occupied the country. For a number of months, Maelgwyn ruled as a tyrant in Lyonesse, punishing the population there for having supported Arthur. In A.D. 538 it was secretly agreed among the people that the dykes should be opened and the country flooded in order to drive the invaders out. This was done, but the disaster turned out to be worse than anticipated, and many were drowned. Lyonesse itself was lost forever beneath the waves.

The Fall of Lyonesse

How, then, was Lyonesse destroyed? Again, the answer is complex because there are two big explanations set several centuries apart. The first is undoubtedly a Christian one, and may have been based on the history of an actual event. The story runs that somewhere in the early medieval period (about the ninth or 10th century), the inhabitants of Lyonesse had become so debauched and depraved that God decided to destroy them. He created a great wave with which He overwhelmed the entire land, consigning it to the ocean deeps forever. Everyone was killed except one man who had remained pure and Godly throughout his days. Here we revisit the story of Trevellyn, mentioned earlier in this chapter. But in this legend, instead of riding a horse, he was permitted to escape the destruction to reach the shore of Cornwall carrying some of the wealth of Lyonesse with him.

This story was popular around the late 1400s and early 1500s, and is clearly a moral fable. Lyonesse perished because of the wickedness of its inhabitants, but one Godly man was spared (similar to Noah in the fable of the Deluge) to perpetuate the line of the drowned country and gain wealth for himself and his family. The tale may also be based on the destruction on the major seaport of Dunwich on the Suffolk coast. In early times, Dunwich was one of the major trading ports in England, boasting a population of more than 3,000 people (big for an early medieval town), eight churches, and five houses belonging to religious orders. It traded wool with the Netherlands and furs with the Baltic region, and boasted a port that could take boats from all over the world. It was mentioned as a major center by both St. Felix of Burgundy and by the *Norman Doomsday Book* in 1086, which mentions it as an extremely important center of trade.

In 1286, however, part of the town was swept away into the sea during a severe winter gale, and the mouth of the River Dunwich was silted up. Trade began to fall away and in 1347, another severe storm destroyed more than 400 of the town's houses (most of which once more fell into the sea). The storms had further changed the nature of the coastline, and throughout the years, many of the houses that were left gradually slipped into the ocean by a process of long-shore drift. Today, Dunwich is little more than a tiny village, which is still being threatened by coastal erosion; and although it still formally has the status of a town, it is not even a shadow of its former importance in medieval times. Only the ruins of a large Franciscan abbey—Greyfriars—together with the remains of a leper hospice serve to give any memory of the town's status in the 13th century. Perhaps some memory of those 13th and 14th century catastrophes (and even others similar to them) found their way into English folklore, and became somehow intertwined with the concept of sunken Lyonesse.

This tale comes from a relatively late period when Christianity was well established in England, and suggests that the sinking of Lyonesse may have occurred somewhere around the ninth or 10th century. Other accounts place the disaster approximately 500 years earlier, in the fifth century.

The List of Kings

The list of the kings of the country, largely taken from Arthurian literature, is suggestive of fifth century Welsh tradition. The list itself, comprising four "known" kings, derives from a number of medieval English texts centred around the legend of Tristan (Tristram), together with a number of what appear to be later Italian works (usually variants on the central theme of the legend), which have all contributed to the *Prose Tristan*. It has been argued that the basis of these texts are Welsh and owe more to Welsh heroic fable than to any kings of a forgotten land. The first of the four "known" kings was Felig (who supposedly took the throne circa A.D. 445). There is great confusion about this particular monarch because he appears in several other guises: Felic, Felec, and Felix. Indeed, he may have also been a saint, as there are references to a St. Felix who may in fact have come from Wales. Is it possible, then, that the saint was also a king of Lyonesse? If so, he also appears to have been married with children. Indeed, the list states that his son, Meliodas ap Felig took the throne of Lyonesse around A.D. 475. He was succeeded by his son Tristan (or Tristram) Fawr, Tristan the Elder, in A.D. 510. This is the famous Sir Tristan who appears in the Arthurian legend, and in the tragedy of Tristan and Iseult. He is described as a "warrior king" and a great hero. The last, and fourth, king mentioned is Tristan's son, Tristan Fychem, Tristan the Younger, who became monarch in A.D. 537 and was apparently on the throne when Lyonesse was overwhelmed that year. There are also hints in English texts about earlier kings of the region, but if there were any, their names are lost both to history and mythology. Gradlon, however, who appears as the last king in the Breton tradition, is not mentioned, nor are any of his predecessors.

Gradlon

The Breton story, however, holds a number of interesting features. Gradlon had only one child, his daughter, Dahut, who was greatly indulged and spoiled. At the time of its destruction, Lyonesse, similar to Holland, was below sea level, but was protected by a series of dams and tidal barriers. Gradlon himself was the only person in the entire kingdom who had keys to the gates and could let the sea in. He was supposedly an extremely good and kind man, and had built the main city of Lyonesse—Ker Ys—into a center of art and culture as well as a notable trading center. His weakness, however, was Dahut. The princess, it is said, was a wilful and spiteful girl. Her mother, according to the legend, had been Malgven, Queen of Hyperborea, who herself had been a wild and temperamental woman. She had died not long after Dahut's birth and Gradlon (described as an old man) had lavished every available excess on his daughter. Moreover, he had turned a blind eye to her tantrums and spitefulness.

A change had come to Lyonesse during Gradlon's reign. Christianity had arrived in the country under the auspices of St. Guenole, who had come from Brittany. Dahut tolerated the saint, but became incensed by the growing influence of another Christian—Corentin, Bishop of Quimper in Brittany—over her father. She accused the Bishop of turning Ker Ys into a dull and boring place. She, herself, favored the old Celtic Pagan ways, and was reputed to take a lover each night from among the male population of Lyonesse in a sort of ritualistic frenzy. During their love-making, she made them wear a silken mask, which, as soon as the rays of the rising sun touched it, turned into iron claws and tore the face from the unfortunate victim before killing him. Angered by the spread of the Christian faith and her father's growing reliance on Coretin, Dahut resolved to destroy the realm and escape to Cornwall. While Gradlon was asleep, she took the keys from him and opened several of the locks on the gates. Water started to seep through. Realizing what she was doing, St. Guenole tried to stop her, but the old man was not strong enough. As the water began to rise, the saint ran to save the old monarch. Taking a swift steed, he pulled Gradlon into the saddle, but the king would not leave without his daughter, even though he knew that she had brought about the disaster. The three of them began to gallop toward distant Cornwall, but their progress was too slow, and the encroaching water

was rapidly overtaking them. Suddenly, Dahout either fell or was pushed by St. Guenole from the galloping horse. Unable to turn and save her, they galloped on, outdistancing the water, until they reach Cornwall. There, Gradlon was granted refuge with his kinsman, King Mark of Cornwall, but his kingdom was lost forever beneath the ocean and most of its inhabitants drowned. It is said that St. Guenole was revered in the region of Landevennec in Finestaire in Brittany, but he may also be known as St. Winwallow, who was worshipped in the area around Landewednag at the Lizard in Cornwall. There is a great religious affinity toward these saints from the fishermen of both locations; they often share worship, sometimes remembering Lyonesse in the course of their prayers. Dahout, however, continued to live—at least in both the mythologies of Cornwall and Brittany—but as a spectre or monster of the sea. She is said to dwell among the rocks and reefs of the English Channel, singing songs that will lure unwary sailors to their doom.

The concept of Lyonesse, the vanished kingdom, had tantalized the imaginations of both writers and poets through the ages and even into modern times. Fantasy writers in particular have sometimes developed the theme of a sunken land lying somewhere off the coast of Britain. The most celebrated of the works incorporating this idea is probably Jack Vance's *The Lyonesse Trilogy* in which he depicts the lost kingdom as part of the Elder Isles. The sunken country also appears in Stephen Lawhead's *Pendragon Cycle*, written between 1987 and 1999, and it may well have served as a model for J.R.R. Tolkein's land of Numenor, a place that coexists with Middle Earth. In the 1995 film *First Knight*, Leonesse is the land from which the central heroine Guinevere comes—she is described in the film as "The Lady of Leonesse," although this is not a sunken land. Rather, it is a buffer zone ruled by her father that lies between the kingdom of Arthur and that of his implacable enemy Maleagant. But the name of the kingdom has obviously been borrowed from the Lyonesse mythology to give it some sort of authentic chivalric and medieval feel.

So does the lost land lie below the ocean somewhere off the coasts of Cornwall and Brittany? It is said that at some future date, one of the signs heralding the return of King Arthur will be when this sunken land rises from the depths of the sea in all its former glory. However, with the threat of global warming and the rise in sea levels along the French and English coasts, it might be more likely that already existing land locations along the shores will one day be joining it beneath the mysterious waters of the English Channel.

9

Davy Jones's Locker

Almost everybody, whether seafarer or landlubber, has heard of Davy Jones's Locker. Recently, the name has become even more relevant with the release of the extremely popular film *The Pirates of the Caribbean: Dead Man's Chest* starring Johnny Depp and Orlando Bloom. Bill Nighy appears as the eponymous Davy Jones. In the films, he appears as a sort of evil, Cthulhu-like figure. He is a commander of the doomed, ghostly ship *The Flying Dutchman*, which is intent on dragging both pirates and sea-travelers to some unknown lair. But just how accurate is the movie representation, and who exactly was Davy Jones?

The Birth of Davy Jones

The name "Davy Jones's Locker" has been used since the 1700s (and perhaps even earlier) to denote the deepest point of the ocean. It was also used as a euphemism for death by drowning at sea (that is, "being taken to Davy Jones's Locker"). The notion of such a place has a strong ideological connection with the concept of the Otherworld because it is supposed to be a region where the spirits of drowned sailors gathered. No real or coherent description of it exists, although some legends have tried to paint a picture of what it might be like. It has been described, for instance, as a great hall in which the spirits of the dead sailors are held in great water-filled glass jars for eternity. In other descriptions, it is said to be a narrow chamber, filled with clutter and ships' tackle in which the sailors' spirits are held in small bottles, thrown among the litter. In other accounts, it is described as a place of eternal torment in which the dead are forced to work ceaselessly, watched over by the terrible Davy Jones—a synonym for the Devil.

The literary history of the term, however, stretches back to the early 18th century. Perhaps the first mention of it is found in a work by the writer Daniel Defoe (more famous for his work *Robinson Crusoe*) entitled *The Four Years Voyages of Captain George Roberts*, which contains the phrase "heaving the rest into David Jones's Locker." This is suggestive of some sort of doom or death, and is probably used to evoke the idea of a mass drowning at sea. A slightly more detailed description of it is to be found in Tobias Smollet's *Adventures of Peregrine Pickle* (1751). Here Smollet notes:

> This same David Jones according to sailors is the fiend that presides over all the evil spirits of the deep and is often seen in various shapes, perching amongst the rigging on the eve of hurricanes, ship-wrecks and other disasters to which the sea-faring life is exposed, warning the devoted wretch of death and woe.

In this case, David (Davy) Jones appears as a harbinger of disaster and death, a figure who, like the Irish banshee, appears to those who are likely to die in order to warn them of their approaching fate. A further reference is made by the American writer Washington Irving, in 1824, in an obscure work titled *The Adventures of the Black Fisherman*. However, here, there is only a passing reference to the Locker:

> He came, said he, in a storm and he went in a storm; he came in the night and he went in the night; he came, nobody knows whence and he has gone nobody knows where. For aught I know, he has gone to the sea once more on his chest and may land to bother some people on the other side of the world, though it is a thousand pities, he added, if he had gone to Davy Jones' Locker.

In the extract, it would appear that the Locker is the eventual destiny of dark and evil seamen who trouble folk both on the sea and land. It therefore becomes a euphemism for Hell or for some region that receives the black souls of the evil drowned.

But exactly who was Davy Jones, and why is his name linked with a dark and destructive Otherworld? And why has he become something of a demon of the sea? Many sailors decline to talk about him, even today, for fear of some supernatural retribution, but there have been a number of theories.

Naming Davy

The first is that the name is a combination of two names: the Devil and Jonah. The latter, of course, was a biblical prophet from the Galilean village of Gath-hepher, near Nazareth, who was instructed by God to preach destruction to the wicked city of Nineveh. However, Jonah disobeyed the instructions and, refusing to go to Nineveh, took passage on a ship bound for the coastal city of Tarshish, in an attempt to escape God's anger. It was a fruitless flight, for God created a storm that threatened to destroy the vessel. Fearing a shipwreck, the terrified sailors identified Jonah, who was asleep in the forward part of the ship, as the source of their danger. In order to save themselves from God's wrath, they threw the prophet overboard whereupon he was swallowed by a great whale. In the belly of the creature, Jonah repented and was spat out on the shoreline. However, among sailors his name became synonymous with bad luck, or with a person who brings bad luck onto a ship. It was therefore believed that if there was a "Jonah" on board, whether a passenger or member of the crew, the ship would ultimately perish on its voyage, or some terrible disaster would befall it and everyone on it. Therefore, the name "Jonah" became associated with doom and death among seafaring folk; even mentioning it invited some form of misfortune. It is therefore thought that combining the name Jonah with that of the Devil, (whose name could also not be mentioned on board) formed a kind of "code" in a proper name—David or Davy Jones. This allowed, according to the theory, the possibility of both Jonah and the Devil to be discussed onboard the ship. The idea that the Devil could claim the souls of mariners who died at sea was also prevalent, and the concept of a chamber or "locker" (as used by a ship's crew to store their valuables) came into play. This was where the Devil stored the souls he had claimed until the great Judgement Day. Thus, Jones became an amalgam of both Jonah, who destroyed boats by visiting

God's wrath upon them, and the Devil, who claimed the souls of the drowned unfortunates; his "locker" was an extension of Purgatory or the Otherworld.

Celtic Beliefs

There may also be a Celtic connection with the figure of Davy Jones. Celtic mariners believed in an entity known as the Fir (or Far) Liath. The name simply means "the Grey Man," and was considered to be a euphemism for a thick fog, sometimes known as "the Grey Man's Breath." Sometimes more deadly than a storm, a deep and clinging fog could ensure that a ship ran aground or onto rocks, and all of its crew drowned. The malign intelligence behind this was the Grey Man, a gigantic, cloudy being (sometimes described as being blind) whose ultimate purpose was the destruction of seafarers. So feared was this entity that sometimes boats in both Scotland and the North of Ireland had holy medals built into their prows to protect them and their crews from harm and malign attentions of the Fir Liath. In fact, even today, boats from Tory Island, off the coast of Donegal, still carry a small jar of soil blessed by the king of the Island (the Kingship of Tory was established by St. Columcille and has remained unbroken to this day) in their prows in order to protect them from beings such as the Fir Liath. And near the town of Ballycastle, there was a rock ledge known as the Grey Man's Path (photographed in the early 1900s by the photographer Robert Welch) along which this entity was supposed to travel when it came ashore. The name of this entity could not be uttered on board a vessel for fear of attracting it; so could the name Davy Jones be used instead?

Welsh Beliefs

Attractive though this theory is, there have also been a number of other suggestions as to the origin of Davy Jones's Locker. The name David (or Davy) Jones sounds rather Welsh, and attempts have been made to link it with St. David, who is the patron saint of Wales. According to some traditions, David, alone among British national saints, struck a bargain with God that each Welshman would know the time and manner of his death, and that the Welsh would be spared the judgement of the Almighty until the actual Judgement Day. Thus, "David Jones" (a combination of the saint's name and a common Welsh name) appears to Welsh mariners as a warning or harbinger of approaching doom or death by drowning, and his "Locker" becomes some place akin to Purgatory where the souls of the Welsh are held until they can be judged and receive their final reward or punishment. Gradually, this concept extended to all sailors, and "Davy Jones" became synonymous with drowning and destruction.

Other traditions, however, suggest that the name and place may have nothing to do with Welshmen, saints, or Christianity. They assert that it has more to do with the West Indies and Caribbean areas than any part of Christian Europe. The name is not "Davy" but "duppy," a Creole word for a ghost, phantom, or dark and malignant spirit. The name "Jones" was simply added by English pirates who prowled through the Caribbean in the late 17th and 18th centuries. "Davy Jones," then, becomes a Creole ghost that often appears during storms and hurricanes, and is closely associated with Caribbean witchcraft and Black Magic. The "Locker" becomes either a remote island in the ocean or an undersea cave where the ghost stores the spirits of its victims and feeds upon them. It preys on boats and ships traveling through the Indies, carrying away the souls of mariners and leaving only destruction in its wake. Somewhere around the 16th and 17th centuries, the Caribbean tradition found its way into more Westernized folklore and took on symbolism and nuances more suited to European maritime ideas. "Duppy" became "Davy" and the surname "Jones" seems to have been added at some later date.

"Captain" Davy Jones and Other Monikers

These are some of the interpretations of the idea, but the name Davy Jones is suggestive of an actual person. So was there ever an actual historical figure who could have given his name to the tradition? According to some sources, there was apparently an actual pirate captain (perhaps a Welshman) named David Jones who operated in the Caribbean during the 1630s. Other accounts place him slightly later, around the 1660s, saying that he operated out of Port Royal, Jamaica, and his main targets were Spanish and Portuguese trading ships bound for the New World. However, he was not a pirate of any great note, and his career was so short that it is unlikely he achieved sufficient status to give him this sort of global notoriety; there is no mention of the infamous Locker.

It has also been suggested that the name Davy Jones is derived from an old English sea chanty (shanty) or work song, sung by sailors on board ships as they performed monotonous duties. The song in question dates from around 1594 and is titled "When Jones's Ale Is Newe." It is said to refer to a pub landlord named Jones who kept a locker full of extremely fine ale, specifically for the refreshment of parched sailors, which he liberally dispensed when they were in port. The thought of this fine ale, immortalized in song, kept the sailors working as their tasks crept into other aspects of their lives— such as a superstitious dread of the turbulent seas. However, this is questionable, as the original song "Jones's Ale" seems to have been a land-based work song (also known as "The Jolly Tinker") that may or may not have transferred to the sea. Certainly in the initial renditions, the occupations referred to are land-based trades.

> There were four jovial fellowes,
> Came o'er the hills together,
> Came o'er the hill together,
> To join our jovial crew,
> And they ordered their pints of beer,
> And bottles of good sherry,
> To carry them o'er the hills so merry,
> When Jones's ale is new.
> When Jones's ale is new me lads…

The four trades referred to among "the jovial fellowes" are tinker, mason, dyer, and soldier ("with a flintlock on his shoulder"). Notice that there is not a sailor among them; this suggests that this was probably a land-based country song in its original form. It is further suggested that the name is not in fact "Jones's Ale," but "Joan's Ale," and that this referred to a brewery run by a woman on the south coast of England.

There is no doubt, however, that some of these songs and ballads would later become sea chantys, and were used to regulate work and boost morale on long and monotonous voyages. It may well have been that "Joan's Ale" became "Jones's Ale," and was used as a "capstan song" (a capstan being a manually operated winch) or a "short drag chanty" used when "hauling a bowline" (pulling on a rope to extend a heavy sail). But it may not have been used on many ships (the favorite short drag chanty of the 18th and early 19th centuries being "Haul Away Joe," a specific seafaring song) and its association with Davy Jones and his Locker is unclear.

The most common suggestion is that the name referred to a notorious pub landlord in Cornwall who worked closely with the Impressment Parties, or Press Gangs. During the 18th and part of the 19th centuries, when England and France were at war and both navies were often short of men, ship captains were entitled to "impress" any able-bodied man they could find in any port into service. This was done in England by offering the "King's Shilling" to young men whom the captain encountered in any English port. The recipient would then go willingly into naval service; however, the reality was far different. When a ship needing crew docked at a port, the captains often sent an Impressment Party, or Press Gang, ashore. This group visited most pubs and alehouses in the area. There they would engage young men in conversation, buy them strong drink until they passed out, slip the shilling in their pocket—a token of their agreement to service—and carry them back on board ship. By the time the young men sobered up, the ship was under sail and bound for some far destination. Many of these unfortunates were destined never to see their wives, sweethearts, or families again. If the young men were able to hold their drink, the bosun usually carried a "belaying pin," a stout cudgel with which he would knock the unfortunate victims unconscious and carry them away. Some of these Press Gangs had arrangements with certain coastal pub landlords who supplied them with likely young men in exchange for payment. David Jones seems to have been one of these unscrupulous tavern-keepers. According to the legend, he had a large ale locker, a vast chamber in which he kept his kegs of liquor. He also used this to imprison young men whom he got drunk on his premises and shut them in the chamber in order to sell them to the Press Gangs. By these means, he made himself a substantial fortune and was able to retire a wealthy man; however, his name was reviled by sailors everywhere who knew about his dastardly schemes. It soon became associated with doom and misfortune and was ultimately linked to that of the Devil. In time, David (Davy) Jones became a foul spirit and an agent of the Devil in his own right.

Locating the Locker

But where was this Locker located? Many sources simply state that it is "in the deepest part of the sea"; other traditions, however, link it with another persistent legend of the sea—that of the ghost ship the *Flying Dutchman*. This was reputedly a phantom vessel that sailed the seas for all Eternity, its captain cursed by God and refused by the Devil. In the film *Pirates of the Caribbean: Dead Man's Chest*, the *Flying Dutchman* is the home of Davy Jones, and a vessel crewed by the damned—those souls consigned to eternal torment. However, this is to misunderstand the context because, although long associated with a ghostly vessel, the *Flying Dutchman* may not be a ship at all, but a person.

The Real *Flying Dutchman*

Bernard Fokke was apparently born near the port of Rotterdam in the Netherlands sometime around the mid-17th century. Later in life, he would become a sea captain in the service of the Dutch East India Company, commanding a number of ships on their behalf. Fokke became something of a legend because of the speed of his voyages between Holland and the island of Java on the other side of the world. In fact, he could usually make the trip much faster than any other captain. Not only this, but he appeared to be able to successfully navigate the particularly turbulent seas around the Cape of Good Hope, which had wrecked many other vessels. There were whispers among his rivals that he had conspired with the Devil to achieve such record speeds. He was nicknamed, however, De Vliegende (Fleigende) Hollander— the Flying Dutchman—and though no name is ever given for his vessel, it was said that as long as Fokke was commanding, it was the fastest vessel on the East Indies route. It is unclear as to exactly when Fokke's nickname transferred to his vessel or as to when it became equated with a ghost ship. This phantom was, allegedly, always trying to clear the seas around the Cape of Good Hope, the route that Fokke himself had traveled many times. In early seafaring tales there is no connection between the Dutchman and Davy Jones's Locker.

The popularization of the Dutchman legend seems to have arisen from a story in *Blackwoods Magazine* in 1821, which made general reference to it as "lore of the sea," and refers to a ghostly ship that had originated in the port of Amsterdam in Holland. It was then used as a central theme in Captain Fredrick

Marryatt's *The Phantom Ship* (published in 1839), which describes her Master as Captain Philip Vanderdecken (meaning "of the decks"). This was amended later to Hendrick Van der Decker, possibly to make him sound more Dutch. Perhaps the most famous rendition of the legend is in the opera "Der Fleigende Hollander" by Richard Wagner, first performed in 1843, which seems to have set the motif of a doomed ship commanded by an undead captain in the public mind.

In his 1855 tale *The Flying Dutchman on the Tappan Sea*, the American writer Washington Irving switches the name of the captain yet again. This time his name is given as Ramhout Van Dam, supposedly a native of Amsterdam. Other names include Captain Falkenbrug, and one tradition even makes him a German (though this may have been amended by the British and Allies during World War I). The story is a simple one: the captain of the Dutchman finds it difficult to round the Cape of Good Hope because of a fearful tempest, and he threatens God that he will attempt the task "should it take from now until the Day of Judgement." God accepts the challenge and the captain is doomed forever to sail the often stormy seas around the Cape. Later, the location was extended to "all the Seven Seas," and many claim to have seen the phantom vessel in many parts of the world—even the future King George V of England claimed to have seen it! Yet at no time was the ghostly ship linked with Davy Jones or given as a location of his Locker—so perhaps the Pirates of the Caribbean filmmakers have got it wrong!

One last point needs to be made: Davy Jones is not always seen as a malignant spirit. During a ceremony known as "crossing the line" (when a vessel crosses the Equator), which is performed on some ships, a figure appears on deck representing Neptune, the Roman god of the sea. Davy Jones sometimes accompanies him as Neptune's son and Lord of the Sea Creatures. This is not strictly true, as Neptune's son was called Triton, and had the power to shift his shape when he chose. Nevertheless, the ceremony serves to underline the importance of Davy Jones.

So do Davy Jones and his famous Locker actually exist? Or are they just extensions of human imagination concerning death and drowning at sea? Similar to many aspects of the Otherworld, such ideas can serve to create a wonderful, speculative world for us—a world in which all things are possible, and which can inspire great literature and film. It is a world that lies just beyond the borders of our perceptions, and which is as timeless and limitless as the ocean itself.

Section 999: Vanished Realms and Cities

Vanished Realms and Cities

Travel, they say, broadens the mind, but in the early and medieval worlds, it also fed the imagination. In these eras, much of the globe was unknown and considered dangerous; consequently, the majority of people did not travel very far. Most had not ventured far beyond their own communities and even when they did travel, it was in limited and prespecified parameters. By comparison, for ancient Greeks or for medieval Europeans, traveling to distant countries and lands would be the equivalent of journeying to other planets within the solar system in the present day. The world beyond the known sphere was both mysterious and hostile. Even lands such as Ireland were incredibly strange and bizarre to the English—even right up until the 18th century. Following a book on Ireland written in 1187 by Geraldus Cembrensius (who had briefly visited the country in 1185), it was widely believed that all Irishmen had axes growing out of their hands with which they attacked their neighbors, that all Irish women had the ability to change themselves into hares or stoats, and that fish with golden teeth swam in several of the lakes and rivers of the country. These may seem strange and impossible now, but for those who had never been to Ireland, they appeared to be true. Even as late as the mid-1600s, pamphlets were circulating in London describing the Irish as cannibals, dressed in skins and living in mud-huts; while these were produced for political purposes (to justify an English military presence in Ireland), such allegations about the country were taken to be true by an English populace who had never been there.

Those who had actually traveled to unknown regions were often regarded with awe by their peers. They had seen things that nobody else had, and they had knowledge denied to everybody else. In many cases, it was believed, they had faced dangers that could barely be imagined by most people. This, of course, gave them an increased status within the communities in which they lived, and it was in their own interests to expand and exaggerate upon what they had seen in order to impress those around them; the limits of these lands corresponded only with the limits of the storyteller's imagination. Thus, fabulous cities began to emerge in far-away lands; fabulous beasts, the like of which were never seen before, started to roam distant forests; bizarre peoples, with even stranger ways and customs, came to inhabit lands in some other part of the world. And in an era when there was little widespread travel, who was there to disprove or challenge such tales? They became widely accepted—a vision of the world that was taken to be a reality rather than a fancy.

Many of these stories were extremely tall. In Greek and Roman times, the unknown oceans that lay beyond the Pillars of Hercules (the Straits of Gibraltar) at the edge of the familiar Mediterranean were filled with monsters and demons that waited to lure sailors into their clutches. And the ancient cultures of the Mediterranean were not the only ones to view the distant areas of their world with suspicion and trepidation. Medieval and early modern Europe, looking toward the Americas, Africa, and Asia, also absorbed tales of monstrous beings, strange civilizations, and bizarre lands across the globe. Far-off cities, it was said, were made of gold; on certain islands in the Pacific, some natives' ears were so long that they could sleep on one while using the other as a blanket; in other towns, the inhabitants hopped about on only one leg. Such places owed either more to the fancies of the traveler, or were crude interpretations of what they actually had seen. Those who did travel to foreign lands—particularly to places such as the Pacific and the

Far East—undoubtedly saw strange and unfamiliar things, which they tried to understand themselves and convey to those in their own communities. In order to do this, perhaps, a little bit of imagination or hyperbole was added. Thus, say, an Indian fakir who stood for a long period on one leg might be described by a traveler as a "one-legged man from a race of one-legged men"; African tribesmen with elongated earlobes might be described as men (and women) with exceptionally long ears on which they might be able to sleep on or use for a blanket. Amazing and imaginative stories concerning distant lands became treated as fact and as part of the geography and interpretation of the developing world.

As exploration and discovery began to unlock the secrets and mysteries of the Earth, some of these tales simply passed into the realm of folktale and story. Some mysteries actually deepened. Who, for example, had built legendary cities, hidden deep in the jungles? What race had erected great constructions in remote mountain valleys? However, gradually the world became a much more familiar place.

The English Victorian age of exploration throughout the 19th century ventured into corners of the globe that had previously been untouched, and which had generated an air of mystery. Victorian explorers (along with American, French, and Spanish) gradually dispelled some of the mystery; even so, some regions remained remote and secret. Some of them even remained so until the 20th century.

Places such as the kingdom of Tibet shut away in the mountains of the Himalayas remained both inaccessible and intriguing. This was a place of magic and wonder where venerable, all-knowing monks in isolated monasteries guarded secrets and marvels that had been long since lost to the modern world. The poverty and hardship of actual Tibetan life were overlooked as this image took hold of the Western mind. During the 1930s and 1940s (even, in some instances as late as the 1950s and 1960s), Tibet was looked upon in both Europe and America as a repository of ancient lore and knowledge. It became an exotic locale—inaccessible and tantalizing, hiding a knowledge that might perhaps revolutionize the world. Even though it was annexed by Communist China between 1949 and 1951, and life there became even harsher and more uniform in nature, Tibet lost nothing of its mystical allure in the Western mind. Remote monasteries, it was believed, had somehow escaped the Communist influence, and maintained ancient ways and traditions, preserving their secrets despite the prevailing regime. In fact, the closure of Tibetan borders by the Chinese authorities only added to the sense of mystery and legend. Indeed, in the 1960s, Tibet became a mystical focus for the "hippy culture" in both Europe and America; many young people followed a "trail" to the nearest large city they could reach: Kathmandu, Nepal. Although some Western views of Tibet have changed throughout the years, some of the mystical associations with that remote country still remain.

A similar perception has also existed regarding South America. Large areas of Brazil and Bolivia still lie swathed in largely inaccessible jungle and, through the years, this too has generated its own mythology. Similar to Tibet, there was much speculation about what might lie deep in the heart of the rainforest, and what secrets the thicket and creepers might conceal. Some stories hinted at lost cities or lost jungle kingdoms that had flourished long before the coming of Europeans, and now retreated into the jungle. There was talk of advanced civilizations that had hidden themselves away and shunned the rest of the world that lay beyond their protective green wall. Some even claimed that these had been founded by survivors from places such as Atlantis and Lemuria.

Interest often focused on areas such as the seemingly impenetrable Mato Grosso region of Brazil. The name simply means "thick forest," and its inaccessibility made it a prime candidate for tales of vanished kingdoms and lost civilizations. Soon, truly imaginative tales of highly technological cities existing side by side with prehistoric monsters, left over from the dawn of time, came to be associated with the area. Much of this vision stems from the writings of the science-fiction and fantasy writing of the early part of the 20th century—particularly Sir Arthur Conan Doyle's *The Lost World* (published in 1912), which placed a group of adventurers on a lost plateau in South America that was inhabited by ape-men and giant, flesh-eating lizards. Other writers had domed cities housing a futuristic society, tucked away amidst the undergrowth. The speculation was further exacerbated by a number of expeditions into the jungle that failed to return. Such failure may have been due to explainable reasons—native or wild animal attack or disease—but they served to fuel ideas of lost civilizations that had somehow captured the explorers and were holding them as prisoners or slaves deep in the South

American fastness. Such speculation was the stuff of adventure stories, and it certainly stoked the popular imagination. Although much of the Mato Grosso and the upper part of the River Amazon have largely been explored today, some of that old mystery still lingers.

South America was not the only place to hold mysterious forests and hidden valleys. North America also had such features in its rich and varied landscape. Even today, certain areas of the country remain largely unexplored. Parts of Wyoming are thickly forested, as are some regions in New England, while along the Kentucky/Tennessee border unused Indian trails lead away into dark forests to deep and remote valleys. In the remote Rutherford Mountain Country, on the border along the Little Piney and Squaw Rivers, for example, many of these trails are almost impassable; communities there tend to be widely scattered and the people claim direct and unbroken lineage from pioneers and Revolutionary War communities. They have, say some accounts, "strange and folk ways." There are tales here of lost "kingdoms" hidden away in the wilderness, dating back to the time when America was born as a nation. Some believe they are still ruled by old close-knit families of European descent. Such places have little or no contact with the outside world. Whether such stories are simply legends, or whether there is a grain of truth to them, the idea of, say, a Puritan society tucked away in some remote valley, living and behaving as it did in Colonial times, has always appealed to writers and filmmakers—one of the most recent offerings being M. Night Shyamalan's *The Village* (2004). Perhaps part of this perception is based on the Amish peoples of Pennsylvania who maintain a 19th century society in Lancaster County just south of Philadelphia, and whose strict Anabaptist religion instructs them to largely shun the rest of the world even today.

Tales of unknown, opulent, and sometimes rather bizarre cities and kingdoms have existed through the years—from the tall stories of medieval travelers to the quasi-scientific investigations of strange and anomalous historical phenomena. And who is to say that some of these realms did not exist? Who is to say that out there, in some remote corner of the globe, there is still an undiscovered country awaiting contact with the known world? Our knowledge of our planet may not be as complete as it might first appear!

10

Shangri-La

In Britain, during the 1960s and 1970s, the most common name for the property to which people retired after a lifetime's work was either "Mon Repose" or "Shangri-La"; the latter was also the name of many seaside boarding houses where people came for a holiday and a rest. The name Shangri-La was suggestive to the popular mind as a place of relaxation, contentment, and peace, away from the strains and stresses of the everyday world. Even today, we still speak of finding "our own private Shangri-La" to which we can escape in time of personal crisis, if need be. But did such a place exist? If so, was it such a haven of peace? Where was it supposed to be?

Early Writings

The popularity of the name Shangri-La comes from the extremely successful 1937 Frank Capra film *Lost Horizon*, which in turn was based on the 1933 novel of the same name, written by Englishman James Hilton (1900–1954). At the time of writing, Hilton was already famous for his novel of English school life called *Goodbye Mr. Chips*, and *Lost Horizon* has been often seen as continuing his theme of "Britishness" and the "stiff upper lip" in times of adversity. The film, which starred 1930's heartthrob Ronald Coleman, told the story of a group of travelers who, fleeing civil unrest in

China, were hijacked on a small plane, which ran out of fuel and crashed in the Himalayas, killing their abductor. The survivors were rescued and taken to an idyllic and peaceful valley, hidden and shielded from the outside world by the mountain chain. There they find peace, contentment, and love, well away from the threat of war that is brewing elsewhere. Shangri-La is a place of tranquility, solitude, and serenity. Is it any wonder that many holiday and retirement places were named after it?

Tibet and Buddhist Folklore

Hilton had, however, based his Shangri-La on the legend of Shambhala (Shambalah or Shambalha), a lost kingdom somewhere deep in the Himalayas, which is mentioned in Tantric Buddhist folklore. This is said to be the source of the Kalachakra Tantra, which is one of the core texts of Vajrayana Buddhism. This form of Buddhist teaching places emphasis on the Yidam or Buddha-form, which can be brought about by the individual through meditation and contemplation; it therefore takes on a slightly more immediate nature than the long meditative route of conventional Buddhism. Some have argued that this particular form of Buddhism originated in Tibet; for others the thinking began in Shambhala or Shangri-La. According to traditional legend, King Suchandra, one of the earliest kings of Shambalah or Shangri-La (then, according to the legend, located in northwest India) requested a special teaching from the Buddha, which would allow him to achieve divine enlightenment while not renouncing some of his worldly pleasures. In reply, the Buddha granted him the Kalachakra, which Suchandra then circulated in parts of Pakistan and Tibet, where it later became a major tenet of Tibetan Buddhism.

Zhang Zhung

Shangri-La was also considered to be one of the great centers of the Zhang Zhung (or Shang Shung) culture of central Tibet. This culture predated the coming of Buddhism and was comprised of 18 kingdoms in what is now central and western Tibet, centered around Mount Kailash (or Gangs Rin-po-cho in Tibetan, meaning "sacred jewel of the snows"). Interestingly, the mountain also appears in Hindu folklore, where it is called Kailasa, and is regarded as Paradise or Utopia, the epitome of everything that is good and pure. The Zhang Zhung culture, however, was served by the Bon religion, a belief system that predated Buddhism in Tibet. This was a mixture of early Hinduism, primitive Buddhism, Shamanism, and spirit worship, and was said to be the religion of the central Tibetan kingdoms since early times. According to tradition, it was certainly the main faith of the Zhang Zhung kingdoms, which had already begun to extend their influence across the mountains and into Northern India. Their capital was said to be the mythical city of Khylunglung Ngulkhak—the Silver Palace of the Garundra Valley (Garundra being an early minor Hindu deity)—a place that has sometimes been equated with Shambhala or Shangri-La.

Historically, the Zhang Zhung culture was overthrown around A.D. 644 by Songen Gampo, the 33rd king of Tibet. In retaliation for the ill treatment of his sister who was married to one of the Zhang Zhung kings, Songen started a war that destroyed most of their cities, and was the first step in the unification of Tibet under one ruler. However, the influence of the Zhang Zhung culture and its Bon religion still maintained an underlying influence on the country and on Tibetan Buddhism, which the later Tibetan kings espoused.

Bon and Buddha

Shangri-La, or Shambhala, may also have its origins in a place where the ancient Bon texts refer to as Olmolunggring, although it is not clear whether this is an actual kingdom, a city, or a complex of monasteries. As the Bon and Buddhist religions began to overlap in Tibet, around the late seventh century, the overall religious picture becomes slightly confused. Olmolunggring was the place where the Buddha (or king) had a number of wonderful palaces, to which he retired during the winter months for prayer and contemplation. His descendants, known variously as the kulika, kalika, or kalka (a series of kings), withdrew from the world and continued to rule there as potentates, espousing a form of Buddhism that was deeply rooted in the Bon tradition. Some scholars have argued that the name is taken from the early Hindu word *Kalki*, meaning "Great Incarnation of the god Vishnu." Olmolunggring was shielded from the rest of the world by mountain walls, impenetrable snow-filled passes, and deep ravines, and was believed to be located in the Kunlun Mountains, which form part of the northern edge of the Tibetan Plateau. It is alternately given as a kingdom whose capital is

Kalapa (also given as the capital for the country of Shambhala) or as a holy city comprised entirely of monasteries in which the lamas (monks) know no death.

The word *Shambhala*, which also applies to Shangri-La, means "pure land," although it is also given as "harmonious valley" or "place of rest and peace." It is probably from these translations that Hilton (and many retired people and bed-and-breakfast owners) took the name. But if such a place existed, where was it? Confusingly, both Buddhist and Bon literature state that it exists both "within and without" the consciousness of an individual. So was Shangri-La largely a concept—a state of mind that could be achieved, perhaps through Buddhist teaching? But if this was so, was there on actual location that promoted this teaching or upon which the individual might focus in order to achieve the perfect state? If this was the case, might it have continued long after the overthrow of the Zhang Zhung civilization? It seems that there might indeed have been such a place.

In the late 14th century, according to tradition, a gyelpo, or ruler of the Himalayan trading kingdom of Mustang, received a deputation of lamas or monks from a remote monastery well outside his kingdom. Mustang had strong ties with Tibet, and its culture was largely Tibetan in nature with Tibetan Buddhism at its center, but the monks brought with them an even older form of Buddhism that taught how to achieve an inner serenity. The place that they came from was a remote lamasery named "the Place of Inner Happiness and Peace," or Shangri-La. No location was given for the lamasery except that it was in a remote valley far beyond the borders of Mustang. However, it was believed that it lay somewhere in the Buddhist region between Tibet and the borders of Northern India. Some have identified the location as the Hunza Valley, lying in what are today the northern provinces of Pakistan, between the Gilgit and Nagar Valleys.

The Hunza, which today lies close to the Chinese border, was at one time an independent principality or "princely state." In fact, it was under the rule of largely independent princes for almost 900 years. A remote and extremely verdant river valley, it was said to have boasted a predominantly Buddhist community, which spread its influence into nearby Kashmir. Hunza was briefly annexed by Kashmir around 1860 during the authority of Maharajah Rabir Singh, but returned to a limited independency in 1888. Today, however, it is part of Jammu and Kashmir, but remains almost inaccessible. Up until the 1950s, there were still extremely strong links between the Hunza and Tibet, which again had profound implications for the region with the city of Ladakh in northern Kashmir being widely known as "Little Tibet." This, argue some, makes it a prime candidate as the site of the lamasery from which the holy monks traveled to the court of the Mustang gyelpo. Moreover, for a good number of months, the Hunza can be cut off from the rest of the world by snowfalls in the mountains, and this adds an element of mystery and magic to the remote monasteries there. It has been suggested that Hilton visited this area when traveling in Kashmir, and that its beauty and inaccessibility served to inspire his vision of Shangri-La in *Lost Horizon*. Certainly he had visited the region (although he had remained largely in Kashmir) several years before the novel was published, but the ideas concerning it are more likely to emanate from the writings of the American explorer and botanist Joseph Rock (1884–1962), who had traveled extensively in Kashmir and parts of eastern Tibet. In the course of his travels, Rock had stayed in various lamaseries and had absorbed many of the tales that the Tibetan monks had told him. He had undoubtedly heard (and recorded in his diaries), certain stories of a lamasery hidden away in a remote valley where all was peace and tranquility. This would later form the basis of Hilton's *Lost Horizon*.

Other sites also existed; for example, several remote and virtually inaccessible river valleys in China were considered to be possible locations for a monastery from which the monks had traveled to Mustang. However, no trace of such a lamasery has ever been found.

Blavatsky and Others

Similar to the legend of Hyperborea, Shangri-La also attracted a number of interested people. As with mythical sites such as Atlantis and Lemuria, the 19th century Theosophist Madame Blavatsky also took an interest in the legendary place and mentioned it in some of her writings. Madame Blavatsky claimed to have contact with a number of Masters (enlightened beings) living in Tibet, and they appear to have had strong connections with Shamballha or Shangri-La. In certain texts, she spoke of what was called "The Great White Lodge" or the "Great White Brotherhood," which appeared to be a grouping of Masters, Adepts, or Mahatmas, all of whom were beings of incredible power and who more or less governed the world through spiritual means, sending their messages through a number of "teachers" (of whom Madame Blavatsky was one). There was a suggestion that this grouping might be based in Shangri-La. This theory was developed and expanded by later Theosophists and neo-Theosophists such as Charles Webster Ledbetter (1854–1930) and Alice Bailey (1880–1949). They put forward the theory that the work carried out within Shangri-La was described as the Ascended Master Activities, which were performed under the direction of a Master named Sanat Kumara, and would affect the direction of history. There were even connections in some theories with the planet Venus, from which a group of Supreme Masters had come in the distant past (one of whom was the Buddha), and there were suggestions that Shangri-La might lie (or may have lain) on that world. Later scientific evidence shows that the Venusian surface is anything but peaceful or tranquil!

Agartha

Agartha had emerged out of a more Westernized tradition than Shangri-La, and was tied into notions of Atlantis and Lemuria. It was a city or realm that existed in a large cavern just under the Earth's crust; the entrance to it could be gained from a cave located somewhere in the Himalayas or Tibet. The idea of an underground city may have been inspired by an old Tibetan legend of a long passageway, which started within the country and supposedly ran under the entire Asian continent and possibly beyond. The entrance to this tunnel was said to lie close to the site now occupied by the Potala Palace in Lhasa. The place had originally been a place of meditation for the early Tibetan kings until King Songsten Gampo had built the original palace there in A.D. 637 as a present for his bride Wen Cheng, a Chinese princess of the Tang Dynasty. At this point, the tunnel entrance was said to have become obscured, but the legend of its existence still persisted within Tibet.

The city of Agartha, according to some Theosophical teaching, was the survivor of a prehistoric war that had almost devastated the Earth. This war had been fought between Atlantis and Lemuria, and had used atomic weapons and other forces that are far beyond our understanding. It resulted in the complete destruction of both ancient continents. However, some colonies survived, one of which was Agartha, just under the Earth's crust or in some remote Himalayan valley. Here, survivors dwelt; they were either the fore-runners of the Masters or else the Masters themselves.

The Nazi Regime

Similar to some other Theosophist theories, stories of Shangri-La also attracted the attention of factions within the German Nazi regime. Taking up some of the confusions that existed within the various strands of Theosophy, the Nazis coupled legends of Shangri-La with those of another mythological site—the lost city of Agartha.

Mixing the two strands of legend, Nazi occultists placed Shangri-La as a possible home for the Aryan race. Those who dwelt there, it was suggested, were not Asian people at all but tall, blonde, blue-eyed god-like humans who were considered by some to be the prototypes of the Master Race.

So strong was the belief that there was something among the Himalayan peaks, that during the 1930s and early 1940s, the Nazis mounted no less than seven scientific expeditions to find it. The purpose of these was to find proof of a non-Buddhist Aryan peoples living in a remote valley, and also recover some of the technology that had been allegedly used in the Atlantis-Lemuria war, which might make Germany an invincible superpower. Several of the earliest expeditions in the 1930s were led by the German hunter and zoologist Ernst Schafer (1910–1992). In 1931, Schafer would lead an expedition into Tibet accompanied by the American explorer and naturalist Brooke Dolan. Dolan's mission was to study rare flora and fauna, but Schafer's was to look for traces of Shangri-La. He found nothing, and between 1934 and 1935, he returned to the Himalayas again, together with Dolan, for a second expedition. Again he returned with nothing concrete, simply several old hill stories. However, this prompted him to return again, this time at the head of a solo German expedition between 1938 and 1939. Again, he found nothing but was still convinced that there was something out there.

Schafer's enthusiasm and conviction prompted another Nazi explorer, the Austrian Heinrich Harrer (1912–2006) to mount his own expedition into northern Pakistan, again to search for the elusive kingdom. In 1939, at the outbreak of World War II, Harrer was captured and arrested by British Colonial forces operating out of Northern India in the Pakistani Nanga Parbat region. Nanga Parbat means "naked peak," and was supposed to be the site of a very ancient lamasery, hidden away among the river gorges there. Harrer was convinced this was Shangri-La, but unfortunately before he could find the site, he was captured and taken to an internment camp in the Uttakhand Province in Northern India, along with another 1,000 "enemy aliens," who were mostly civilians.

In 1944, Harrer managed to escape in the company of another Austrian, Peter Aufschnaiter, and two Germans. Convinced that Shangri-La lay somewhere in what is now a region of Pakistan, he made his way back toward Nanga Parbat, but his way was blocked by British patrols, and both he and Aufschnaiter made their way instead to Tibet and the city of Lhasa. There, Harrer was to spend the next seven years, and during that time, befriended Tenzin Gyatso, the 14th (and present) Dalai Lama. The two remained friends until Harrer's death. Although his book *Seven Years in Tibet* (later a film) was published after the Chinese formal annexation of the country in 1950, Harrer was never to find the elusive monastery that he sought, nor did any other Nazi expedition, including one acting on direct orders from Heinrich Himmler.

Although the Nazis mounted the last serious (and heavily funded) expedition to find Shangri-La, there have been a number of others. Several American-led expeditions entered the province of Kham on the Chinese-Tibetan border during the 1970s. For several hundred years, Kham had maintained a certain degree of independence from both China and Tibet (although part of it encompassed an area of central Tibet), and it was said to be the location of several "mysterious cities." None of the American expeditions were particularly well equipped or scientific, and it was little surprise that they did not find anything. The same result came about on a number of further, hastily arranged expeditions into parts of nearby Nepal. However, the name of Shangri-La continued to live on in folklore.

Someone who was greatly taken with the legend was the president of the United States, Franklin D. Roosevelt. The president had often declared himself a fan of James Hilton's writing and of *Lost Horizon* (both the book and the film), and actually named his summer retreat—now known as Camp David—Shangri-La. At a press conference, following an attack on Tokyo by U.S. military planes during World War II, Roosevelt jokingly stated that the

aircraft had taken off from bases in Shangri-La, thus turning the legendary kingdom into a strategic U.S. outpost in the Far East. One newspaper actually took him at his word and printed that the planes had taken off from the aircraft carrier *USS Shangri-La*. Bizarrely, the mythical kingdom became a part of the United States Navy.

Not only is the location of the actual realm something of a mystery, a certain element of controversy and speculation surrounds the film location of Hilton's book. The cast was, apparently, sworn to secrecy, but the location is often given as the Ojai Valley in Ventura County, California, near Westlake Village and Palm Springs. This was the land of the Chumash Indians, who themselves were considered to be a rather mystical people. However, there were disputes that the film was not filmed there at all—no trace of the "lamasery" used in the film has ever been found at the Californian location— but rather, somewhere in Montana. Just as many arguments continue about this as they do about the existence of the lost realm.

Throughout the years, the name "Shangri-La" has come to mean a place of rest, contemplation, and reflection. It is also strongly associated with tranquility and personal fulfillment. And perhaps, apart from the discovery of an actual place, that might be its lasting legacy. In this particular instance, the ideal might be much more important than any actual location.

11

The Kingdom of Prester John

In the year 1165, a mysterious letter sent from the East caused something of a stir in Western Europe. Addressed to the Byzantine Emperor, Manuel I Comnensus (1143–1180), it was translated into a variety of languages and was circulated widely. The letter asked for urgent help; somewhere in Eastern Asia, there was an almost magical kingdom of Nestorian Christians, ruled over by a good and wise king who was a direct descendant of one of the Magi—the three Wise Men who had worshipped the infant Jesus. His name was Prester John. According to the letter, this mystical kingdom was under threat. Expansions among surrounding Muslim and Pagan peoples had led to frequent attacks on its borders, and Prester John himself had written personally to the emperor requesting his aid. Already a large force of Muslims were pressing down on his country, ready to attack; therefore, the Eastern king begged for help from the Christian West before he was overwhelmed.

Who Was Prester John?

No one knows what Manuel's response was. As a ruler, he was extremely interested in extending his empire, and a link to another Christian monarch farther east would give him a toehold among the Muslims there; however, he was also extremely cautious. He certainly did not mount an army to offer the requested aid, but it is likely that he referred the matter to Pope Alexander III in Rome to see if he could help. Alexander was equally cautious and probably with good reason. Nobody had ever heard of this Prester John or of his kingdom. There had been no accounts of such a king from the merchants who had traveled eastward, and his realm seemed to trade with no recognized country. The letter might be no more than a hoax or, more dangerously, a trick designed to draw the Church into a protracted and bloody conflict against the Eastern Muslims, which might ultimately enable the latter to gain new territories in the West. Alexander had to be aware of the political ramifications of his decision.

The fact that Prester John might be a Nestorian king may have also provoked papal caution. Nestorianism had grown out of Gnostic Christianity, and taught that Jesus was not one being but two: the human who had died on the cross and the Divine Logos, which had existed from before the foundation of the world. The baby to which Mary had given birth was the Son of Man, but not the Son of God. This theology had been condemned as heretical by the powerful First Council of Ephesus in A.D. 431. While recognized as Christians, the Nestorians (named after Nestorius, patriarch of Constantinople [386–451] who had first put the doctrine forward), were treated cautiously by mainstream Christians. However, many Nestorians had formed communities in the East, and some of their churches were thought to espouse teachings that might today be considered elements of early Buddhism. The pope may have been reluctant to offer aid to a king who, although a Christian, might not readily hold traditional Roman beliefs.

According to some sources, Alexander did nothing at all, but in other traditions, he sent a letter expressing solidarity (but offering no assistance) to Prester John, using his own personal physician, Philip, as the envoy. Philip reputedly left for the East on September 27, 1177, and from then on vanishes from the pages of history. If he did go, it is unlikely that he returned. Prester John's letter, however, continued to circulate among the courts of Europe and to generate interest and excitement.

A Mystical Realm

The country it described was incredibly wealthy. Here there were many mines that yielded abundant gold and precious stones; the climate was temperate and the land was watered by several rivers. Under Prester John's beneficent rule, it had enjoyed years of peace and stability, and its populace was incredibly content and happy. There were also many wonders within its borders. There was said to be a pool within the royal courts where, if one were to drink the water, it would extend that individual's lifespan by many hundreds of years. There were young women attending the monarch who were more than 200 years old! And there were exotic creatures and beings there too. For instance, part of the royal retinue was made up of men with horns in the center of their foreheads; there were creatures living in the royal forests that had three eyes and fish swimming in the rivers that had teeth made from pure gold. The county was also supposed to be the location of the legendary Gates of Alexander. Reference to these—also latterly known as the Iberian Gates—appear in a collection of writings dating from between the third and sixth centuries concerning the alleged exploits of Alexander the Great known as *The Alexander Romance*. These "gates" were mighty barriers, constructed by Alexander's men and designed to keep out the barbarians from further east. Their location had been lost since before the first century, but they were believed to lie in the eastern Caucasus. Some have identified them with the Caspian Gates in Derbent, Russia, and others with the Pass of Daniel, or Danal, in Russian Georgia. Wherever they were, they were supposed to mark a kind of demarcation between East and West. In the letter to Manuel, they were identified as lying within the realm of Prester John. Here, too, was the "magnificent tomb of the Patriarch Thomas," a figure who was identified with St. Thomas, one of Jesus' disciples, who had supposedly gone east. The letter appeared to be a mixture of both Pagan fable and Christian myth. Much of it is undoubtedly medieval invention, which was probably inserted to the main text much later, but it created the idea of a magical and mystical kingdom far away in the East.

Discovery

Where was this kingdom located? Initially, at the time of the letter, the consensus was that it lay somewhere in India. The basis for this idea lay in another Christian legend. According to some traditions, a shadowy and mysterious figure known only as John the Presbyter, or John the Elder, had carried the Christian message to India where he seems to have disappeared in the early days of the Church. Little is known about this shadowy person, and in fact they reference him in only one fragmentary document—the text known as *The Exposition of the Sayings of the Lord*, a second century work attributed to Papias, bishop of Heiropolis in southwest Turkey. Even here, the reference is only a fleeting one. One of those who claimed to have met him was the teacher Ireneaus of Lyons, who claims that John the Presbyter was a friend of his own tutor, Polycarp of Smyrna, but reveals little information about him. Attempts have subsequently been made to connect him with the Apostle John, the writer of the Gospel and other various documents, but the figure is too vague to attach any early Christian writing to it. However, tradition says that the Presbyter was instructed to carry the Gospel to the lands of the East, and so he set out for India where he may have founded a church or churches. No evidence has ever been found for John or his mission, and he left no writings or texts behind. Whether or not this mysterious Presbyter John was a king somewhere in India is unknown. An obscure reference to him does appear in an allegedly fragmentary work ascribed to an equally mysterious writer known as Peter of Syria, dating from about the second century. This describes him as a "patriarch," but does not elaborate any further. Could Prester John then have been some sort of Church leader somewhere in the East, perhaps even in India?

Crusades and Christians

The mystery arose from an extraordinary and secretive meeting in 1122, when Pope Calistus II is recorded as having received a visit from an eastern patriarch named John who had come from a "land far away." Nothing is known of this leader except that he was not wholly of the persuasion of the Roman Church, nor is anything known of the purpose of the meeting between the two men—it may well have been an attempt at a political alliance. If so, it came to nothing. No attempt was, however, made to link this mysterious patriarch to Prester John until 1145 when Bishop Otto of Friesing recorded in his *Chronicals* that Prester John was indeed John the Presbyter. Was the communication of 1165 a call for aid, promised by the pope at that meeting, or did it relate to something else? Scholars have been unable to ascertain its true nature.

Although the famous letter continued to circulate, and was no doubt embellished throughout the late 1100s, nothing further was heard from this mysterious Christian king. However, in 1248, it received a surprising resurgence of interest.

In that year, Crusader bishop of Acre, Jacques de Vitry, returned to the West with the welcome news that "King David of India," the son or grandson of Prester John, was building an army to take on the forces of the Saracens and so defend Christianity. This was the time of the Fifth Crusade (1217–1221), preached by Pope Honorius III, and things were going badly for Christendom. In 1141, however, even better news reached the West—King David had defeated the powerful Moslem Khwarezmian Empire as well as the Seljuk Turks, and was planning to aid in the building of the Holy City of Jerusalem. However, de Vitry had made a mistake—"King David" was not the son of Prester John at all; he was not even a Christian. In fact, he was a Mongol warlord named Temujin, whose name would one day be infamous around the ancient world as Genghis Khan. His "kingdom" was no exotic Eastern realm, but instead, the harsh land of Steppes of Central Asia. Nor was he particularly well disposed to Western Christendom, although he did open a number of Eastern Christian shrines to pilgrims. The move to recognize Genghis Khan as a descendant of Prester John, however, was a political one. The fledgling Crusader states in the East were constantly under Muslim threat, and to ally Christendom with an emerging force such as the Mongol Empire might work to their advantage. The kingdom of Prester John then, became the center of the Asian Steppes.

As the reign of Genghis Khan became ever more ruthless and bloody, and as the allegedly promised aid in the rebuilding of Jerusalem failed to materialize, the mantle of "son of Prester John" passed from Genghis's shoulders to that of his foster-brother Toghrul, king of the Keraits, who the Chinese Jin Dynasty had named as the Wang Khan. Several medieval writers, such as William of Rubruck, speak of Toghrul as being "King John's" brother and a ruler of a Kerait kingdom that had been defeated by Genghis Khan. He seemed well able to become the dynastic successor to Prester John. Toghrul's reign proved no less violent than that of his foster brother, and soon Christendom was distancing itself from the Mongol Empire as the possible kingdom and dynasty of the legendary Prester John. What is interesting, however, is that Toghrul was in fact a Nestorian Christian, and roughly correspondeds to some of the attributes accorded to Prester John.

Political Presence

By now the figure of "Prester John" was becoming something of a political one. Desperate to gain and maintain a presence in the turbulent East, the Western Church began to play up the idea of a brave Christian king, holding out against the encroaching forces of Islam and Paganism. And if the Mongol Empire was not the ideal template for a Christian kingdom and a potential ally in the East, there were others. The French Crusader historian Jean de Joinville (c. 1225–1317), for instance, mentions several Christian missions to a number of Tartar kings, none of which appear to have been very successful. Some of the Tartar leaders seemed just as bloodthirsty as the Mongols, hardly the descendants of a wise and beneficent Christian ruler. Further medieval texts concerning the region, such as *The Travels of Sir John Mandeville* compiled between 1357 and 1371, detail an attempt to find this king, all of which resulted in failure. Among the Asian races, Prester John remained as elusive as ever.

In his travels in the East, the Italian explorer Marco Polo mentioned a county that he called Abascia in which he claimed there was a substantial Christian population whose needs were served by capable patriarchs. However, it is thought that he was referring to Abyssinia, where there were indeed substantial numbers of Christians and several churches overseen by patriarchs. His writings did nothing to explain the mystery.

The Christians of St. Thomas

In the 15th century, however, the legend was to receive yet another twist. In the mid-1400s, word began to reach the West of a previously unknown group of Christians living on the Malabar Coast in Southern India. They called themselves "the Christians of St. Thomas," taking their name from a leader known as the "patriarch Thomas." Attention was once more turned to the letter that Manuel I had received from Prester John. One of the sites in his fabulous kingdom mentioned in this communication had been the tomb of the patriarch Thomas—did this give some credibility to the communication?

Even more startling, these Christians (who were thought to be Nestorians), claimed that prior to Thomas, their leader had been "the Patriarch John of India." To add further confusion to the tale, the patriarch John was also described as a great ruler who had presided over a land that had encompassed "the Three Indias." Great speculation arose as to what these lands might be and as to the identity of the patriarch John (might he indeed be the legendary Prester John?) and attention was turned toward certain ancient Chinese writings, which were now appearing in Europe for the first time.

First and foremost was the *Chu-fan-chi*, an early Chinese geographical work by the scholar Chau Ju-kua written around 1225. Together with another work by the same author—the *Ma-tua-lim*—it gave an impression of the medieval East, which had hitherto been unknown by those in the West. The work spoke of two great kingdoms, lying in part beyond both China and India. These were the kingdoms of Sanfotsi and Zabag (which included an area that Arab seamen referred to as Sirandib, and which we know today as Sri Lanka). There is also mention of another kingdom known as Tuopo, or Shopo. There has subsequently been great debate about the actual areas covered by these kingdoms, although it is generally agreed that at least part of them contained lands controlled by the Chola Empire of Southern India—a Tamil dynasty that had ruled in the 13th century. Some commentators believe that Sanfotsi in particular ruled areas such as present-day Malayasia and Burma, the Korean Peninsula, and parts of the Philippines, which encompassed a substantial realm. Could these kingdoms have been "the Three Indias" over which Prester John ruled?

It was suggested in various parts of the West that although nominally Christian, these Christians of St. Thomas were in fact more Buddhist than Christian, and Buddhist elements featured strongly in their forms of worship. This led to the assertion that the patriarch John, while perhaps initially being Christian, had converted to a form of Buddhism and had become a lama. Some accounts suggested that he had been a lama from the outset, and his "kingdom" lay not in India at all, but in remote Tibet. In fact, in some respects, Prester John became equated with the ruler of legendary Shambhala, as a kind of lama-king who espoused Eastern religion rather than Christianity. His "kingdom," therefore, some claimed, lay somewhere among the peaks of the lofty Himalayas, and was more or less inaccessible to Westerners. Such theories kept the idea of Prester John firmly in the East, but already the identity of this mysterious figure and the supposed location of his mythical kingdom was shifting.

As the Mongol Empire began to crumble due to internal disputes, the idea that Prester John might be a Central Asian king began to fade. Besides, there was new evidence as to who he might have been. India was often mentioned as the location of his kingdom, but "India" was so vague a concept to the medieval mind that few were completely sure as to where it actually was.

Proving and Disproving the Legend of Prester John

In 1306, more than 30 representatives from the court of Wadem Arad of Ethiopia attended a Christian Council in Rome. Wadem Arad was a ruler of the Solomonic dynasty, which held a very special place in the Middle East and also in Christian folklore. The dynasty traced its roots to an alleged union between King Solomon and the Queen of Sheba. The founder of the dynasty, Menelik I, claimed to be issue of that union, and therefore claimed the biblical Solomon as his father. The legendary country of Sheba was defined as being in the south of Ethiopia, which had engendered it some prestige among Christians. The representatives stated that the foundation of their country had also originated from the patriarch John who had been appointed by God to oversee them. This patriarch was also known as John the Presbyter. This established Ethiopia, already a Christian country, as a possible location for the realm of the mystical monarch, and gave him a direct connection into biblical writings. Might "the Third India," some argued, not have been in Asia at all, but in Arabia? The theory was a tantalizing one. And it built on an old legend that circulated throughout the 13th century.

It was said that in 1248, French knights returning from the Seventh Crusade had brought back from the Middle East a "great secret" that had never been disclosed. Some said that it was a relic that they had found among the Arabs. While there is no actual account of what this relic was, it was said to be the skull of Prester John, a Christian king of Arabia, who had been "betrayed" by the Church in the West. When his kingdom had allegedly been threatened by the Saracens, he had contacted the West for aid, and the Church there had ignored him. Consequently, his kingdom had been overrun, and he himself had been slain. All that remained was his skull, which had been secretly venerated as a relic by Christians in the Middle East. It had been "liberated" by Crusader knights and brought westward. What became of the skull when it came to Europe is unknown—it is even possible that such a relic never existed at all. However, it was enough to connect the idea of Prester John with the Middle East and with Africa.

Medieval writings linking Prester John with Ethiopia first appeared in 1329 in a document written by a French Dominican monk named Jordanus known as *Mirabilia Descripta*, which records a number of fanciful tales linking Prester John with the Ethiopic dynasty. Their emissaries hailed the Ethiopian king Dawit II as "Emperor of Ethiopia; a descendant of King Solomon and of Prester John." The move was, of course, a political one, and designed to secure Portuguese interests in Ethiopia. As far as Prester John went, however, the Ethiopians knew nothing about him. They never used the title "Emperor of Ethiopia," and although they made some reference to the patriarch, they did not generally regard him with the immense importance that the Portuguese accorded him. When this salutation was used in 1441 by a Portuguese envoy to the court of another Ethiopian ruler, Zara Yaqob (1399–1468) the king gazed at him questioningly. In fact, the idea of attaching the name of Prester John to the Ethiopian kings was to foster military and trading links with the Christian West—just as earlier generations had attempted to link the name with Temujin (Genghis Khan) or Torghul (the Weng Khan).

Gradually, however, the idea of Prester John and his kingdom began to fade. There seemed no prospect of ever finding evidence of an early Christian king in the deserts of Arabia, and through the years the connection to the Ethiopian lineage was disproved. At best, the whole thing assumed the air of a Christian myth; at worst, of Church propaganda for political purposes. Nevertheless, similar to most legends, its mystery and romance continued to inspire writers and poets throughout the centuries.

Did Prester John exist? Was there really a legendary Christian king somewhere in either the Far East or in Ethiopia? Or was the whole idea simply an elaborate trick, designed to ingratiate Western powers with Eastern rulers, or, inspire the populace of war-torn Eastern countries in their faith? We will probably never know. In any event, the idea of the mysterious, mystical Christian king has echoed down through the centuries and still forms as much of an intriguing legend today as it did far back in medieval times.

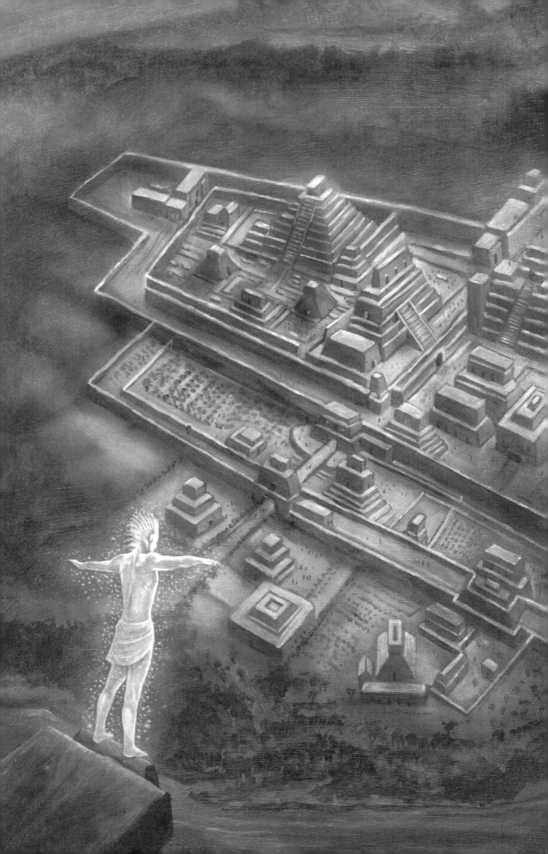

12

El Dorado

On the morning of the April 22, 1540, a large company of armed men (mostly Spaniards) and pack animals marched out of the dusty city of Culiacán in Northern Mexico, heading north into what would one day become the United States of America. The expedition was led by Don Francisco Vasquez de Coronado, governor of Nueva Galicia, who set out to find the Seven Cities of Gold—a network of golden citadels—rumored to lie somewhere in the unexplored hinterland. Ahead of them was their guide, an Italian Franciscan monk, Fray Marcos de Niza, who was following a trail that had been laid out by an earlier explorer Estevanico (Black Stephen), the Black Mexican of the Zuni.

Legends of Gold

Since the middle of the 12th century, there had been stories of marvelous cities in the American interior, some of them resulting from European legends. From the early 1100s, the wealthy and holy city of Mérida in southern Spain had been constantly attacked by Moorish invaders before being finally destroyed in 1150. Before that happened, however, tradition says that seven bishops fled the city, taking with them part of the municipal wealth and a good number of religious ornaments. They fled, it is said, to a "far land" where they encountered an already thriving civilization of dusky-faced foreigners who welcomed them and allowed them to stay. Using the wealth they had brought with them, and the inordinate wealth of the foreign civilization that came from mining (mainly gold), the bishops founded a number of cities of opulent splendor. The land to which these clerics had fled was generally taken to be America, and the cities that they had established were reputedly deep within that continent. Legends persisted of settlements deep in the hinterland, some supposedly ruled over by the descendants of Europeans. These were the cities that the incoming Spaniards were trying to find, and the most persistent of these legends—that of the Seven Cities of Gold—was what Coronado's expedition was trying to prove.

According to the legend, one of the major golden cities, Quivara or Qiviria, lay in the unexplored wilderness beyond an area known as the Jornada del Muerto (the Journey of Dead Men). This was a desert-like basin in the north of Mexico and few Spanish explorers had ever crossed it. It was said that on its northern edge lay an area known as "Tejas," or "Techjas." This was a name used by the Hasinai Confederation of Indians, and was used to refer to another confederation of tribes to the north. The name meant "those who are allies," and would later be changed by European tongues "Texas," and it was here that Coronado expected to find the golden city. Bearing the Cross of Christ in front of them, he and his men marched from Culiacán into unknown territory.

He gruelingly marched his expedition across the Jornada del Muerto into southern Texas. No fabulous city, however, awaited him, only a region that Coronado himself would name Llano Escado, or the Staked Plain. This was a seemingly endless sea of grass—a huge plain stretching away for as far as the eye could see. Most historians believe that Coronado gave the area its name—Staked Plain—because of the geological formations that surrounded it that resembled a stockade or military fortification, usually made of wooden stakes. Some say that he drove stakes into the ground to guide his expedition across the seemingly unending grassland. On the other side of this "grassy sea," de Niza assured him the city that he sought would be there, and so Coronado marched on, drawn by the legend. He crossed what is today Texas and parts of New Mexico and Arizona without finding anything. Still, de Niza assured him, according to local Indian tales, the city lay somewhere on the other side of the horizon.

In mid-1541, with his expedition decimated by disease, desertions, and attacks by Indian bands, Coronado crossed the Wichita River in present-day southern Kansas. Just beyond this river, Zuni guides had assured him, lay Cibola and great wealth. Coronado, however, found nothing but the squalid mud pueblos of the Wichita Indians and more grassland. Defeated and disillusioned, he turned back and retraced his steps to Culiacán. Although he was to remain governor of Nueva Galicia until 1544, Coronado was a shamed and broken man. The failed expedition had almost bankrupted him; finally with the title of governor, he retired to Mexico City where he died on September 22, 1544. Marcos de Niza was to survive him by another 14 years before also dying in Mexico City, shamed and penniless, in 1558. The main memorials to the tragic expedition are a monument in Sierra Vista, Arizona, and the Coronado Shopping Mall in Albuquerque, New Mexico. Nevertheless, stories of fabulously wealthy and infinitely mysterious cities located somewhere in the American hinterland persisted.

Aztec Gold

When the Spanish had first arrived in Mexico in 1518, under the leadership of Hernan Cortez, they had found a relatively advanced and reasonably wealthy civilization there, which greeted them more or less as gods. This was the Aztec empire, ruled over by Moctezuma II. Impressed by the lavishness of golden gifts, Cortez and his men would take Moctezuma II prisoner and eventually overthrow the Aztec civilization. However, Tenochtitlan allegedly traded with other cities in the hinterland where there were gold mines and places where precious stones could be found; stories of these settlements piqued Spanish interest. Stories concerning them circulated widely among the Spanish conquistadores and may well have formed the basis of the legend of Cibola. There was another intriguing aspect to the tale as well. When Cortez arrived among the Aztecs, he was feted as a god. This was because the Aztecs believed that one of their chief deities—Quetzalcoatl (whose main incarnation was a plumed serpent)—would visit them in the guise of a bearded European. For Cortez, this may have been significant, as it might have been suggestive of the Spanish bishops who had fled from Merida in the 12th century. The Spanish leader remembered the legend that they had founded cities somewhere in a "far land," and he may well have believed that these were indeed the cities with which Tinochtitlan traded. If so, they might be fabulously wealthy. This idea was probably passed on to Coronado (who had met Cortez) and formed the basis of the governor's expedition to find Cibola.

And the legend concerning the Seven Cities of Gold was not the only such tale among the early Spanish explorers. Two other conquistadores, Garcia Lopez de Cardenas and Pedro de Tobar had heard Hopi Indian legends of a great city situated on a river somewhere in the north. De Tobar led a small expedition early in 1540 (shortly after Coronado's expedition had departed) to try to locate it, but had to turn back because of disease among his men; de Cardenas, however, marched another expedition north and crossed into what is today Colorado. His plan was to find the river, which the Hopi legends had described, and follow its course, hopefully, to the lost city. And although he did indeed find the river, he failed in his attempt to locate the legendary metropolis. However, what he did find was the Grand Canyon through which part of the Colorado River flowed, and which remains today as one of the "wonders" of the American continent. Naming the river Tizon, de Cardenas found he could advance no further, as there was no way down the sheer walls of the river canyon. Tired and exhausted, he returned to Spanish America to stake his claim, only to find that the river he'd "discovered" had been visited and claimed in September 1539 by one of Cortez's generals, Francisco de Ulloa, who had crossed it several hundred miles further down near the coast. Nevertheless, de Cardenas claimed that somewhere, just beyond the point where he had turned back, lay the fabulous city. Of course, more modern exploration of the Colorado Plateau has shown he was wrong, and no such city existed. But still the legends persisted, and there was talk of further expeditions, none of which actually came to fruition. However, interest in finding such places remained great.

Exploring South America

By the end of the 1500s and the beginning of the 1600s, the legend of lost cities in America had merged with another legend—that of El Dorado. It is this name that is most associated with lost cities, and has almost become a by-word for an unattainable goal. In fact, the name does not refer to a city at all. It can be roughly translated as "the gilded man" (or more often "the golden one"), and may refer to a statue or, more probably, an actual person.

It may not have concerned the hinterland of North America, but rather the region of the Andes Mountains in South America.

The legend began to circulate as Spanish explorers began to push into Colombia in the 1530s. In 1537, the conquistador and explorer Gonzalo Jiménez de Quesada, made contact with the Muisca, a nation of the Chibcha culture in the Colombian interior who told him a story of a tribe high up in the mountains, whose great chieftains covered themselves in gold dust before leaping into a freezing cold-water mountain lake as an offering to their gods. These chieftains could only emerge from the waters when the gold had been washed off. The Spaniards referred to this person as el indio dorado—the gilded Indian. Legends surrounding golden offerings to the gods—particularly those of mountain lakes—became widespread among the conquistadores. One of the favored locations for such offerings was Lake Titicaca, high up in the Altiplano region of the Andes Mountains, between present-day Bolivia and Peru. This is one of the highest navigable lakes on Earth, boasting several islands, and thought to be the center of worship for the Inca people since ancient times. The deity who was allegedly worshipped there was Pachamama, also called the Mamacuna, who was supposed to be a Mother Nature–like figure who ensured good weather. However, she demanded tributes every year, including human life, but many of which were of gold. Her temple was on the Isla del Sol, far out in the lake. This notion of giving gifts to the spirits of rivers and lakes was not unique among the Aztecs; many other ancient peoples (including the Celts) did exactly the same. There was also a widely held belief among the worshippers that the Aztec race had sprung from Titicaca, and there were ancient ruins on what is now the Bolivian side of the lake, suggesting that there had been a city there at one point—almost 1,500 years before the Aztec civilization flourished. This has been given by some commentators as one of the locations for the legendary city of Atlantis, and it is certainly suggestive of an extremely antique settlement.

By the early-to-mid-1600s, the Spanish empire was starting to wane slightly in some areas, and it was left to English explorers to link the notions of a lost city high in the mountains and the idea of the golden man rising from the cold-water lake. One of these explorers, much given to exaggeration, was the one-time English Royal favorite Sir Walter Raleigh. Raleigh enjoyed something of a reputation as an explorer, and did nothing to play down his exploits. Having made several expeditions into the South American interior, Raleigh announced that during one of them in 1596, he had visited a city, far up on the Orinoco River, which had been ruled over by a king, swathed in sheets of gold and known as "The Golden King," in Spanish El Ray Dorado or El Dorado. The location of this city had been on a large lake somewhere in Guiana, now part of Venezuela. Moreover, this city owned a massive realm of gold and jewel mines (mainly emeralds), which made its king and inhabitants inordinately wealthy. Such stories, of course, echoed the old Spanish legends of Cibola and Quivira, and piqued English interest in the idea of mysterious cities on the American continent.

Raleigh had apparently not been the first to encounter this mysterious king. In 1534, conquistadores from the Colombian expedition of Sebastian de Belalcazar, an explorer who had sailed with Francisco Pizarro, conqueror of the Incas, had also heard legends of the "Golden King," and had allegedly seen him in a magnificent city in the middle of a great lake. However, they placed the city somewhere on the Cauca River in Central Colombia. Another account had been given by a shipwrecked sailor who had sailed in 1531 with Diego de Ordaz (one of Cortez' generals) who had spent some time with El Dorado himself, although he located the city somewhere in present-day Honduras. There were also tales of a golden king brought back to Europe by German explorer Philipp von Hutton who, together with Geog von Speyer had traveled some way up the Orinoco and had heard Indian tales of a city further north ruled by such a person. Raleigh no doubt built on these accounts and had moved the river slightly in order to fit in with the route of his own expedition. His account was widely accepted, and for nearly 200 years the fabulous city and its lake appeared on all maps of the Orinoco until its existence was disproved by Prussian naturalist and explorer Alexander von Humboldt in the 1700s.

With the decline of the Spanish Empire and Spanish exploration in the New World, the legend of El Dorado began to assume slightly less importance. From time to time, explorers might return with old Indian tales of fabulous Indian mines (and undoubtedly there were some) where gold and precious stones abounded, but no large-scale expeditions were mounted to find them. When such expeditions were mentioned, the authorities simply pointed to the expense and failure of Coronado's journey and such proposals were usually shelved. Nevertheless, such tales continued to keep the idea of a lost civilization alive in the public imagination. The Andes Mountains seemed

a reasonable place for such a civilization to exist, as did the steaming jungles that bounded on the mighty River Amazon, which cut into the heart of South America. As North America opened up to more and more exploration and colonization, South America still maintained an air of mystery that pulled on the imagination. The location of the mythical city therefore moved southward, and it was here that some of the later explorers turned their attentions.

The legend of El Dorado gradually became entwined with other legendary locations somewhere on the South American continent. One of these concerned the Ciudad de Los Cesares—the lost City of the Ceasars. This fabulously wealthy metropolis lay somewhere in the hills of present-day Patagonia, and had been reputedly founded by survivors from a Spanish ship (or ships) that had been wrecked there during a storm. The ship had been carrying great treasure that the crew had managed to save, and they carried it with him into the jungle-covered hinterland. There they had established a settlement, trading with local Indians who allegedly mined gold in the hills. This settlement grew into a massive city, reminiscent of those back in Spain, and was inhabited by a half Indian/half Spanish people who now shunned much contact with the outside world. The original crew had taken umbrage with Spain for not having sent ships to rescue them. Again, this story had overtones of the founding of the Seven Golden Cities by the fleeing Spanish bishops in the 12th century. The fabulous City of the Caesars took on some of the legendary characteristics of El Dorado in the popular mind, and soon legends concerning the two were virtually inseparable.

Another persistent legend that became entangled with that of El Dorado was that of the Sierra del Plata, which seemed to be located somewhere in either the present-day countries of Uruguay or Bolivia. The name meant "mountain of silver," and it was supposedly a great range of river-veined mountains that the Indians mined for their inordinate wealth. Located at the base of this range was a city in which the silver ore was processed and wonderful ornaments and trinkets were made. Part of this legend may well have been born out of the gifts given to the Spaniards and English explorers by native tribesmen. The merging of the Uruguay and Parana Rivers (both thought to originate in the Sierra) was given the name Rio del Plata (literally River of Silver), which was later changed to River Plate—where the German battleship *Graf Spee* was scuttled at the outbreak of World War II (during the naval Battle of the River Plate). In legend, however, the wealthy Indian city, which processed the silver ore, was equated with El Dorado and the legend grew.

Metaphors and Discoveries

For a time, the mysterious city became something of a metaphor. It was the symbol of distant and unattainable wealth, and of something valuable that perhaps lay just beyond the limits of an individual's reach. It was also used as something of a metaphor for a glittering prize that only persistence could attain. The reality of the lost city, however, was given a fresh impetus in the mid-19th century.

In 1860, Henri Mahout walked out of the Cambodian jungle and into the main street of an overgrown city of magnificent temples. He had discovered Angkor Wat, a lost religious city of the Khmer people that had flourished more than 500 years before. Soon after, another such city—Angkor Thom—was also discovered amid the encroaching jungles. Both cities had lain, forgotten and undetected, deep in the jungles for many years. If such massive and wonderful places had been hidden away for years, the argument went, might not El Dorado? Some expeditions were mounted once more, and at least one bore fruit. In 1911, the American explorer and archaeologist Hiram Bingham, following old Indian legends, found the ruins of a city high up in the Andes. The ruins that he had discovered were those of the lost Incan city of Machu Picchu (the Old Peak). This was located on a height above the Urumbamba Valley in Peru, northwest of the city of Cusco; it was not a city as such, but more of a summer retreat for the Inca nobility. Nevertheless, it sparked much theory once again about the actual existence of El Dorado. If Machu Picchu existed, might not other Inca or Aztec cities?

Speculation was rife, and it was assumed that the almost impenetrable Matto Grosso region of the Brazilian rainforest might hide the remains of another ancient city. So alluring was the premise that it soon drew in another explorer to follow the legend of El Dorado. Colonel Percy Fawcett was an adventurer and trailblazer in the South American jungle (particularly in the Amazon region), and he was convinced that somewhere deep in the wilderness lay the ruins of a vast city, which he simply named Z. Between 1906 and 1924, Fawcett made seven expeditions to Brazil, tracing the courses of rivers and visiting jungle settlements. He became well known for his courtesy among the river tribes, and established a reputation for himself with the Brazilian authorities. However, listening to native tales, he became more and more convinced that an ancient city lay somewhere deep in the Amazonian jungles. Fawcett also claimed to have unearthed a map and some notes allegedly attributed to Cabeza de Vaca or some other conquistador showing the location of such a city (this was, of course, highly suspect). In 1925, together with his son Jack and another friend Raleigh Rummell, he led an expedition, partly funded by the National Geographic Society in London, along the Amazon and deep into the Matto Grosso. They were never heard from again. Fawcett had left strict written instructions that if they did not return, no rescue expedition was to be mounted, and his wishes were respected. He had also telegraphed his wife from Brazil, stating that they were about to enter unknown territory, supposedly the haunt of cannibalistic and head-hunting tribes. It is quite possible that his expedition, which was last seen crossing the Upper Xingu River, was attacked, and Fawcett and his companions were killed. It is also a possibility that they died from disease somewhere in the jungle. Indeed, one of the Xingu Indians is alleged to have seen a white man, presumed to be Fawcett or one of his expedition, dying of fever in a native village, somewhere beyond the river.

Fawcett's disappearance sparked fresh mystery and speculation. It was claimed, for instance, that his expedition had found the lost city, but that the inhabitants there might have killed them; or he might still be living there, away from the world. Once again, stories of El Dorado began to circulate through the Western world. This continued sporadically for some time with notions of a lost civilization somewhere in the Brazilian jungle. In turn, El Dorado became a city of gold, a futuristic city of an immensely advanced culture or a colony built by aliens from space. However, if it did exist, it always remained tantalizingly elusive, just beyond the furthest point of exploration.

Today, El Dorado has returned to being something of a concept. Among the Muisca of Colombia, it is still the name for vital energy, and is believed in folk religion to be the name of one of the creators of the Universe. It has appeared in literature as something fabulous, but virtually unattainable. It has served as an inspiration to the American writer and poet Edgar Allen Poe, who wrote four stanzas on the subject, and also to Joseph Conrad, who referenced it in his *Heart of Darkness* (published in 1902). To many people, however, it still represents a distant ideal, something that appears just beyond their reach, but which will one day be discovered and attained.

13

The Kingdom of Prince Madoc

The discovery of the North American continent is usually credited to Christopher Columbus, an Italian working in the service of Spain. The date given for this important discovery is 1492. But although this is generally accepted, even today, this was not always the case, and the "discovery" created much unrest among European monarchs. Indeed, the Stuart king of England, James I, described it as "Tudor propaganda" designed to keep peace with Spain. And throughout the years, there have been hints and suggestions of earlier discoverers, and of different "empires and kingdoms" (many of them from Europe and Asia) within the continent.

There have been tales of a Turkish kingdom in parts of Tennessee and Alabama, perhaps before Columbus arrived. In fact, some of the racial speculation concerning the curious Melungeon peoples of the Cumberland Plateau and parts of eastern Kentucky is that they are of Turkish descent. And of course, some have argued that the name of the state itself is Turkish—Allah Bhama, allegedly meaning God's Cemetery. Others, however, have argued that it was the name of an Indian tribe that once occupied the area, or a word from the Muskogee dialect that means "Resting Place" (although no similar word has been found in Old Muskogee). This story, and others like it, have lived throughout the years.

The Kingdom of Alabama

One of the most persistent of such legends, however, asserts that part of Alabama was actually a medieval kingdom ruled by a Welsh prince. The kingdom had existed in the region during the 12th and 13th centuries, and there were allegedly still descendants of those whom the prince (whose name was given as Madoc) had brought with him from Wales, dwelling there. The legend seems to have originated in part during the mid-17th century. In 1660, a Welsh missionary, the Reverend Morgan Jones, was captured by a tribe of the Tuscarora nation, known as the Doeg. Believing himself to be condemned to death, the preacher uttered a prayer in Welsh, and was amazed when an old Indian answered him—in Welsh. It transpired, the old Indian stated, that this was the sacred language of the tribe that had been given to them by a great leader, long ago in their history, who was known as Modok. Jones (and many of those who came after him) was convinced that the area had been once inhabited by the Welsh and, talking to the Indians, seemed to trace the arrival of the "great leader" back to the 12th century. Subsequent researches have suggested who this "Modok" or Madoc might have been.

The Gwyneth Brothers

Both history and tradition name a Madoc as one of the 17 sons of Owain Gwyneth, ruler of Gwynedd, a northern kingdom of Cmyru (Wales), who took the throne in 1137. Although Welsh, it is quite possible that Owain also had some Norman blood in his veins as well, and may have ruled Gwynedd with some Norman support. However, his large family was to cause problems for the country when he died around 1166. The eldest legitimate son, Jarwath (Edward), suffered from a facial disfigurement, which immediately eliminated him as heir. Celtic law dictated that only an unblemished king could rule for fear of transferring his weakness into his people (an old Celtic superstition). Another contender, Howell, although older than Jarwath, was illegitimate, and was considered to be "basely born" because his mother was Irish. Nevertheless, Howell seized the throne by force and ruled for several years until his mother died. He then briefly left Wales to lay claim to his mother's estates in Ireland and while he was gone, his half-brother Daffyd (David) seized the throne and had Howell murdered upon his return. Daffyd ruled as king until Jarwath's son, Llywelyn, came of age and tried to claim his father's birthright. It is thought that he appealed to the Normans, who occupied England, and they granted him aid in exchange for his support against the southern kingdom of Powys. Gwynedd erupted in warfare.

Madoc, who was probably also illegitimate, became fearful. Daffyd was regarded as extremely ruthless and had ordered the death of at least two of his brothers. Llewellyn, however, was considered extremely treacherous, and had tried to murder another of his uncles. Hearing rumours of a vast new land beyond the sea to the west, Madoc decided to "cut and run," and in 1170 set sail with an intrepid band of followers.

Sailing only by the stars, they continued westward, eventually reaching the Gulf of Mexico and dropping anchor in Mobile Bay. The land that he found was temperate and lush and very much to Madoc's liking. He set up a colony there, farming the lands around Mobile and venturing slightly further inland. However, he was soon homesick, and in 1171, according to the legend, he returned home to Wales.

A few days in his native country was enough to cure him of his yearning. Gwynedd was still in turmoil and the war between Daffyd and Llewellyn had turned most of it into a wasteland. The Normans now conquered Powys and were threatening from the south. Madoc decided that his future lay on the other side of the ocean. His ship, the *Gwennon Gorn*, accompanied by his half-brother Rhyrd, set sail for America once again. The legend says that he was also accompanied by two of his sisters—the first Welsh women to set foot on American shores. Some commentators have stated that even if Madoc had made landfall in America, he could not have found his way back to Wales so accurately and then back to America again. However, some Viking ships used primitive compasses, and Greek ships used a navigational instrument known as a lodestone (which continually pointed northward) from which they could take bearings. Besides, Madoc was reputedly an extremely good seaman and navigator himself. According to legend, he had taken part in the actual building of the Gwennon Gorn (which means *stag's horn*) using nails made from stags' antlers. It has also been stated that he knew the winds, and so he was able to guide the boat back to the American continent.

From this point, Prince Madoc and his group disappear into history. It has been suggested that he landed further south than the site of his original expedition and reached Mexico where it was he (and not later Spanish) who was feted by the Aztecs and Quetzalcoatl.

Stories of Madoc's voyage lived on in song and poem back in his native Wales. A manuscript dating from the time of the English king Edward IV (1451–1483) and attributed to the Welsh bard Gutyen Owen, mentions Madoc's departure from Wales and his journey to an unknown land. In 1589, the voyage was also mentioned in the Tudor historian Richard Hakluyt's collection of early maritime voyages. Hakluyt was probably drawing on Owen's work and a number of other works that were in turn based on the manuscript—such as Dr. David Powel's *History of Cambria*.

Another manuscript, now stored in the British Museum and dating from around 1477, details the lineage of the kings of Gwynedd. It mentions that one of the sons of Owain Gwyneth was "an explorer of unknown lands," and gives the date for the departure of one of his expeditions as 1171. Parts of yet another manuscript (badly deteriorated) supposedly dating from 1255 and titled "The Romance of Madoc" were found in a monastery in Poitiers, France, during the 17th century. This manuscript seems to have disappeared once more, although a record of its discovery has been kept. The text is attributed to a Flemish poet known as William the Minstrel, and it spoke of Madoc's voyage to a sunken Paradise far beneath the waves. This may have been an interpretation of the prince's journey to America.

So widespread was the story that it had even reached both the English and Spanish Royal Courts. The Spanish in particular were intrigued by the story during the 1500s, particularly because a number of explorers had returned from the New World with stories that some of the Indian tribes they had encountered had spoken a language that was not unlike Welsh. It was also noted that some of these tribes had lighter colored skin tones than some of their neighbors, giving them the title "gente blanco" (white men). In 1557, the Spanish sent Parda de Luna into the Mobile River country to look for some of these Indians but, apparently, the results of his expedition were inconclusive. Later, in 1624, another expedition was mounted, this time into what is now Georgia; though several strange anomalies appear to have been found, nothing significant was discovered to link the Indians with the Welsh.

Still the Spanish did not give up. As late as 1711, expeditions were still being mounted to locate Welsh-speaking Indians. Part of the brief was also to find Indians with beards that would suggest European descent. Around this time, the Sieur d'Iberville arrived on the Alabama coast to found a new settlement. He chose a place known locally as The Mad Dog River (known as the Dog River today). In local parlance this was actually known as The Madog River which, some have argued, is a corruption of the name Madoc. Further up this river, it was claimed, lay the remains of an ancient stone fort (although this had been cleared away by local Indians by the time explorers arrived), which had been built by a great chieftain in times long past. Might these, it was argued, have been the ruins of a castle reminiscent of those in Wales?

In 1782, the explorer and Indian agent John Sevier (later the first governor of Tennessee), stumbled across the ruins of several stone fortresses in Tennessee and Kentucky while conducting a number of campaigns against local Indian tribes. Asking an old Indian, Chief Oconosoto, what these were, he was told that they had once belonged to a fair-skinned race of Indians, descended from a people known as "Welsh" who had come across the sea in a great boat and had landed at the mouth of the Alabama River near Mobile. They had settled there, but had been driven out through conflicts with local indigenous tribes, pushed back further inland and across the Hiwassee River just inside the present-day Tennessee border. Oconosoto claimed that his forefathers had engaged the "foreigners" in a massive battle near what is today Muscle Shoals, and drove them further back along the Mississippi River. They later settled along the Missouri and Ohio Rivers. However, he also said that these "foreigners" had married among local Indian tribes, particularly the Mandans, who were now in the upper reaches of the Missouri. Sevier revealed this information in a letter to Major Amos Stoddard, who had written to him enquiring about Welsh Indians. He also included the story related by a French trader who had lived for a time among the Cherokee. The French-man told Sevier that the Cherokee had traded with a tribe of light-skinned Welsh-speaking Indians who told him that they had sprung from a nation of white settlers.

The explorers Meriwether Lewis and William Clark also told about a light-skinned tribe of Indians, supposedly related to the Mandans, who had exhibited a style and manner that amounted to "European superiority" when compared to the tribes around. Clark, who was in charge of Indian affairs in the St. Louis area between 1822 and 1838, later stated that some Mandan women were "exceptionally pretty" and bore a distinct European cast to their features. This impression was borne out by other adventurers who met branches of the Mandan, and many assumed that at least some of these Indians boasted European ancestry.

Another writer, Francis Lewis (Welsh by birth), and one who signed the Declaration of Independence, had been captured by Indians after the fall of Oswego (August 1756) in present-day New York state, and was held prisoner by them for a while near Albany. He states that his captors often spoke to each other in a Welsh-like dialect, and when they spoke to him in English, they phrased it in a particular way—as "Welsh people might speak English." He eventually spoke to them in his own native Welsh and they let him go.

Today, the Mandan would make a fascinating study and the roots of their language might be explored. Unfortunately, between 1836 and 1837, many of the tribes were wiped out by a severe epidemic of smallpox. A tribe of 15,000 was shrunk to a few hundred, which were quickly assimilated into other surrounding tribes. The Welsh-speaking Indians seem to have disappeared completely as stronger, harsher dialects took over.

Evidence of Madoc

Apart from the language, what else could Madoc and his followers have left behind? The strongest evidence of their presence were a number of stone fortifications that closely resemble medieval Welsh strongholds. Whereas Indians may have built their forts on the plains where they camped, many of these fortresses are built defensively on unassailable clifftops and heights as European soldiers might have done. The overgrown ruins of such forts have been found in Tennessee, Alabama, and Georgia. What is interesting, too, is that, given the age of these ruins, the stone appears to have been cut using a form of chisel—a tool that would not have been available to the Indian tribes of the area. The geometry of the structures is also highly unlike anything the Indians might have constructed and instead resembles a medieval English or Welsh castle; in Tennessee, these forts form a defensive pattern. In 1823 a local judge, John Haywood, wrote down some history about Tennessee, and claimed that at least five of the forts near Chattanooga were designed to protect a white European people who were living in the Tennessee hinterland, many centuries ago. Some of these are surrounded by a deep ditch or moat, reminiscent of Norman or medieval fortifications, which suggest that Haywood might be right.

In 1540, the Spanish explorer and conquistador Hernando deSoto led an expedition across Alabama and Georgia in search of the fabled Seven Cities of Gold and Indian gold mines that were reputed to be in the area. He is alleged to have recorded a number of stone fortifications (then abandoned), which he claimed had been "built by the English or by an English prince," according to Indian legend. Could he have meant Welsh? There are certainly the remains of such a stone fortification at DeSoto Falls near Mentone, Alabama, where the Spaniard and his men made camp. The size and positioning of the fortress suggests that it may have been an important site, perhaps the camp of a great chieftain. Intriguingly, it has been noted that there are many architectural similarities between the fortress at DeSoto Falls and Dolwyddelan Castle in Gwynedd. These include low entrances, exactly the same arrangement of moats and defenses, and the same method of construction for the outer walls. Dolwyddelan lay in Madoc's homeland, and was a castle with which he would have been familiar. Is the coincidence too close? It is possible that in 1171, the Welsh, having failed to return to their original encampment on the Gulf of Mexico, made their way inland using the main river systems, primarily the Alabama and Coosa, until they reached what is now De Soto Falls where they built their first major castle? The ruins of another such castle lie not all that far away, at Fort Mountain, which displays many of the same architectural characteristics as the one at De Soto Falls. It is worth noting that none of the Indian tribes in the locality—principally the Cherokee—built stone fortifications; the engineering skills demonstrated in both these forts and a similar one at Old Stone Fort, were far beyond their competence.

These are not the only such forts to be found in the States. There was a large fort at the mouth of Chickmauga Creek that has now been submerged in an irrigation scheme; another stood at Pumpkinville (now part of Athens, Tennessee) on the Hiwassee; and another still on a high precipice above the Duck River, near Manchester, Tennessee. On the map, these forts form a network—some connected by waterways—and are in keeping with the medieval idea of building small castles in order to keep power and law in a district. They would therefore be consistent with the establishment and maintenance of a small kingdom in the region. Did Madoc rule the lands around Alabama, Georgia, and Kentucky as a kind of Welsh feudal king? On the suggestions of the physical evidence, it would appear so. Although the major fort above De Soto Falls is now gone (locals carried away its stones to build barns and walls), we have enough description of it to identify it as a medieval European prince's stronghold. An Alabaman historian, Albert Picket, who visited the site around 1851, remarked on how well the complicated system of defensive ditches had been designed, suggesting that their skills were advanced for any of the local Indians of the time.

Also near the De Soto Falls site is yet another intriguing piece of evidence. About three quarters of the way down the bluff, above the nearby Little River, is a series of five caves. Initially, these may well have been natural caverns, but, at some point, they had been extended and developed as defensive fortifications. In fact, there may have been a defense wall of earth and rubble in front of the caves' mouths. A single path up the side of the cliff, suitable only for one man at a time to climb, leads up to them. All the caves have been extended and widened, once again by using chisel-like implements, which, it is argued, would probably not have been available to the local Indians. The area is quite clearly a defensive position, consistent with those found in medieval France and England. On this defensive position, an armed group of men could hold off the advance of an enemy as they tried to climb to attack the castle above. Most commentators and historians agree that this was not an Indian tactic, but the mark of European warfare. Some have argued that Hernando de Soto's men constructed the defense themselves, but others state that the cave extensions are far older than the Spaniard.

Perhaps de Soto himself had heard of Prince Madoc, as there is rumored to be an old map of Alabama, Georgia, and parts of Kentucky attributed to the explorer (which several claim to have seen) on which one word appears. That word is "Madoc." For centuries, it was thought to be the name of a tribe, but might it be something more? A copy of this map is still said to be extant in Seville, Spain, today.

Despite such a crushing weight of circumstantial evidence, there is still no recognition of the Welsh kingdom in Alabama, or of its medieval ruler. Most historians today tend to regard the Madoc story as a popular myth or medieval romance without any foundation. And yet, of all the stories of lost realms and kingdoms, arguably the legend of a Welsh prince ruling in some parts of Alabama and Georgia during the 12th century seems to be the most credible. And even if it were only partially true, it gives a fascinating and intriguing insight into a history of the American continent which has, in many respects, been all but ignored. Whether or not he truly existed as a medieval king of America, the story of Prince Madoc provides an enduring and intriguing mystery that certainly deserves further investigation.

14

Hyperborea

Fans of Robert E. Howard's Conan the Cimmerian series or other "sword and sorcery fiction" will perhaps be familiar with Hyperborea. In much of the writing, it is simply a land that is unimaginably far away, and which seems to be permanently locked in winter—a place of intense cold and solitude. It is a place of glaciers and snowstorms, where the wind whistles continually across frozen plains. Its only inhabitants are said to be tribes of ferocious, fur-clad warriors who eke out a harsh and violent existence in the desolate wasteland. This, of course, is the fictional version of the countryside, but did such a place actually exist? If so, where might it have been?

In a Land Far, Far Away

For the ancient Greeks, Hyperborea was the furthest point in the world that they could possibly imagine. And for some, it was as different from their own pleasant and temperate Mediterranean homeland as could be conceived. Even the name Hyperborea ("the land behind Boreas, or the north wind") suggested desolation and bleakness to them. Yet, for others, it was an earthly Paradise where the inhabitants didn't have to work, lived in splendid towns and cities, and made no war against each other. The picture of Hyperborea across the Greek world was therefore an extremely confusing one.

Its location, too, was a matter of some dispute. For some Greeks it lay far to the North, beyond the lands of Scythia. The Scythian kingdoms comprised areas of what is now today Kazakhstan, Belarus, and parts of Russian Georgia. It was also taken to include parts of the Ukraine. To its north lay the land of Hyperborea that was either a frozen wilderness or a wonderful sun-drenched country. In both mythologies, it was a land where the sun never set. This idea may have come about through descriptions of the extended winters and summers in northern climes when, indeed, the sun shone continually for almost six months of the year. To those living around the edges of the Mediterranean, it must have seemed as though the northern lands lay in perpetual daylight. Within this daylight lay either endless, sparkling snow or a wonderful lush green country, punctuated by flowing rivers.

Other Greeks, however, took a different view regarding Hyperborea's location. They described it as a massive island-continent beyond the Pillars of Hercules in the Atlantic Ocean. According to Plato, such a country had been visited by the Carthaginian explorer Hanno the Navigator around 570 B.C. Hanno had spent most of his career mapping out the coasts of North Africa, and had even traveled further south. However, he claimed that Hyperborea contained a number of significant Berber-like kingdoms similar to those that had already been established in Morocco and Algeria. The continent, he claimed, lay not far from the North African coast and traded with Morocco and the Iberian Peninsula (present-day Spain and Portugal). Other explorers, however, disagreed, and placed the Hyperborean continent further north. Around 325 B.C., according to Pliny the Elder, a Greek explorer named Phytheas of Massilia sailed through the Pillars of Hercules, following a course that took him well to the north of Ireland. After several days' sailing he made landfall in a warm and temperate place that he named Thule (which others have declared was Hyperborea), where the inhabitants were extremely jolly and pleasant, and seemed to spend most of their time holding large festivals in honor of Greek gods. This was where, it was said, Apollo wintered and took his ease among such pleasant and generous people. His description of these inhabitants has led many to believe that they were a Celtic people and has caused some, including the philosopher Aristotle, to suggest that this was where the Druids (Celtic holy men) came from and where the "mysteries" of Celtic religion began. It is possible that Phytheas had actually visited the

Outer Hebrides, an island chain far off the coast of northern Scotland, and had mistaken the peoples there for the mythical Hyperboreans.

The notion of this land in the Northern Atlantic was taken up again around 55 B.C. by the Greek historian Diodorus Siculus. He spoke of an island far beyond the Pillars of Hercules, no bigger than Sicily, on which there was a wonderful round temple dedicated to the moon. The "temple" that Diodorus describes may well have been the impressive stone circle at Callanish on the Isle of Lewis in the Hebrides, which was supposedly raised by a proto-Celtic peoples and may have been dedicated to both sun and moon worship. Although Diodorus had never been there, he was probably relying on another, earlier work written around A.D. 300 by the Greek geographer Hecataeus of Miletus, which mentioned an island, slightly smaller than Sicily, lying in the northern oceans. It was said that Latonia, the mother of Apollo, had been born here, and so the god had a special association with this land. The people there worshipped him in his incarnation as the sun—perhaps reflecting the old Celtic sun-veneration of the Northern Isles.

Others in the Greek world disputed the location of Hyperborea. How, they argued, could such a delightful and temperate climate exist in the North when the lands there were covered with snow and ice? Hyperborea therefore must lie in some warmer part of the world, such as Thrace (parts of Turkey, Greece, and Bulgaria); some even placed it on the other side of the Black Sea, while others still gave it as a warm valley somewhere in the Ural Mountains. Although Pliny the Elder (A.D. 23–79) tried to resolve the problem by establishing a belief in various climatic zones, much doubt as to the location of such a temperate area remained.

To add further confusion, Hyperborea was often linked with another distant, mythical land that the Greeks named Thule (later Ultima Thule in medieval times, although it was also mentioned as such by the Roman poet Virgil). This, for the Greeks, was another far-away point, one of the most distant they could imagine, and it was also the name that Phytheas had given to the country on which he had landed beyond the Pillars of Hercules. Later, Thule was actually believed to have been in the British Isles, although some also identified it as Scandinavia or some of the Baltic isles. Explorers of the 15th and 16th centuries would identify it with Greenland or Lapland. Some of the early Greek writers even doubted whether Hyperborea actually constituted land or not. Polybus, writing in his *Histories* (written around 140 B.C.)

suggests that, as a landmass, it was neither solid, water, nor air, but a combination of all three, and it had the consistency of jellyfish and could not be walked upon. Most of the early peoples, however, agreed that Hyperborea/Thule was an island-continent far to the north that could only be reached by an impossibly long sea-journey.

But what of those who lived there? What sort of people were they? The remoteness of their country, it was said, did not stop them from trading with other people, and the Hyperboreans sent gifts to Greek centers such as Athens, Delos, and Delphi. The Delphic Oracle of Apollo was said to frequently receive gifts and offerings from that far-away country in honor of the god. One of the earliest references to Hyperboreans comes from the Greek scholar Hesiod, writing in 700 B.C., who makes reference to them. Later Greek and Roman writers such as Herodotus (484–425 B.C.) generally regarded as "the Father of History," and the Roman poet Cicero (106–43 B.C.) also mention them, stating that the people of Hyperborea were extremely fit and healthy, and lived to almost 1,000 years old. They also lived in a state of complete happiness in a pleasant and temperate land and were extremely wealthy, having much gold that they had won from griffins, which inhabited part of their country, and had guarded large treasures left by former races. The celebrated Greek heroes Theseus and Perseus were supposed to visit them, and found them to be extremely able warriors although they refused to be drawn into the wars of other races.

But what did the Hyperboreans actually look like? According to Hanno, who had visited them around 500 B.C., they resembled a people who would later come to be known as Moors, inhabiting much of the North African coast and parts of Spain. They were, reputedly, dark and swarthy skinned, but lighter in color than the Africans who lived further south and, according to some accounts, smaller than many Europeans. Some descriptions are suggestive of Berber peoples while others seem to point to a Semitic-type race. Hanno, of course, located their land not far from the North African coast, so at least some of these descriptions would seem to be fairly consistent with the region.

But here again, we find conflict and confusion for some later Greek explorers, for example, Phytheas, describe them differently. In some accounts they are described as being practically giants, pale-skinned and fair or red haired, perhaps reflecting something of a more Nordic influence. They were

rather civilized, living in both towns and cities and trading with other peoples, but they were also very proud and fierce, willing to attack those who threatened them or who transgressed their laws at the slightest opportunity. Although they traded locally, they took little to do with the Mediterranean sphere of influence.

The Guanches People

Diverse theories regarding Hyperborea were later used to explain the origins of a number of races scattered around the Atlantic area. The most celebrated of all these "explanations" concerned the mysterious Guanches peoples who were the original inhabitants of the Canary Islands, and who were later ousted (or exterminated) by Spanish and Portuguese settlers. The name "Guanch" or "Guanchinet" comes from a mixture of ancient terminologies and actually means "man of Tenerife" (*guan* for "man" and *Chinet* for "Tenerife"). Although these people were considered to be reasonably primitive (they had not advanced far beyond the Stone Age) when the first European explorers arrived during the medieval period, there seems to have been some evidence to suggest that they may have been the descendants of other, more advanced inhabitants. Either that or the islands were previously inhabited by another race who subsequently abandoned them to the Guanches. Some have claimed that this race was the Hyperboreans. Hanno the Carthaginian explorer visited the islands in the 500s B.C. and claimed that he found them to be largely uninhabited; but he also found evidence of great ruins, as in those of mighty cities there. It is suggested that the Guanche might have migrated from some part of northwest Africa, taking over these ruins about which they knew little, and making them their homes. Some accounts of early explorations of the Canaries state that they were living among the remnants of dwellings that they could not possibly have built themselves. Were these the ruins of Hyperborean cities?

Pliny the Elder, relying on the testimony of King Juba II of Mauritania, a North African coastal Berber kingdom, claims that there was indeed a fairly advanced civilization on the Canaries that preceded Guanches settlements, and that these may indeed have been Hyperboreans or the inhabitants of Thule. He points to a curious tongue that many of the Guanches spoke, and which they were said to have picked up from survivals on the Canaries. In the later 1300s and early 1400s, the incoming Spanish and Portuguese eradicated this language and more or less eliminated the Guanches by massacring them, enslaving them, or allowing them to marry into Spanish society; all traces of these people have therefore been eliminated, including their language. There is now no way in which we can check Pliny's theories. But the origins of the Gaunches people remain an intriguing mystery—some have even connected them to survivors from the destruction of ancient Atlantis or even Lemuria.

The Aryans

The Guanches were not the only ancient people supposedly to have originated in Hyperborea—another such race was the Aryans. Aryan was initially an Indo-European language form that probably started out among some of the early tongues of the Far East. However, by the late 1800s and early 1900s, scientists and anthropologists were already developing ways to explain differences in various races and dispersal of prehistoric races. One of the determinant factors, it was argued, might be language. Language identified and unified a people, and shaped the course of their culture. It also set them apart from their neighbors and defined them as a people. Thus, the Aryan language became identified with an early people, and the phrase "Aryan race" was born. The word *Aryan* may come from a mingling of ancient Persian and Vedic Sanskrit (the form of Sanskrit used in the holy Vedas of northern India), and is taken to mean spiritual or noble. It was first used to describe, in a generalized way, a culture that had sprung up in ancient Iran, which contained elements of both early Persian and Indian thinking. Later, as more language groups were discovered, further elements of the Avestan tongue (the most ancient language in Iran/Iraq and used in the Gathas—the most sacred texts in Zoroastrianism) were added making the term mean "superior and skillful." The anthropologists of the early 20th century, eager to make distinctions between ancient peoples and to show the origins of some more modern races, referred to this culture as "Aryan," although it is not exactly clear if indeed these were a homogenous people or they saw themselves as such. Soon, however, an entire ideal had built up around this grouping including a point of origin that some argued might be Hyperborea or Thule. Based on alleged cranial measurements, this race was considered to be different from, and superior to, other emerging races such as the Semites and the forerunners of the African peoples. This led to the idea of a pale-skinned race that might well have spread out from Hyperborea into Europe and some of the more northerly lands of Scandinavia. Others, however, argued that the Aryan race had originated in the Caucasus Mountains in southern Russia, and this was where Hyperborea had lain. From this idea would emerge the term "Caucasian," which came to be applied to any white European or those of white European descent. This, in some ideologies, was tied in with the notion of beauty. The ancient Greeks had held that the goddess Aphrodite was fair-haired and blue-eyed, and this was symbolic of her purity and beauty. This would later transfer itself into the perceived characteristics of the Aryan race.

Such notions would, of course, inevitably lead to the development of a racist philosophy. This ideal was fuelled by the writings of H.P. Blavatsky under the alleged direction of her "Secret Masters" in Tibet. In her book *The Secret Doctrine* (published in 1888), Madame Blavatsky identified Hyperborea as being the home of the second "root race" dwelling on Earth, and stated that it was located somewhere in the vicinity of Greenland. This gave the land a sense of the occultism that was associated with Blavatsky's movement, and suggested that Hyperborea might be connected to ancient mysteries long forgotten.

This concept of an ancient, mysterious, and culturally superior people springing from a lost land, now disappeared, found its expression in Nordic-Aryanism, a philosophy that developed the idea of a "Master Race," which had been the forerunners of blue-eyed, blond-haired humans—mainly in parts of Germany. These had been people with a slightly different cranial development to other species of man, and were therefore much more "skill-ful, spiritual, and noble" than other races around them—as the term Aryan had now come to suggest. The theory of Aryanism was based partly on the work of the French anthropologist Joseph Deneker (1852–1918), who coined the term "Nordique." It was generally agreed that a white-skinned, fair-haired race had come into Europe from an unknown origin somewhere in the north, and had a profound affect on the people there. These people, it was suggested, were Aryan. Occultists claimed that they had come from Hyperborea or Thule (which were now rapidly becoming one and the same). Such theories were widely accepted throughout Europe in the era following the first World War, but in the mid-20th century, they took on a much more sinister tone.

In 1918, a German occultist, Rudolf von Sebottendorf (or Sebottendorff) founded the Thule Society also known as the Thule-gesellshaft, the Teutonic group or Studengruppe fur germanisches altertum (Study Group for German Antiquity) that was supposedly an occult and folklore society. The "folklore" element of the group concerned itself with a highly romanticized view of German history. Much of it concerned itself with the rise of the Aryan people who had originated in Hyperborea or Thule. Von Sebottendorf was not all he appeared—his name was actually an alias; he had been born Alfred Rudolf Glauer (1875–1945), and he was something of a noted con man. Some of his interests lay in German freemasonry, and he often portrayed himself as an "occultist," privy to hidden mystical knowledge. His ideas regarding Hyperborea, some of which he had culled from Madame Blavatsky, were especially suspect, but that did not stop them from being accepted by some very powerful advocates.

One of the groups that Glauer's theories attracted was the NSDAP (the National Socialist German Worker's Party) or Nazi Party. Nazi mystics viewed Hyperborea as the birthplace of Aryan "ubermenschen" (supermen), and the blonde-haired, blue-eyed German people as their descendants, constituting a "Master Race," which would one day dominate the world. They took the name "Ultima Thule" (that was the name with the Roman poet Virgil had used to describe a city at the furthest point of human geographical knowledge) to be the capital of Hyperborea and the epitome of early civilization. The Nazi leader Adolf Hitler was also greatly in favor of such theories as they matched his own ideas of racial superiority, which would eventually lead to the horrors of World War II. Many senior Nazis—for example Heinrich Himmler—also held such views regarding Hyperborea/Thule, theories that were swept away by the defeat of Nazi Germany and the end of the War. As for Glauer himself, he is supposed to have committed suicide by leaping into the River Bosporus in May 1945, although it has been suggested that his death was faked by Turkish Intelligence for whom he was working at the time, and that he actually died in Egypt in the 1950s, still maintaining some of his beliefs concerning the Aryans.

Perhaps as a result of its close connection with Nazi ideology, theories regarding Hyperborea began to diminish following the end of World War II. It was revived slightly in the 1960s and 1970s by science-fiction and fantasy writers who used it as a setting for some of their stories and novels. It has also been mentioned by certain heavy metal bands as part of their song lyrics, and there are even computer games that make reference to it. Today, however, the actual land remains little more than a vague memory, a theory that has more or less vanished into time.

Did Hyperborea truly exist, somewhere among the snows close to the North Pole, or was it just an idea to denote the furthest point to those living in the Mediterranean cultures could possibly imagine? Or was it simply a description of some parts of Scandinavia by those who lived in more southerly countries? Whatever the answer, the name Hyperborea has entered our language as meaning something incredibly far away, perhaps unattainable or unreachable, and maybe, for many of us, this is the most enduring image of this mysterious and unimaginable land.

15

Irem: City of Pillars

Anyone who is reasonably familiar with the works of the American horror writer H.P. Lovecraft (and those who emulated him) will be familiar with the dark city of Irem. This was a hideous, shadowy place, located somewhere in the deserts of Arabia, built in some distant pre-historic time, and now inhabited by the ghouls and afreets of Arabic folk-lore. It was the place deep in the sandy wastes of the Sahara, visited by the mad Arab, Abdul Alhazarad, author of the text *Al Azif*, which, translated into Latin, became the blasphemous *Necronomicon*, a staple of Lovecraft's dark fiction. Here, among the dark and towering pillars of that terrible city, Alhazarad learned awful secrets that actually drove him mad and formed the source for a dark lineage that seems to have extended all over the world. Irem then became a dark and sinister place in horror writing, initially appearing as The Nameless City deep in the desert, in Lovecraft's eerie story of the same name. But had Lovecraft (and those who came after him) based this mon-strous city on an actual location that Mankind had forgotten or else blotted from its collective mind? Strangely, both historical fact and myth are closer to the Lovecraftian tradition than one might imagine.

Afreets and Fiends

In Lovecraft's Mythos, Irem is the haunt of djinni and afreets, creatures that have inhabited the world in some former time. Before the consolidation of Judaism and the coming of Islam (and even long after), there was a widespread belief in spirits and disembodied forces all across the Arab and Semitic worlds. Animistic entities dwelt in rocks, pools, streams, and caverns far out in the desert and beyond the dwellings of humans, making their presence known only in the vaguest of ways. They were recognized in the minor whirlwinds that swept across the desert plains from time to time, or by eerie sounds emanating from remote hollows and valleys. Mostly, they were inimical and hostile toward Mankind, and sought to do humans harm when they could. These were the djinn or spirits who had no real corporeal form, but were nevertheless extremely powerful. It was widely believed that they were beings who had existed since before the foundation of the world and they were heirs to the ancient magics that had formed the Universe. They could create fierce sandstorms that could lay to waste an entire city, or floods that could devastate a fertile valley; they could create solid objects out of air and smoke, and inflict disease and pestilence upon those who had angered them. The genie in the story of Aladdin is such a being (although often set in China, the story had Middle Eastern origins). However, only certain men could communicate with them or in some cases control them.

Muqarribun

These were the muqarribun, or Ghost Priests, of Bedouin folklore, who dwelt in Arabia in pre-Islamic days, and who were regarded as magicians and sorcerers, usually leaning toward the Black Arts. Indeed, all who had dealings with the djinn were regarded with intense suspicion. The muqarribun, however, often allowed themselves to be possessed by such spirits, and this was often regarded as the source of their magical powers. They were also interpreters, listening to the "voices of the desert" (voices of the djinn) and deriving meanings from them. As well as this, they were the guardians and recorders of old lore, which had allegedly existed from a time before the world was formed.

The muqarribun knew of Irem or Iram, and mentioned it in those fragments of their writings that survive. Their lore states that it was built several generations after the Flood (some accounts say five) and that it was built by the tribe of Ad, who were direct descendants of Noah through his son Shem. According to tradition, the Ahd-al-Jann were a race of giants—"more than men"—similar to the Nephilim of Semitic folklore, who had close links with the djinn or "formless ones." At the time of the building of Irem, their king was Shaddad of the bloodline of Shem, and it was he who conspired with the djinn, to build a large city for his people. Since the Flood had scourged the world, the survivors had grown lax in their ways and in their worship of Allah (God). They now consorted with the djinn, who had also survived the Deluge and, encouraged by the latter, had given themselves to witchcraft and magical practices. With the aid of the djinn, Shaddad built the city of Irem as his capital, and it became a haven of necromancers and practitioners of the devilish arts. The location of this city lay on the Arabian Peninsula in an area known as the Rub-el-Khali, or "Empty Quarter." According to the tradition of the muqarribun, the location had a "hidden meaning"; "the empty quarter" referred to death and decay, and a kind of dark void within the soul of Mankind. It was a gateway to the lands of death, which lay beyond the senses of most mortals. This, of course, made it a fitting home for a city such as Irem. Some traditions say that Irem was built by the djinn themselves before the time of Adam, and was later inhabited by men. This tradition stems from the name "Irem of the Pillars"—the ancient Arabic word for "pillar" corresponding to another meaning, namely "Old One." The name, therefore, was a city of the Old Ones (that is, djinns).

The City

As activities in Irem became more and more blasphemous, Allah sent the prophet Hud to warn the people there to behave. However, the populace ignored the warning and so Allah punished the city, first by a drought, and secondly by a monstrous sandstorm that buried the dark metropolis. Irem vanished beneath the sands of the Empty Quarter, apparently lost forever. However, even though it was covered in sand, its baleful influence still crept out like a shadow across the desert to affect large parts of the Middle East. These were the legends of which the muqarribun spoke, and they were quite clearly pre-Islamic.

So strong a tradition was this story of Irem that it even found its way into Islamic holy text as a warning in the style of Sodom and Gomorrah in Semitic teaching: "Seest thou not how thy Lord dealt with the Ad of the city of Irem with the lofty pillars The like of which were not produced in all the land" (Holy Qu'ran: Surah Al-Fajir 89 1–89:14). This seems to have been an absorption of ancient muqarribun lore into mainstream Islamic teaching. It also appears in a collection of folktales from the Middle East known as *The Thousand and One Nights*, which has given us many other tales such as Ali Baba and Aladdin (Al-Haddin).

Folklore in the Middle East

More traditional Bedouin folklore spoke of a city that had been erected by an ancient civilization that had ruled part of the Middle East about 3,000 years before the coming of the Prophet. It had been extremely wealthy and had traded in spices and unguents with the rest of the world. However, the inhabitants had always been interested in the occult and the dark sciences. They encouraged the muqarribun and kahins (oracle mongers—men who also allowed themselves to be possessed by spirits in order to see the future) to live within their walls and to practice their questionable arts. Irem or Iram (the spellings only differ slightly) became a by-word for occultism throughout the lands of the Middle East. In the end, Allah would tolerate it no longer, sending a mighty sandstorm to swallow up the entire city. Allah's anger stemmed from the fact that the principal god of Irem was the entity Moloch or Molech. In the center of Irem lay the great Tophet, or enclosure, which was dedicated to this fearful god, and in which, it was whispered, child sacrifice was carried out.

Moloch

Moloch appears in both Semitic and early Arab mythology. It is a complicated deity, taking on a number of guises such as a man with the head of a bull. The name is thought to have derived from the words *molech* (king) or *boseth* (shame), and is usually taken to refer to a dark and barbaric entity (although this may not strictly be the case). In Semitic folklore he is portrayed as one of the enemies of Yahweh (the chief god of the Israelites), and is sometimes equated with Ba'al, the corn/fertility god of the Canaanites. It was thought that Moloch demanded human sacrifice from his followers to ensure good harvests (perhaps something similar to the sacrifices offered up to the Crom Cruach in pre-Christian Celtic Ireland), especially the sacrifice of children. In Semitic tradition, it was said that such worship took place in the valley of Gei-ben-Hinnom (Gehenna), the Valley of Hinnom's son, which lay near the city of Jerusalem. The steep-walled valley had a particularly sinister reputation and was said, at its most northerly end, to contain the Tophet, a large enclosed area in which small children were ritually burned to death in honor of Moloch. Unsurprisingly, the name Gehenna soon became equated with Hell. Arab mystics asserted that the Tophet was an area where the world of men and the Otherworld overlapped, and where the god could take burning children to himself. This had overtones of muquarribun lore that said the Rub-el-Khali was also the "gateway to Hell." Because the Tophet was supposedly located in the very heart of Irem, according to Bedouin folklore, it suggested that the city itself might also be somewhere in the vastness of the Empty Quarter.

Another god that was said to have been traditionally worshipped in Irem was Khadhulu, the Abandoner or Forsaker. There is supposed to be a reference to Khadhulu in a rumored, fragmentary text known as the al-Kadiff, or al-Khadiff, although no trace of such a work now appears to exist. However, the reference would seem to be only a passing one, and the name Khadhulu may be no more than another Arabic name for the Semitic Moloch. Yet another given name is Shaitan (enemy) from which our name Satan derives. Whether or not Khadhulu is one of the djinn or not is unclear, but its significance in Arab mysticism is twofold. The main thrust is that Khadhulu will promise Mankind great things, but will ultimately abandon or forsake him; the second, that the entity will cause Mankind to abandon or forsake the true faith that is Islam. According to some Arabic legends, Khadhulu had his soul in Irem, and the king Shaddad was his physical embodiment. In Semitic folklore, Khadhulu seems to have been a "fallen angel" or "son of God."

Readers cannot fail to have noted the similarity between the names Khadhulu and Cthulhu in Lovecraft's fiction, and the resemblance between the legendary Al-Khaddif in Bedouin lore and the Al-Azif among his list of forbidden books. Is it possible that Lovecraft himself picked up on some of the Arab and Semitic mythologies, adapting them for his fiction? And that part of that mythology became embodied in the sinister city of Irem, the image of which haunts some of his work?

The dark and sinister city, then, certainly exists in Arabic folklore, but is there anything in the history of Arabia that might link with it? Indeed, there would appear to be, but the location moves a little from the Rub-el-Khali or Empty Quarter of the Sahara Desert and further down onto the Arabian Gulf.

Sodom and Gomorrah

Of course there are a number of stories of mysterious Arabian cities that have been overwhelmed by natural disasters—either by sandstorms, or even by the sea. The two most famous cities, of course, are Sodom and Gomorrah, which are said, according to legend, to lie somewhere under the Dead Sea. Similar to the story of Irem, they were destroyed by God because of the wickedness and perceived "unnatural practices" of their inhabitants. For example, in Sodom it was said that widespread homosexuality was prevalent; leading to the derivation of the word *sodomy* in modern times. The fate of the two cities served as a warning to others. Only one righteous man—Lot—was spared, but his wife was supposedly turned into a pillar of salt for looking back to witness their destruction. Although mentioned in the Bible as historical sites, many scholars today argue as to whether Sodom and Gomorrah actually existed or whether the tale is simply a cautionary fable.

Ubar

The name Iruma (Irem) appears in connection with another vanished city, significantly also located in the Empty Quarter. This was the trading city of Ubar, and it is known that such a place existed. Ubar was an extremely wealthy metropolis that lay on a main trade route between the desert kingdoms and the sea. Its major trade was frankincense, from which it had derived most of its prosperity. Frankincense is an aromatic resin, initially used in Middle Eastern perfumes and was derived from the bark of the boswellia tree, large acreages of which grew in Yemen. Although it is named as frankincense (from the Franks who first introduced it to Europe), it was also known as olibanum throughout the Middle East (from the Arabic al-luban—"the milk"), and was prized among the elite and wealthy of the Arabic society. Indeed, in the biblical tale, it is one of the gifts offered to the infant Jesus in the manger by the Three Wise Men. Much of its production was based in Yemen, but its popularity means that it was exported to both the Arab and Asian worlds. Ubar, which lay near what is today the borders of Yemen, was a major center for such trade.

Scholars knew of Ubar's existence from records found in the ruins of another city. This was the city of Ebla in Syria, 20 miles south west of Aleppo. In its heyday, Ebla maintained a large and extensive library of cuneiform texts, mainly relating to economic matter (Ebla itself was a trading city) and it is here that Ubar is mentioned. Ebla seems to have traded with Ubar and refers to it from time to time as Iruma. It also clarifies the phrase "of the pillars." The word "pillars" would appear to be a mistranslation, and the word should in fact be "towers." Ubar, it would appear, was heavily defended— perhaps against desert raiders—and had prominent fortifications consisting of a number of high towers. This also gave protection to camel trains coming across the desert and seeking shelter within its walls. It is described as a place of inordinate wealth and culture, trading with Asia and the Arabic world.

Around A.D. 1000, all reference to Ubar suddenly ceases, as if the city had disappeared. It was generally assumed that because of some natural catastrophe, it had been abandoned and claimed by the desert, although some legends state that it had be "swallowed up by the earth" (this turned out to be literally true). However, the general consensus was that it had been overwhelmed by a terrible sandstorm, and it still lay there, somewhere under the desert. This gave it the nickname "The Atlantis of the Desert."

For a long time, Ubar remained an intriguing myth, and noone really knew what had befallen it or why it had been abandoned. In 1984, however, the orbital Challenger satellite, monitoring the old Middle East spice routes as part of a historical research program, picked out what appeared to be the remnants of an old road system, which appeared to have been designed for camel trains in the Dhofar Province of southern Oman. Further investigation using X-Ray scanning revealed the surrounding area was the roof of a large underground limestone cavern, filled with a huge subterranean lake that had formed a water-table for a city built above it. However, as the inhabitants of the city drew water from the cavern through a series of wells, the water table within the cavern had lowered considerably. Deprived of its buoyant support, the cavern roof weakened and collapsed, swallowing the city above. The gaping abyss was subsequently covered by the encroaching desert. The city that had literally fallen into the hole was Ubar. Although ruins remained, they were soon depopulated, and the inhabitants were scattered throughout the Middle East and parts of Asia. Challenger also picked out traces of other lost cities along the frankincense route, dating from as early as 2800 B.C.; it was estimated that by its location, Ubar acted as an important center for that trade. The date of the collapse is estimated at around A.D. 500 or even slightly later, which would tie in with the disappearance of the city from all records. The camel trains simply went elsewhere.

The area, according to tradition (and perhaps with some foundation) was believed to be the center for a branch of Islam not found anywhere else (although it has since spread to Algeria and Libya). This was Ibadism, distinct from both Sunni and Sh'ia factions, taking its name from Abdullah Ibn Ibad at Tamini (although he may not exactly have been the sect's founder) who was a prophet less than 50 years after the death of Mohammed. Rumor has it that this strict branch of Islam, which regards the Sunni and Sh'ia traditions as kuffar (unbelievers or "those who deny God's grace"), has a more mystical branch that is perhaps tinged with some of the beliefs of the Asian continent and may contain elements of older pre-Islamic faiths that have been modified. At one time, this Islamic tradition was only found in Oman, and seemed to be centered where Ubar had once stood. Given its trade with Asia and other parts of the East, had new philosophies crept in to slightly influence Islam in this area?

The notion of Irem then—the monstrous city that haunts the shadows of Lovecraft's fiction (and which, through Alhazared is central to the idea of the Necronomicon)—is a complex mixture of folklore and history. Was it the frankincense-trading city of Ubar, which fell into an underground cavern and was lost for almost a thousand years? Or does it relate more to the lore of the muqarribun, the Ghost Priests who traced it back to a monstrous pre-Adamite metropolis raised by the "Old Ones"?

Whatever the answer, Irem seems a strange, terrible, and shadow-haunted place; perhaps its actual location lies somewhere in the darkest depths of the human imagination. This maybe is the truth of the fabled City of Pillars.

16

Bimini and the Fountain of Youth

Few mythical places have actual locations formally named after them. El Dorado County in California is one such place. Bimini, a present-day district of the Bahamas administration, is another, named after an earthly and mystical paradise in Arawak folklore. Today the district of Bimini is comprised of a chain of small islands in the Bahamas, but in folklore, it was the Arawak equivalent of the Garden of Eden, and the place from which human life had sprung. The name means "The Mother of Waters," and it was thought that in Bimini, the rest of the world was created from the ocean. But it held another secret: Bimini was believed to be the location of the fabled Fountain of Eternal Youth. And, similar to El Dorado, it was the Spanish exploration of America that brought Bimini to its legendary prominence.

Since earliest times, the idea of living forever or of being forever young has both excited and entranced the human imagination; such a concept has often been associated with water. An ancient legend, perhaps even predating the Sumerian civilization, tells of the Sons of Parthalon, a prehistoric king who rode out questing for the fabled Waters of Oblivion, which held the power of life and death over mortals. Such Waters, it was said, gushed out of the rock in a great fountain, and those who drank from them would either die instantly or, using the proper incantations, live forever. Such a geyser was located in an arid barren land "where no man dwelt," and was sometimes equated with the Land of Nod, to which Cain was banished after killing his brother Abel. According to the legend, all the Sons of Parthalon were killed either in the quest or, when they located the Fountain, by drinking from the waters, without the proper incantations; and in despair, the old king killed himself by slashing his own throat while seated on his rock throne. The story may of course be simply a metaphor for the transition of power from one dynasty to another in the prehistoric world. Later, as similar legends grew up, the waters lost their deadly properties and granted only eternal youth to the drinker. However, the location where they gushed forth from the Earth remained unknown.

Bethsaida

The idea of the Fountain of Youth became entwined with legends concerning other healing fountains, wells, or pools. For instance, one of the most famous healing pools was at Bethsaida in the Holy Land, and is mentioned in the New Testament where Jesus healed the man who could not walk. However, the Pool of Bethsaida did not heal all the time, but only when the waters there became "disturbed" (when an "angel troubled the waters"), and then only for a brief period. According to the Gospel, the crippled man could not make it into the waters in time, so Jesus healed him in situ as it were.

Perhaps taking their lead from the Bethsaida tradition, and an equally famous healing Pool at Siloam, the location of the Fountain of Youth was placed largely in either the Middle East or Eastern Europe. Part of this belief stems from a series of texts dating from the second and third centuries that have been accorded the title *The Alexander Romance*. These are a collection of tales and myths concerning the hero Alexander the Great, where he often plays a central role, although some of the stories may well predate Alexander's time.

Alexander and the Quest for Eternal Life

In one of these stories, Alexander and a servant go on a quest to find the Fountain of Life, which is located in a mysterious country on the eastern shores of the Black Sea. It is referred to in the story as Abkhazia, or the Land of Endless Night, and it is continually in darkness or wreathed in a perpetual fog. There are, however, people living there—this is born from the people in the surrounding lands who can hear voices emanating from the dark or mist. These are believed to be the guardians of the Fountain of Youth and are known as the Hanyson, who have given their name to a district known as Hamshan in present-day Turkey. They were allegedly the descendants of an army of the Persian king Shapur II who, according to an old Christian fable, persecuted a number of Christians who were living in the area and stole their lands. In retaliation, God punished them by cursing the land with perpetual darkness and mist, preventing them from leaving their territory. In the story, Alexander crosses this misty land and finds the Fountain, but does not drink from it. His servant, however, does so and becomes immortal, but finds that he cannot leave the Land of Endless Night. He continues to live there forever among the Hanyson. Whether or not Abkhazia was an actual kingdom bordering on the Black Sea is unclear, but it appears to have been far enough away and perceived as such an exotic location as to be the site of the Fountain of Youth.

Finding the Fountain

As time went on, however, the actual location of the Fountain of Youth seemed to shift as new tales about it began to circulate in the West. Such tales seem to have been at their high point in Europe around the 13th or 14th centuries, and this probably coincided with slightly greater travel among the wealthy (who often went on pilgrimages to distant holy sites), and a general rise in the secretive practice of alchemy. Besides, trying to discover the Philosopher's Stone (which was supposed to turn base metal into pure gold), these early scientists were also concerned with finding the Emerald Tablet (if mixed in a glass of wine would confer immortality upon the drinker). Whispers of such study, of course, generated a popular interest in the notion of living forever and of eternal youth.

In the 1100s, for example, it was thought that the Fountain lay somewhere in Ireland—then a mysterious and largely unexplored country. Writing around 1185, the scholar Geraldus Cambresius (Gerald of Wales), firmly asserted that somewhere in the Wicklow Mountains there was a lake where if a man washed his hair, "though it be white as snow," it would return to its natural color. Other writers, such as the monk Jocelyn of Furness, based at Inch Abbey in present-day County Down, stated that there were lakes in the Mourne Mountains famed for their restorative powers.

Another location that were given for the Fountain were the eastern Caucasus Mountains in Russian Georgia. Here, during the mid-15th century, several ruins of defensive towers had been found bearing a legend carved into the stone that they had been erected by Prester John. Apparently, the purpose of these fortifications had been to protect the West (and the Fountain of Youth) from the advancing hordes of the Tartars. Thus, the gushing Fountain was located somewhere among the high passes of the frowning mountains.

Not only this, but the Fountain was also supposedly located somewhere in the Arabian deserts. This belief was largely due to a number of stories told about the mysterious Al Khidr, a sage and early Moslem holy man (in some branches of Islam, he is revered as a saint), who was supposedly a contemporary of the biblical patriarch Moses. A number of tales are attributed to him including the formation of a number of magical and restorative springs in the desert. One of these was said to be the Fountain of Youth. Later, some of his "miracles" would be attributed to Moses himself—in one instance, Moses is said to have struck a rock with his staff, causing water to gush forth and so restore and refresh the Israelites. The stories of Al Khidr and the Fountain of Youth were at one time extremely popular in Moorish Spain where the storytellers may well have had contact with early explorers and seamen coming from the New World.

The linking of the mysterious personage of Prester John with the restorative Fountain, however, served to move its location even further East. The enigmatic Christian king had been thought, during the early medieval period, to be a ruler somewhere in either China or India, so thinkers began to believe that the Fountain lay there. Even in the late 1400s, it was said by some to be found somewhere among the Himalayas where Prester John ruled as a lama-king of a mysterious land. Some even claimed that the Fountain had been mentioned in the alleged letter that the ruler had sent to Emperor Manuel I to encourage requested aid. It was also mentioned in the rather spurious *Travels of Sir John Mandeville* as being located somewhere in the Far East and in the realm of Prester John.

For many years, alchemists in places such as Prague bought vials of water from travelers who claimed that this was indeed a sample taken from the Fountain in a far-away place. Some of these were then used to prepare the elusive Emerald Tablet without any success. The notion of the restorative waters, then, remained an intriguing and romantic mystery, which lay somewhere beneath the surface of formal legend.

Similar to many other legends, the idea of the Fountain of Youth became entwined with a number of other fables, and in this case, an actual historical expedition. This was to move the legend back into the Western sphere and to the New World—America. It was also to link the idea with a historical name, that of the Spanish conquistador and explorer Juan Ponce de Leon.

Arawak Legends

Before looking at Ponce de Leon's contribution to the legend, it is necessary to look briefly at the Arawak Indian legend of Bimini. In Arawak folklore, Bimini was both a place and a person. Although mentioned in the Arawak tongue, linguistic historians have traced it to Tiano, a form of language used by pre-Arawak Indians in the Caribbean. It referred to an ancient Arawak (or perhaps pre-Arawak) goddess who had risen from the primal waters to give birth to the world. The land that she had given birth to was ill defined, but was considered by the Arawaks to be sublimely beautiful—akin to the Garden of Eden in Semitic and Christian mythology. It is not clear as to whether Bem-min-eee (Mother of Waters) was actually a land or an island, but, it was generally agreed that it lay far beyond the reach of most mortal men. The general consensus seemed to suggest that it was a very lovely island that lay just beyond the horizon, and could only be reached by the strongest of rowers in a very fast canoe. If Bimini was indeed an island, then it was considered to lie in the Bahama chain, not far from the coast of Florida.

As the tradition developed, the concept of Bimini began to change slightly, moving away from its original Arawak origins and more toward another tradition, that of Atlantis. No longer was Bimini island an earthly Paradise of Arawak legend, rather it was the center of an ancient and highly advanced civilization that had existed before the Arawaks had come. And indeed, there may have been some evidence to suggest that this might have been true. The mysterious and submerged Bimini Road—a series of what appear to be manually cut limestone blocks that lie just below the ocean surface off the coast of Northern Bimini Island—is suggestive of some form of ancient construction. Although some have argued that it is no more than a natural underwater rock formation, others—notably the American occultist Edgar Cayce—have suggested that it might be the outer defense wall of an ancient harbor or part of an ancient road, which at one time connected the entire chain of islands. According to Arawak tradition, those who lived in Bimini were immortal and retained their youth forever. This concept also transferred into legends concerning the super-civilization. The city of Bimini was inhabited by immortals who owed their endless lives to a great fountain, which gushed in the center of the island, and was considered to be sacred to ancient gods.

Ponce de Leon

Such stories traveled all around the area, and were repeated in places such as Cuba and Mexico where the Spanish had established colonies. The tale of Bimini and the lost Fountain of Youth soon reached the ears of Spanish explorers and conquistadores. The early 1500s were a great age of Spanish exploration when the existence of many things was considered possible, and Spanish adventurers were soon setting out to look for the sacred place. It is here that the name of Juan Ponce de Leon first appears.

No other name is more closely associated with the Fountain of Youth than that of Ponce de Leon. According to legend, this intrepid Spanish explorer actually discovered this wonderful land with its miraculous Fountain on the southern tip of the North American continent (Florida) and claimed it for Spain. However, the truth concerning the discovery and Ponce de Leon's mission was slightly different.

In 1493, Ponce de Leon had traveled with Christopher Columbus on his second journey to the New World. When Columbus elected to return to Spain, Ponce de Leon remained behind on the island of Hispaniola, where he planned to settle. However, he also had a number of political ambitions as well. This was a new territory where a man might make his name at the Spanish Court as a representative of a far-flung dominion. After holding a number of small governorships, he was immensely successful and ruthless in putting down a number of rebellions among the natives of the Bahamas, and was appointed as the first Spanish governor of the important port of Puerto Rico (then called Boraquien) in 1509. However, events elsewhere were conspiring against his new-found position. Columbus had died in 1506, and his eldest son, Diego, made representation to the courts in Madrid for control of all the lands that his father had claimed for Spain. The courts upheld his claim and in 1511, Ponce de Leon found himself replaced as governor of Puerto Rico by Diego Columbus.

It must have been a galling moment for such a proud and arrogant man who now found himself sidelined in the developing colonial politics of the New World, but Ponce de Leon had a plan to restore his political fortunes. While governor of Puerto Rico, he had heard a strange legend that had been brought to the island from Cuba. It was an old Arawak legend concerning an ancient chieftain named Sequene, who had set out in a canoe with a number of rowers bound for a mystical land named Bimini, which was an earthly Paradise and where no one ever grew old. Here, too, was an amazing restorative fountain, the waters of which could heal any wound and bring back youth to an aged man. Sequene and his men had never returned, and it was imagined that they were still living, ageless and in luxury, in that fabled land. The tale intrigued Ponce de Leon and he resolved to find this mysterious Bimini with its wondrous Fountain and claim them both for Spain.

In 1512, Ponce de Leon applied to Ferdinand, king of Spain, for permission to seek out and colonize Bimini. The king considered the request sympathetically and replied that he could do so on the understanding that he was to finance and equip his own ships. And so in February 1513, Ponce de Leon set sail to look for the wonderful land and its Fountain of Youth.

According to Arawak legend, the country lay somewhere to the north of Cuba, and therefore, this was the route that the expedition took. On March 27, 1513, they made landfall on an unknown shore that Ponce de Leon called "La Florida," because they had landed during the festival of Pascum Florida ("the flowery Passover," or the Spanish Easter). He had landed on the shores of what is now the modern state of Florida. Where exactly he set foot on Florida soil is unknown, but some have suggested that it was somewhere near present-day Cape Canaveral. The land was not at all pleasant—not the wonderful island of Bimini—and was largely covered in forest and swamp. Ponce de Leon made several forays inland, exploring parts of several rivers and fighting with local Indians before returning to Puerto Rico. He had discovered Florida, but he had failed to find either Bimini or the legendary Fountain of Youth. However, in 1521, he made another attempt, sailing from Puerto Rico to the Florida coast once more, this time with the intention of founding a settlement there and resuming his quest for the Fountain. However, the land he chose was unsuitable for a sustained community, and was under frequent attack from the Calusa Indians, which prevented Ponce de Leon from venturing too far inland. Riddled with disease and injuries, the colony collapsed. Badly wounded by an Indian arrow himself, Ponce de Leon sailed to Cuba where he died, all but bankrupted by the expense of his failed expeditions. Others would explore and develop his discoveries, but none would find the fabulous Fountain.

In legend and folklore, Juan Ponce de Leon is regarded as the Spaniard who hunted for the Fountain of Youth in an attempt to regenerate himself as a young man; but to make such an assertion is to misunderstand what Ponce de Leon was actually doing or indeed the personal enormity of his failure. He was seeking regeneration, but it was the regeneration of his career as a colonial politician at the Spanish Court rather than any personal quest for youth. Perhaps the wonderful land of Bimini and its Fountain had become a metaphor of his ambition.

Maybe, like the quest of Ponce de Leon, the quest for the legendary Bimini is more about human ambition and endeavor than trying to find an actual place. Similar to the Garden of Eden or Shangri-La, Bimini represents an idealized state, the summit of human struggle. And perhaps that is the true meaning of that legendary country.

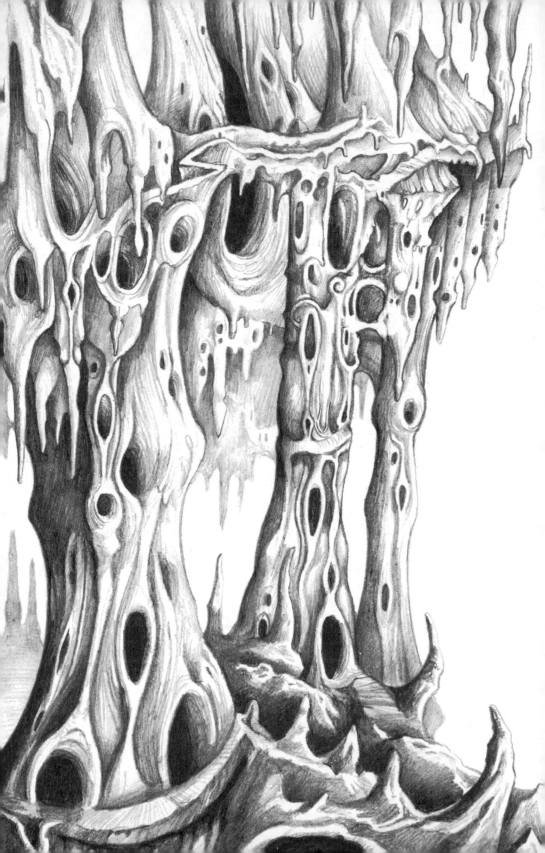

Section IV:

Subterranean

Worlds

Subterranean Worlds

Having explored much of the planet's surface, Mankind is now looking toward outer space as the next unconquered region, waiting to be discovered. However, perhaps a more fascinating world might lie beneath the surface of our own world. Lands of wonder and mystery could be lying somewhere beneath our feet.

Since earliest times, stories of subterranean kingdoms have been the staple of the legends of many cultures. There have, for instance, been tales concerning survivors from the Deluge who fled underground when the Flood waters rose and formed a civilization in the depths of the Earth. This story not only appears in Semitic legend (from which the Biblical story of the Deluge originates), but also in Greek, Assyrian, and Roman cultures. References to people living under the ground, and to subterranean civilizations, therefore appear in many places. For example, in the Christian Bible there are several passing (but nevertheless curious) references that have intrigued scriptural scholars through the years; for instance: "No man in Heaven, in Earth, neither under the Earth was able to open the book, neither to look there on" (Revelation 5:3) and "Every creature, in Heaven, on Earth and under the Earth, saying....Glory and power be to the Lamb" (Revelation 5:13).

Semitic folklore taught that the Underworld was the place where evil dwelt. The "Sons of God" (mysterious beings who had existed at the foundation of the world), who had disobeyed Yahweh (Jehovah) Himself, and had mated with the daughters of Men, were exiled for their disobedience to the lower depths. The Lake of Fire, into which the arrogant renegade angel Lucifer was finally cast, also lay in the Underworld. The subterranean realm then became a by-word for darkness and malignancy, and it is no coincidence that medieval Christians located the Kingdom of Hell, where the Devil ruled, deep below the surface of the everyday world.

And yet, for some, the Underworld might be a Paradise. In some Semitic tales it was the location of the Garden of Eden. It was a place where the seasons held, and day and night in the surface world mattered very little. It was also a place of inordinate wealth; gold, jewels, and semi-precious stones were dug out of the Earth, so why should they not exist in abundance in the subterranean realm? In some versions of the apocryphal book of Enoch, there is a description of an underground Paradise—a place of great beauty and wonder where myriad precious stones are to be found. Enoch compares this to a world that existed before the Fall of Man, and this would later translate into visions of prehistoric worlds existing somewhere beneath the Earth's crust. Such places, it was suggested, might contain dinosaurs, mammoths, and other extinct creatures as well as flora and fauna no longer existing on the Earth's surface. They might also contain creatures that had never walked on the Earth's surface, but had perhaps evolved in the lightless caverns underground.

And the rumors of a civilization somewhere in the depths of the Earth continued to intrigue and fascinate Mankind. There was much speculation about the origins of such a civilization and as to how advanced it was. If somehow, as some believed, dinosaurs and prehistoric fauna had been trapped beneath the Earth's crust, then this civilization might also be fairly primitive. The idea of cavemen living in great caverns beneath our feet was quite a common theme. Others believed that the civilization might be fairly advanced—perhaps even more advanced than that which was on the surface. Far below the crust might lie wonderful cities, maybe boasting high technology. They might be survivors from Atlantis or from some other advanced prehistoric race, all but forgotten, who had perhaps lived on the surface, but who had fled underground to avoid some catastrophe. There were tales of Roman, Greek, and Mesopotamian-like cultures somewhere far below the ground. Some of these people ignored the surface dwellers; others, it was imagined, were incredibly hostile toward the human race.

Could the lands that they inhabited be accessed from the surface world? The general consensus of opinion was that they could. In various places scattered across the Earth, it was believed, lay entrances to these underground kingdoms. Many believed that the entrances to these inner worlds lay somewhere within the Poles, which at the time such theories were current, still remained a largely unexplored and mysterious area of the globe. Sailors in the northern climes had returned with strange stories concerning great maelstroms and whirlpools in the icy oceans, which were suggestive of water being drawn unto vast underground caves. This, it was argued, was proof that the Earth itself was hollow, and might even boast some form of internal atmosphere in which men and animals could live. Such an idea lives on today in groups such as The Hollow Earth Society. This was based on theories that proposed that the Earth is merely a hollow shell with an interior atmosphere. Works following this train of thought include William Reed's *Phantom of the Poles* (1902) and the writings of Marshall Gardner (1913). Following in this tradition, the Hollow Earth was believed to be the home of civilizations much more advanced than ours.

But if these underground civilizations existed so closely with us, why are we so unaware of them? How could such an advanced culture remain hidden, perhaps for centuries? Did they give any indication as to their presence? The answer that is frequently given is that they wish to keep their existence secret from us, or that when they intervene in our world we don't recognize it as such.

For example, there have been stories since earliest times concerning fairies and "little people." These, argue some of those who believe in a Hollow

Earth, are not supernatural beings at all but the inhabitants of an interior world who have come to the surface. Similar strange beings are said to have been encountered in various parts of the world (in Tibet or in the Amazonian rainforests—there are said to be entrances in both locations). And there are other beings that have been encountered and described as visitors from outer space. This, argues the theory, is to misunderstand—these are not aliens from other planets, but from subterranean worlds. Indeed, some UFOlogists argue that "flying saucers" are craft from the Hollow Earth and that they enter and exit their own sphere somewhere around the North and South Poles. And some more fanciful notions actually combine the ideas of extraterrestrials and subterranean dwellers by claiming that the Hollow Earth is in fact no more than a base for aliens from beyond the stars who are observing us. Some strands of thought even go so far as to claim that Mankind is actually no more than a massive genetic experiment carried on by aliens from beyond our Solar System who are monitoring the results from inside the Earth.

Theosophy, too, has made connections with the idea of interior worlds, and some branches have claimed that the Inner World is actually the home of Ascendant Masters who are secretly controlling and guiding Mankind's destiny. In the end days of the world, it is suggested, the Masters will emerge to guide the planet to its final end. Such Masters, some assert, are connected to the planet Venus, but have established their main base in the interior of our world. Scrolls known as the Hedon Rogia, purportedly either found in India or else dictated through a "communicator helmet" operated by a believer, reveal an extensive inner world that the Masters benignly dominate. And there are, of course, stories of these Masters sometimes coming to the surface as they are said to do at Mount Shasta in California, only here they appear as survivors from Atlantis or Lemuria. No matter how we may view such claims, they are nonetheless indicative of an interest in a world that lies somewhere far below us.

And there is little doubt that an interior world, populated perhaps by prehistoric cavemen, an advanced civilization still holds a wonderful speculative interest for the human imagination. It has proved to be inspiration for theorists and writers across the ages. Witness Jules Verne's *Journey to the Center of the Earth* (originally published in 1871), which set the tone for many subsequent works. Somewhere below, worlds of wonder, beauty, and adventure await the intrepid traveler if he or she dares to go there. The future may not lie out in the stars, but down in the depths.

17

Miners of the Lost Worlds

From time to time, queer stories concerning underground realms are recounted by miners or surveyors engaged in geological work. Tales of prospectors and mining engineers unexpectedly finding cavern systems with unusual flora and fauna, and even small animals, some boasting their own internal atmospheres (some of which have been proven to be toxic), have come down to us throughout the years from many parts of the world. However, because it has such a rich history of mining and gold-hunting, many of these stories tend to proliferate in North America—particularly in the West. The Cascade Mountains of northern California and the Monterey Peninsula seem to be especially rich in such stories, particularly around the times of the California Gold Rush, although some of them date back to the Spanish period.

Underground Vikings

An example of such a "discovery" concerns two miners looking for an allegedly lost silver mine near Carmel in Monterey in the late 1800s/early 1900s. The two—Jim Elliot and Henry Paris—were supposedly searching for a reputed vein of pure silver somewhere in the Carmel Valley's Cachagua country when they entered a lonely ravine, allegedly located in the Trampa Canyon area, which seemed to bear the marks of ancient workings. They entered a large, uneven cave that seemed to slant downward into the Earth. At its far end, Paris scrambled through a gap in the rock and found himself in a kind of tunnel, which seemed to lead even further down. With Elliot following, he descended a kind of rock "chimney," eventually emerging in a large, stinking, underground cavern. In fact, the cave was so vast that neither man could see where it went, just the total darkness stretching away beyond their meager lights.

Much of the place seemed to be taken up with a vast underground lake or "sea" that stretched into a dark infinity. The men walked down to a tiny "shore" where a stagnant water swirled around their boots. The "sea" seemed to be teeming with small, pale fish that seemed to glow with a faint phosphoresce and that swam away as soon as they stepped into the water; it unsettled both men greatly. Everywhere the rocks seemed to be coated with a strange type of fungus that made them slip and slide, and giving the place a "bad air" with its vapors. Directly in front of them, however, was a staggering sight. The remains of what appeared to be a Viking longship had been drawn up on the "beach." The men looked in astonishment at the great wooden head carved on its prow and examined metal areas in which oars had been positioned. They could not see any trace of life, nor did there seem to be any further immediate evidence of Viking visitors. Nevertheless, the two were convinced that there might well be treasure lying out there, somewhere in the darkness of the vast cavern. However, they were beginning to feel sick as the foul air from the fungi started to affect them, and, fearing that they might be poisoned by the toxic atmosphere, they decided to return to the surface and fetch help.

The experience had left them both badly shaken, and when they returned to Carmel, the first place they went was a saloon in order to get a drink to steady their nerves. One drink led to another, and soon they became embroiled in a brawl in which a man was injured and both were arrested. They were sentenced to a rather harsh 30 days in jail, and so it was well over a month before they got out and gathered together some helpers. By this time, they were unsure of the entrance to the underground world—all they could really remember was that it was somewhere in the area of Trampa Canyon. They searched several locations but could not find the gap in the rock; when they thought they'd found it, it seemed to have been blocked by a recent rock fall. The underground sea with its rotting Viking ship and possible lost treasure would remain down in the darkness for many more years to come.

Big Sur

One of the most famous "Lost Worlds" is said to lie in the Big Sur area on Monterey's south coast. The region known as "the Big Sur wilderness" lies about 25 miles south of Carmel Mission and is presumed to take its name from the Spanish who passed through it in the 16th century—*El Grande del Sur*, meaning "big river in the south." According to legend, Indians living along the Little Sur River would sometimes lead Spaniards into the Pico Blanco (White Peak) area of the wilderness from which they would return several days later with their burros laden with raw silver. However, the Indians insisted that they go into the region alone, much to the displeasure of the Spaniards who wanted to see where the silver mine might be.

In the latter years of the 19th century and the early part of the 20th century, a mining engineer named Alfred K. Clark came prospecting in the Big Sur area, trying to find the Indian mine. Clark, or Uncle Al, as he was known, was something of an eccentric character; he was a Union Army war veteran who had spent some time prospecting in the West before heading for Monterey. He built a cabin and homesteaded on the South Fork of the Little Sur River. He befriended the last surviving members of the Little Sur Indian tribes and gained the confidence of one who is said to have revealed the location of the silver mine. However, the mine was not where the old man said it was, and on his return from Big Sur, Clark found the Indian had died. Nevertheless, he had enough details to begin a search through the area, which was to take up the remaining years of his life. Searching in the area of the

Pico Blanco, Clark found some traces of silver ore and, dreaming of finding the lost mine, he headed northward to seek some financial support for his venture. In San Francisco, Dr. Clarence H. Pearce met with Clark and soon after became his foremost backer. However, after months of back-breaking labor at the place where Clark had found the traces of ore, nothing further had been discovered. Disheartened, some of the backers pulled out, but Clark declared that he would dig on until he found the silver lode. For the rest of his life, he would work around the area of the Pico Blanco, well away from civilization and only coming to town when he needed supplies or to briefly work for local ranchers when he needed money for supplies. He became a legend in the style of the Lost Dutchman—a crazed recluse who lived out in the wilderness.

"Uncle Al" had, however, made a few friends in the Big Sur area—one of whom was Al Greer who, with his family, had given the old man supplies from time to time. When Clark fell sick, Greer took him into his home and tended to him, suspecting that the old man was dying. What had started out as a fever rapidly developed into pneumonia and, as Greer had guessed, as the spring of 1930 came round, Uncle Al was breathing his last. He gathered the family around his bed and told them that he wished to reveal a secret to them in return for their kindness—a secret that might make them rich.

He admitted that he'd never found the lost silver mine nor in all his diggings had he ever struck a silver lode, but what he had discovered out in Big Sur was more valuable to historians than silver could ever be. One day while working on some old Indian diggings, Clark had suddenly broken through the wall of an underground shaft that seemed to lead directly into the Pico Blanco. He followed it deep into the mountain where it seemed to split into several tunnels. He followed one that led him into a mysterious room-like chamber, which he began to explore, holding his light in front of him defensively. The cavern was one of a series through which Uncle Al walked cautiously. Stalagmites and stalactites were everywhere, and curiously shaped rocks rose up around him; looking closely, he saw the marks of ancient mortars and picks on the rock walls. Part of the cave had been made by men, he reckoned. He also noticed strange, pale flowers, the like of which he had never seen before, sprouting from between the stones around him and, in a shallow river that he crossed, small pale fish. He touched some of the flower petals and thought they were made of stone.

Most wondrous of all, he suddenly emerged into a great cavern where there were traces of human or humanoid habitation. Here, the rock walls were covered with curious drawings of all kinds. In fact, one wall seemed to be covered with what looked like a representation of the sky with various constellations marked. Here, too, were drawings of what looked like prehistoric animals and men fighting with sabre-toothed tigers. There were pictographs of what looked like woolly mammoths as well. On the walls and scattered all around were evidences of some sort of settlement, which seemed to stretch back into the darkness; but Clark did not pursue these. Instead he returned to the surface and mentally marked the entrance to the strange underworld.

Uncle Al died leaving the location of the spot to the family gathered around his bed. However, there was a problem in that the Greer family didn't believe him. Al Greer simply put it down to the ramblings of a very old man in the grip of a raging fever and dismissed it as a fantasy. Much later, they moved on, but some others who heard the story decided to hunt for the strange lost world on the slopes of Pico Blanco. The tale corresponded with stories of "lost worlds," large caves in the mountain ranges that might have once contained life. The "stone flowers" that Uncle Al had found in the underground world might well be "gypsum blooms," called that because of their petal-like appearance, which is produced when a substance known as selenite exudes from the cracks in cavern walls. The small pale fish were probably troglobites, or "blindfish," which had lost their body pigment due to dwelling in the darkness away from the light. However, although the search was extensive, the entrance was never found. One tunnel might have fit the bill, but that had long caved in. To date, there is no real evidence of Uncle Al's strange underground world, but it has become so famous that from time to time people still search for it.

Explorers of the Lost Worlds

The Monterey Peninsula is rich in such stories of underground realms, mainly cave systems and some allegedly containing fabulous treasure. Such fortunes have often been linked to Californian and Montereyan badmen such as the robber and rustler Joaquin Murieta ("The Robin Hood of El Dorado") or, slightly earlier, the dreaded Pacific pirate Hippolyte Bouchard. Bouchard, who had served in a number of naval campaigns under the celebrated Guillermo Brown, the Irish-born first admiral of the Argentinean Navy, was reputed to know the location of many of these interior worlds, and used them to store his loot. In November 1818, he attacked the coastal fortress of El Castillo where three Spanish treasure-ships were supposedly sheltering. After a brief defiance, the garrison commander and de facto governor of Alta California, Pablo Vincente Sola, withdrew his forces to Monterey and left Bouchard to loot the ships at will. What became of the riches that he plundered from them is unknown, but there is a legend that he took them to a cavern system somewhere further along the coast, where he concealed them, and where they still lie to this day. There is a persistent story that in the early 1920s, a geologist, exploring somewhere near Cypress Point on the northern end of the Peninsula, blundered into a series of vast underground caverns, one of which held three skeletons, some old, rusted flintlock rifles, and several large strongboxes. As is usual in these tales, he is said to have returned to the surface, but when he came back with help, he couldn't find the spot. It has been suggested that the strongboxes held part of the treasure that Bouchard had pillaged from the ships at El Castillo, although some others argue that it was the haunt of another adventurer, the English pirate Francis Drake. Similar stories are attributed to Murieta, who raided and plundered through both California and Monterey, stealing money and cattle which he then sold. Although he is sometimes portrayed as a kind of "robber philanthropist" in the style of Robin Hood, there is little doubt that he was a villain of some stature. Together with his band, known as the Five Joaquins—Joaquin Batellier, Joaquin Carrillo, Joaquin Ocomorenia, Joaquin Valenzuela, and the fifth "Joaquin," Manuel Garcia ("Three-Fingered Jack"), he was responsible for the majority of the murders and serious robberies in the Sierra Nevada region of California in the early 19th century. He was allegedly killed around 1853 by Captain Harry S. Love of the California Rangers (although this death is frequently disputed—it is also said that he died in bed in Mexico), but not before he had deposited vast amounts of loot in underground "worlds" (cavern systems) all across the Californian Sierras. From time to time, there have been claims of miners finding these "stashes" (together with the loot accumulated by another Californian outlaw Tiburcio Vasquez), and the "lost worlds" in which they are hidden.

There is also the persistent Indian legend of the "Lost Caves (or Lost Worlds) of the Golden Quills." This refers to two huge caves reputedly located near Carmel Mission, which had reputedly been extended by Indian labor. They were said to contain ledges that held the hollowed-out feather quills of many birds, into which the local Indians had poured large quantities of gold dust and flakes of pure gold. (This was also done by the Indians of New Mexico in an attempt to hide their wealth from their enemies or from invaders.) However, legend says that these "Lost Caves" have long been stripped of their wealth by robbers and adventurers, and interest in the legend has therefore long since waned.

J.C. Brown

The most famous of all the Californian "Lost World" stories however comes from the Cascade Mountains in the north of the state and hints that there may indeed be some sort of subterranean civilization lurking down there. The tale concerns a rather suspicious individual named J.C. Brown.

No one is sure what Brown's profession really was. Some sources state that he was a geologist, others a mining engineer, and others a prospector. In 1904, he was hired by the English-based Lord Cowdray Mining Company to scout in various areas of the Cascade Range in order to site prospective mines. It is also unclear as to what he was looking for—it may have been gold, coal, or something else. Brown made at least two visits to the Cascades— the first seems to have been uneventful, and he found nothing; the second seems to have been much more surprising.

In a lonely mountain area, Brown entered a narrow canyon that ended in a large and curiously shaped rock. A recent landslide in the area had moved this boulder slightly, and as he came up the canyon, Brown was aware of something like a wind blowing out of the cliff ahead. Imagining it to be an old Indian mine, he investigated further. Squeezing between the edge of the boulder and the cliff face, he suddenly found himself in a man-made tunnel that led down into the Earth. Still believing that he was in Indian workings, he made his way down only to find that the tunnel ended in a narrow chimney, which went down into the dark. Once again, Brown continued downward, easing himself down the chimney and into another short tunnel. He stepped out into a mammoth that extended away in front of him. Amazingly, the entire cavern seemed to be lined with sheets of beaten copper and contained a number of seemingly ancient artifacts. Here were shields, swords, necklaces, and large statues of what seemed to be ancient men. The copper-lined walls also seemed to have pictures on them showing ancient battles and cities on fire. It was the most amazing thing he had ever seen, and yet as he stared at it, Brown had the distinct feeling that he was being watched. Nevertheless, he ventured further and into a second cave. Here lay the bones of what appeared to be gigantic men, the remains almost twice the size of an ordinary human. Some were dressed in fragments of armor and some seemed to be clutching ancient weapons with their bony hands. The feeling of being watched grew ever stronger as Brown progressed even further. Beyond the cavern of skeletons, another rock shaft descended into the darkness and, as he stood on its rim, Brown thought that he detected a faint movement far below. He turned, retraced his steps, and fled to the surface.

Although he told a few friends what he had found, he did not report his discovery to his employers, the Lord Cowdray Mining Company. Similar to so many other people, he may have been afraid that they would lay claim to the find themselves. Astonishingly, he left California and did not return to resume his quest for 30 years! He returned to the region in 1934 and apparently there were still some people living there who remembered his strange story, although none had gone up to check it. Brown went up into the region to check his location and then returned to gather together a party and purchase some mining tools.

He agreed to meet with a company of speculators late one evening in the middle of summer, but he never showed up, and he was never heard from again. His room (in a local rooming house) was checked, but nothing was found. All his clothes and possessions were still there and wherever J.C. Brown had gone, he had departed in a hurry. There was one curious twist to the tale, however. Brown's room was on the second floor of the building and, as no one had seen him leave by the door, the only way he could have left the boarding lodge was through the upstairs window. By this time Brown was now an elderly man and crippled with pains, so nobody could see how he could have done it. There was another ominous clue: Under the window of Brown's room was the footprint of a giant man etched into the soft soil! It was as if some giant had simply stood outside his window and had drawn him out of the room. To this day, the fate of J.C. Brown remains an unsolved mystery.

Of course, cynics may say that Brown hadn't found anything at all up in the Cascades and that when he was put "on the spot," he slipped away unseen, perhaps aided by an accomplice. But those who spoke to him in 1934 stated that he was determined to return to the mysterious cavern, and had even hired several armed men to go with him.

Some have said that the location of the entrance to Brown's "Lost World" lay somewhere in Siskiyou County—famous for coal mining—and that it is somehow connected to Mount Shasta, which lies close by.

So, are there giants—either cavemen or advanced survivors from a sunken realm—living in some lightless kingdom beneath our feet? Certainly there are great caverns down there—caves that can perhaps boast an internal atmosphere and perhaps some form of plant and animal life. And who knows, maybe once in a while they can carry away some of us who dwell on the surface, taking us back to their underground world, just as they may have done with J.C. Brown.

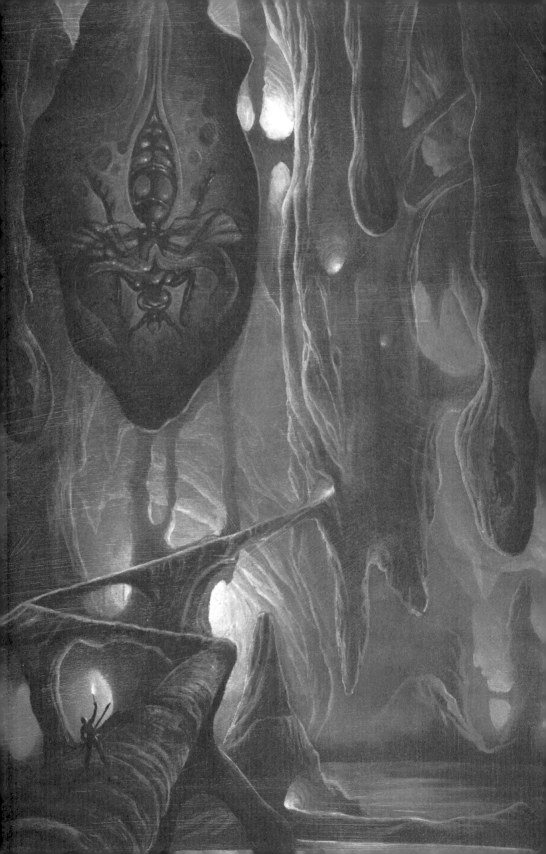

18

The Lair of Judaculla

W hile, according to several tales and legends, numerous civilizations may lurk in the depths below us, there might be something else down there as well. Deep caves, dark holes in the ground, and deep, gloomy gullies have long been the abode of monsters and awful supernatural things. Such places are the home of dragons, monstrous worms, and even flesh-eating ogres who terrify, attack, and devour those who venture too close. If these caverns are in remote or isolated areas (as many of them tend to be), then this lends an additional sense of mystery and terror to them, and it seems to make their supposed denizens even more fearsome. Thus, the brave hero goes off to fight the monstrous creature in some near inaccessible and blasted place well away from the haunt of humans. The idea of a remote and largely unknown area where monsters dwell is well established within the human psyche.

Although today we tend to think of America as being a highly technologically developed country, there are still such remote and frightful areas scattered all through its landscape. Lonely lakes in the Rockies, or dark swamps deep in Louisiana are said to harbor terrible creatures that are often hostile toward man. Indeed, many such areas have become the subject or horror and monster films through the years. In many instances, such locations have acquired fanciful names that link them to supernatural entities of places— Hell's Gutter, The Devil's Courthouse, Devil's Hole, Satan's Gatehouse, and so forth—and are regarded with awe and trepidation by those who live around them. Strangely shaped trees and rocks often add to the air of threat and danger around such places and give an edge to their supernatural reputations. In a number of cases the term "Devil" not only refers to the infernal ruler, but to some terrible monster that is supposed to dwell in such locations—the Jersey "Devil," the "Devil of the Mammoth Cave" (in Kentucky), or "The Devil's Lake" (the Rockies and several other locations). Sometimes this creature takes on physical shape and sometimes it is just an invisible presence that might be nonetheless rather frightening. In some cases, the monster was even worshipped as a god or supernatural figure at the place where it was supposed to dwell.

Such a location lies in the North Carolina woods, where it is known locally as "The Devil's Tramping Ground." It lies in the woodlands about 10 miles to the west of Siler City in Chatham County off a rural highway near Harper's Crossing. The "Tramping Ground" is an area of clear ground, set in a perfect circle and measuring about 40 feet in diameter on which nothing will grow. It is tucked away in the woodlands and is said to cover an entrance from which the Devil is said to emerge from the Underworld, from time to time, in order to march back and forth while he contemplates what wickedness he can do in the world. There is supposedly an underground chamber deep beneath this patch that leads directly to the Infernal Regions and the clear area is created by the sulphurous fumes seeping up from below. That is the tradition anyway. In old times, it was said to be a worshipping place for the Cherokee Indians who worshipped some ancient creature or deity there. This entity emerged from an underground lair, though exactly how it did so is not clear. However, it had the power to rip an individual to shreds if it so chose. The grassless area in the center of the clearing is said to be the result of thousands of mocassened feet dancing in honor of their "god."

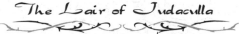

The site has a particularly sinister reputation, perhaps allied to the eerie creature from the depths, together with a dark history. It was from somewhere in this area that the notorious David Fanning led his attack on the Guilford Court House during the Revolutionary Wars of the mid-18th century. He was backed by a band of ruthless pro-English "Tories," who both laid waste to and terrorized the Chatham countryside. Perhaps he is the "monster" that was said to abide in the area and is somehow connected to subterranean caverns that are said to exist there. There is, however, no real evidence, other than folkloric fable, for such caves.

And, of course, there may be good natural reasons for the grassless area in the center of the woodland clearing, rather than being a result of the sulphurous fumes of some concealed subterranean world. There are a number of other such areas on the tops of hills scattered all through the area and known as "Balds" (for example, "Grier's Bald," named after the mysterious murdered Appalachian hermit—and religious fanatic—David Grier, or "Big Bald"), and some years ago the North Carolina State Museum, under its director Harry Davis, conducted a soil investigation of the area together with Dr. J.J. Stuckey, the state geologist. They concluded that the area of the Tramping Ground was sufficiently loaded with sodium chloride—salt—to prevent ordinary vegetation from thriving there. Nevertheless, stories of some sort of infernal entrance there persists in the rural folklore of the region.

North Carolina seems to be one of the most consistent spots for entry into some underworld. At the Nantahala National Forest Reserve, part of which lies on the slopes of Whiteside Mountain, just off Highway 64 between Cashiers and Highlands, the creature concerned is known as Spearfinger, a vicious witch who is based on Cherokee folktale, and who dwells in a cave system that extends deep into Whiteside Mountain.

The sides of the Mountain are littered with rocks, each said to be hiding various entrances to subterranean realms. The most prominent is a jutting formation on the eastern slopes of Whiteside known as The Devil's Courthouse. A large outcropping is said to be the throne on which Satan will sit when he judges the world and claims the evil people who dwell therein. The throne itself is said to be an entrance to subterranean worlds, and it is here that Spearfinger was said to emerge. In her true form, she is a monstrous old woman with yellow-grey skin, turned slightly pale from living in the darkness, who has outlived generation after generation of Man. She is described as a giant with skin that is harder than rock itself, and so dense that it was impenetrable by either spear of axe. She took her name from a long, pointed forefinger on her right hand, which was shaped like (and as sharp as) an awl. This she used to stab individuals who had the misfortune of venturing too close to her. When on the surface, Spearfinger could be identified by a heavy, unpleasant, and sickening musk (said by the Cherokees to be the stench of the Underworld), which she could nevertheless sometimes mask in order to disguise herself. This caused her to be crawling with flies and other creeping things that were drawn by the stench. Her teeth were also said to be rock-hard and more like stalactites and stalagmites than anything else. These she used to rend her prey like an animal, tearing at the flesh with rock-hard fingernails. Legend says that she was one of an elder race who lived in the area long before the Cherokees came, but was forced underground by the coming of Man. She is the last of her kind left alive and she is seized of a terrible hatred toward humans. At times, she takes on the appearance of an old human woman and in that guise she goes about the countryside stealing children which she then eats in the underground darkness of her lair. Ancient Indian wisdom frequently states that it is advised to avoid the rocks and stone scattered across the mountainside in the Nantahala for each one may hide an entry to Spearfinger's world, and those who investigate too closely are never seen again.

Judaculla

But Spearfinger is not the only legendary figure that emerges from the Underworld to haunt the region around the Nantahla. On the Chaney Fork Road, a little more than 3 miles off Highway 107, south of East Laport, lies a large stone, known locally as the Judaculla Rock, which has up until the present day presented a curious enigma for both scientists and passersby.

The Rock, which is roughly the size of a small boulder, lies in a field on the farm of James Parker in Jackson County near the Tuckasegee River. What makes this rock so interesting is that it is inscribed with the oldest petroglyphs (markings or drawings on stone) anywhere in America and probably elsewhere—possibly more than 10,000 years old. No one is sure whether the spidery inscriptions (obviously done by some intelligence) are drawings or writings or indeed a combination of both, but nothing similar to them has been found anywhere else.

The markings clearly invite all sorts of interpretations. Some people see fish, others see owls, some see men, and others still see a rudimentary map of the Heavens. And there also seems to be the imprint of a giant hand with seven fingers. Some old Cherokee legends state that the rock was carved by a gigantic race of creatures who had emerged from an underground kingdom, and who briefly dwelt on the surface long before the Cherokees came to that country. The name "Judaculla" is thought to be an Anglicized version of the name of a mythical Cherokee giant Tsul-Kalu, which means "His eyes are slanted," suggesting that he had almond-shaped eyes. Judaculla's race allegedly left the stone behind as a marker when they returned to their subterranean domain as the Cherokee began to proliferate across the land.

Once again, various interpretations have been offered to explain the curious designs on the Rock. It is said, for example, that the drawings represent a battle between the Cherokee and the Georgian Creeks in 1775. However, others strongly disagree saying that the carvings were made long before the Revolution. Recently, a Cave Art project conducted by the University of North Carolina Office of Archaeology suggested that the designs/writing might be somewhere in the range of 4,500–5,000 years old, although this is once again disputed by others who claim that they are even older. Some commentators say that the Rock is some sort of boundary marker used by ancient men to warn others away from their hunting lands while others still declare that they are in pictograph language perhaps similar to Egyptian hieroglyphics and long forgotten by Man, carved by some subterranean civilization.

To emphasize this latter point, there is also a deep cavern known as Judaculla's Cave on the southwestern side of Richard Balsam Mountain (also known simply as Balsam Mountain), the highest point on the Blue Ridge Parkway. It is from here that the slant-eyed giant and/or the subterranean race were said to have emerged into the surface world, and into which they returned. Indeed, there is said to be a cave system that extends under the Mountain (and all through the area), which leads to an underground world far below. Such a theory has been used to explain a number of mysterious disappearances in the countryside throughout the years. The Judaculla Rock, then, presents both an intriguing and controversial mystery that may never be satisfactorily solved.

Throughout the years, the Judaculla story has become entwined with other Cherokee Indian legends, and even the person of the mythical slant-eyed giant has metamorphosized into something else. In some version of the tale, he is not a humanoid figure at all, but a monstrous insect, living somewhere deep underground and only emerging at certain times of the year. In addition, the location of his lair shifts slightly, from Jackson County to the thickly forested Nantahala Gorge in Macon and Swain Counties, just off Highway 19, between Nantahala and Wesson. This is probably the most primal and spectacular scenery in all of western North Carolina, but it is also the most mysterious. The bottom of the Gorge in cloaked in dense woodland, and it is said that down there in the darkness are entrances to several subterranean worlds where terrible monsters are said to dwell. One of these, according to some traditions, is another version of Judaculla that maintains several "nests" somewhere in the forest gloom.

It may be that the Judaculla legend has become mixed up with another Cherokee tale—that of Ulagu, the giant Yellow Jacket. Yellow Jackets are a type of Vespid (family grouping Vespidae) or stinging insect—in fact they are the smallest of such types found in North America that can actually fly. Nevertheless, some can grow quite large and can easily resemble bees or wasps. They construct large nests out of a paper-like substance known as carton, and these nests are invariably underground. Some of them can be quite extensive. Many of these Vespids have a taste for human perspiration, which they find sweet (probably due to exuded sugar content), and can therefore deliver an extremely nasty sting when feeding or when alighting on an individual.

According to Cherokee tradition, such insects were at one time enormous, and terrorized early men with their attacks. Ulagu (the name is derived from the Cherokee word for "boss," "chief," or "leader") and his "wives"

are the last of these ancient insects and have—like Spearfinger and Judaculla—outlived many generations of Men. Its underground nest system is said to stretch throughout the Nantahala Gorge with many entrances down among the thick tree clusters there.

In times past, according to Cherokee fable, the great Yellow Jacket developed a taste for small children, and would frequently swoop down to carry away infants who were sleeping in cribs or playing in front of tents or houses. The appearance of the mighty insect, with a body almost as large as a house, often shocked observers into immobility, and so Ulagu/Judaculla was able to make off with its prey unhindered. The creature flew so fast that no man could track it or see where it went; and though a number of searches were carried out, no trace of the entrances to its nest could be found. Then a Cherokee chieftain came up with an idea.

Meat was left out in the open with a long white rope tied around it as a bait for the aerial predator. The Cherokee hunters believed that they would follow the dangling rope and so trace the beast more easily. The initial attempts, however, were fruitless, and the Yellow Jacket swiftly carried off the meat before the hunters could track it. So they increased the size of the bait— a whole deer was offered—and also put extremely long ropes around it. The giant insect returned and seized the bait, which was now so heavy that it slowed down Ulagu's flight and made it easier to follow. The ropes dangling from the meat remained in the sight of the hunters. They pursued the creature until it disappeared into a small cave high up in the cliff face above the deepest part of the gorge. They memorized the location where the white rope had disappeared into the cliff face and returned to it later with a massive hunting party. There they found a large cave opening from which a strong breeze seemed to be blowing. This, they discovered later, was the air from the moving wings of Ulagu and his wives as they moved about their interior world. Timorously, they made their way into the cave, which seemed to stretch down for a long way, almost in several deep shafts. Suddenly they emerged in a series of incredibly high, interconnected chambers deep underground, all of which seemed to be lined with some form of thin, papery material, set in six chambered rows. The walls seemed to be teeming with massive wasp-like creatures, which paid them little attention. These were

Ulagu's "wives," going about some unknown business. The caverns also seemed to be filled with smaller wasps—some form of offspring perhaps—which crawled on the hunters' skin. The world around them seemed endless and filled with insects. Of Ulagu, there was no sign, and it was presumed that he had retreated deeper into the cave system. Terrified that they might be stung to death, the hunters made their way back up the tunnel to the cave above and out into the open air once more. They decided that they must rid the world of such a place, and destroy the danger by filling the caverns below with smoke.

On the side of the gorge, they constructed a great fire—possibly the largest fire that had ever been lit in the Cherokee Nation—and sent the smoke down into the cave. From far below came an angry and confounded buzzing sound as the fire smoke overcame the insects in their cavern. Finally, says the legend, the vapors killed Ulagu, his "wives," and many of the larger insects. However, some of the smaller insects escaped from the cave and out into the world, where they multiplied and spread. And that, according to Cherokee legend, is how wasps and yellow jackets came into our world from a terrible land far below. And the tale continues, the wasps still remember that day and, in revenge, will try to sting the humans who, they believed, murdered their great lord. For many Cherokee, the appearance of a wasp is indeed an evil omen, and all flying insects are to be avoided. Of course, in some versions of the tale, Ulagu did not die, but still lives in his subterranean world, somewhere beneath the Nantahala Gorge. Those who visit the woods around the location often comment on the numbers of stinging insects to be found there, and this has, in some eyes, given credibility to the tale.

Throughout the years, the legend of Ulagu, the gigantic Yellow Jacket, has become intertwined in Cherokee mythology with the tale of Judaculla, the great slant-eyed giant in the Cherokee mind. Some will state that Judaculla is a massive insect, the size of a small aircraft, lying in wait in a massive cavern somewhere below the Devil's Courthouse on the slopes of Whiteside Mountain. Others will state that he was the leader of a subterranean tribe who had lived on the surface for a time before the arrival of the Cherokee drove them underground once more. The tales are greatly confused and are sometimes contradictory, but they all share a central theme: There is something huge and monstrous lurking in some lightless world far beneath us; something which may, on occasion, visit our surface world and cause us harm.

19

The Green Children

If relatively advanced civilizations lie somewhere beneath our feet, have they ever made any form of contact with us? There are some who claim that they have and, from time to time, stories of encounters with often small, otherworldly people or beings have been reported. Similarly there have, in certain remote areas, been alleged meetings with God-like individuals who claim that they originate from within our planet. However, such encounters are usually few and far between, and most are not well recorded. There is no sustained and cohesive story regarding those who have come to the surface from some subterranean land—or is there?

In order to find such a tale, it is necessary to go far back into English history, probably to the 12th century because the story of the Green Children was recorded during the reign of King Stephen (1135–1154).

The story, which must have been quite widespread, is recorded by two important medieval writers—Ralph of Coggeshall (Ralph was the sixth abbot of the Cistercian abbey at Coggeshall in Essex between the years 1207 and 1218) and William of Newburgh (1136–1198). It was also repeated by Roger of Wendover (d. 1236) who served for a time at Coggeshall Abbey. In its time, then, the legend of the Green Children must have been extremely common and, perhaps, there might have been an element of truth to it.

The reign of Stephen was one of almost perpetual civil war as the king struggled for power with Matilda, daughter of Henry I, also known as the Empress Maud. Nineteen turbulent years were described as a time "when Christ and his saints slept" and, as with many other such periods, it was a period of great uncertainty. While the story of the strange visitors from "St. Martin's Land" was only one of a number of "marvels" said to have occurred during that time, it seems to have persisted throughout the ages.

The story is a reasonably straightforward one. A number of hunters, setting traps along the edge of a forest near the hamlet of St. Mary-by-the-Wolfpits (later rendered as "Woolpit") in Suffolk, suddenly came upon two children—a boy and a girl in their early teens—sheltering under a tree. There was nothing unusual about this, for as the conflicts raged back and forth between Stephen and Matilda, houses were burned and families were dislocated. Children wandered here and there throughout the battle zones, often looking for their parents. However, there was something unusual about these children: Their skin was bright green in color! The huntsmen were, of course, terrified and, on capturing the children, took them to a local knight whose name is given as either Richard de Colne or de Calne. Sir Richard owned the lands around and was the main benefactor of the "little church" of St. Mary's in the hamlet beside some old pits where wolves fought for local sport.

Supposedly a supporter of King Stephen, Sir Richard initially feared that this was some sort of trick, engineered by the followers of the Empress Maud, but the huntsmen told him a rather strange story. On the previous night there had been a storm, which had uprooted several large trees in the area; this is where the children had been found. Beneath a great oak that had been pulled from the earth was a deep hole that seemed to lead into some sort of underground cave, and it was assumed that from this, both the children had emerged. The huntsmen had attempted to question them, but they spoke an unknown tongue, and could not understand or make themselves understood. They had been offered food—a piece of cooked hare—but neither of them would touch it. The boy had attempted to eat some apples, but it made him sick. They seemed unused to the food, which the others ate, and viewed anything that they were given with great suspicion.

Both children were brought into Sir Richard's presence for questioning. Their skin was indeed a deep emerald green, and they appeared to have an Asian look about them (their eyes may have been slightly almond-shaped). When they spoke, they did so in a high fluting tongue, which Sir Richard found "shrill." Once again, he attempted to get them to eat, assuming that food would provide some form of common language between them. A portion of cold beef and a chicken leg were given to each of them, but the children simply peered and prodded at them curiously, seemingly repelled by the cooked flesh; nor did they attempt to eat any of the apples, berries, or nuts that were placed in a bowl in front of them, seemingly unfamiliar with any of them.

Halfway through this curious experiment, an old serving woman came into the hall bearing a basket of long green beans. As soon as they saw these, the children commenced a loud and fluting racket and rushed toward her. With a scream she dropped the basket and fled, but the children pounced on the wicker container and began to cram the raw beans into their mouths.

What was to be done with them? Sir Richard took them as his wards and brought in a priest, Father Anthony, to teach them at least some measure of English. The knight fed them as well, although for long periods they would eat nothing but green beans. However, over a period of time, their tastes seemed to change and they began to devour cooked meats with relish. The girl seemed more eager to sample new foods than the boy, but she had always seemed the more adventurous of the two in any case.

An expedition was mounted to explore the hole from which the two had crawled, but although there was a large cavern-like space under the roots of the tree, it was impossible to advance any further. The storm had also dislodged soil and several great stones that had blocked off parts of the underground chamber, and it proved impossible to shift them. Any access that might have been available was now thoroughly sealed. Where the two children had come from still remained something of a mystery.

As time passed, both children began to lose their greenish tinge and began to interact more and more with those around them. The boy still remained rather sullen and uncommunicative, but the girl was quite chatty, and as she learned the language, communicated readily with those who wished to speak with her. The first question, of course, concerned where they had come from. Had they actually come from the Underworld?

They had lived, the girl told those who asked, in "The Land of St. Martin," which was very far away. Here, she went on, the sun never rose beyond a certain point on the horizon, and the land was consequently very dark, although there was faint light. It was a land that had been populated by Celtic peoples who had ruled England before the coming of the Saxons, and there had once been commerce between the upper world and St. Martin's Land in times long past. That trade, however, had gradually fallen away, and now the two dominions existed in isolation from each other. In her country, the girl said, everything was green—the land was green, the people were green, the animals were green, and even at times the very sky seemed green. There was little distinction between day and night in St. Martin's Land, and the people there slept as they saw fit. Nevertheless, the countryside was very much like that around St. Mary's—the people lived by farming and dwelt in small villages along the sides of great rivers, which broke up the landscape.

There was no formal religion among the people of St. Martin's Land, although from time to time, they could hear a sound reminiscent of church bells, but nobody could tell from where it came. Still, some of the people often measured their days by it and the sound told them when it was time to stop work. At certain times there were heavy rains, but thankfully those occurred only infrequently, and most of the rain was no more than a light drizzle.

The people of St. Martin's Land had a great veneration for living things, similar to the beliefs of the early Celtic peoples, and treated their animals, no matter how lowly, with great respect. They found it abhorrent to kill or devour any animal, hence the children's aversion to cooked meat. Much of their food consisted of pulses, most of which had been planted during their season of rains.

Father Anthony found it interesting that there was no formal religion in St. Martin's Land, and pressed the girl further on the matter. She told him that there was neither priest nor prelate among her people, nor was there a church of any description. There were, however, ancient stories saying that the people had once worshipped old gods such as the Celts had worshipped. Indeed, there were many ancient forts, monuments, and standing stones throughout the land. There were still some among her people who followed old ways.

Through climbing up to the summit of certain high hills, the girl claimed that she could see another, much brighter domain cut off from her own country by a broad, swift-flowing river. She had never been to this country, nor had anyone else in her village, and she claimed to know nothing about it.

How had the children come to the surface world, Sir Richard asked. The girl replied that she did not rightly know, but that she and her brother had been tending their father's sheep on a very high hill in their own country. She herself had been trying to see the bright country from the summit of some very tall rocks, and they had actually allowed the sheep to stray. Fearing their father's anger, they began to look for them and round them up again. One, however, had strayed into a very deep cave on the mountaintop, a large cavern that neither of the children had noticed before. As they went into it, the cave seemed very deep and dark, and as they advanced they heard the familiar sound of bells once again, ringing out from the gloom. They decided to go further into the cavern and to find out where they came from.

The ground beneath them, which had formerly been flat, now began to grow steeper and steeper, and they found themselves climbing upward. The sound of the bells grew louder and louder and then far away in front of them; they seemed to see a bright light—faint first but growing steadily as they approached it. Eventually, they stepped out into the brilliant light and, as they did so, the sound of bells stopped just as suddenly as it had begun. The light that was all around them now was so white that it nearly blinded them. They climbed out of a hole and found themselves on the edge of a forest near St. Mary's-by-the-Wolfpits. Frightened, they attempted to crawl back into the hole from which they had emerged, but were suddenly set upon by hunters and captured.

The story was an incredible one, and all who heard it were amazed. The girl further revealed that although she liked the surface world, her brother was most unhappy and pined for his own world, which she assumed was far below. He still found the surface world very strange. In her own world it was generally the women who were the stronger gender, while men, though the rulers and elders in each village, were generally much weaker. Thus, her brother was constantly sick and wanted to go back home. If local people found them strange with their green skin, then think how strange it was for them to be surrounded by pink-skinned men and women. If he did not return to St. Martin's Land soon, she was afraid that he might die.

She had, therefore, searched for a way back to the underground kingdom, but had been unsuccessful. Sir Richard did not tell her that he had given orders to have the hole that they had crawled out of sealed up. He was frightened that a troop of armed knights might also emerge from it in order to retrieve the children, and was taking no chances. The children were therefore trapped on the surface world and there seemed no way back for them.

Father Anthony insisted that the children be baptized as Christians, and so they were, at a secret service that only Sir Richard attended. Even so, they seemed to find the religion rather strange and seemed extremely unsettled at Mass and other sacred events. They continued to live at Sir Richard's castle, and though the girl seemed to settle into the routine of everyday life there, the boy still seemed morose and withdrawn.

Two years after they had been discovered, the girl's dire prophesy came true; the boy seemed to become even more listless. He wouldn't eat, he took no part in his lessons with the priest, nor did he engage in play of any kind. Sometimes, he was to be found down by the Wolf Pits looking longingly at the ground. And, as winter drew in, and the ground hardened like iron, he began to seriously sicken. Father Anthony did what he could—he offered prayers and sent to the Abbey at Bury for sacred water from the Well of Our Lady—but to no avail. As Christmas Day approached, the boy took an inexplicable fever and died.

His sister continued to live at the castle of Sir Richard de Colne for a time. Unlike her brother, she seemed to have adapted well to the world around her—she now ate foods that everyone else ate, she spoke English much better, albeit with a peculiar accent, and she also took with gusto to drinking and dancing. Her hair became fairer, and as she grew older she became more beautiful. And as she grew to womanhood, she became more forward and flirty in her ways. There were whispers that she'd actually become Sir Richard's mistress, thus antagonizing the knight's wife, but these were simply rumors.

In time, she left Sir Richard's castle and married one of his squires. They went to live at Lenna, near King's Lynn, but from time to time, she would leave her husband and return to St. Mary's-by-the-Wolfpits, looking rather lost and lonely. She, too, now seemed to be pining for her former home in St. Martin's Land. Then, one day, she simply vanished.

Many rumors circulated about her disappearance. Some said that, although married, she continued to be Sir Richard's mistress, and this is why she returned. It was also said that she had borne several children to him in secret, and that in revenge, his wife poisoned her and made away with the body; others said that she'd been swept up in the savage conflicts that were still rampant throughout the countryside. Others affirmed that she'd managed to find a way back to the underground kingdom of St. Martin's Land, but others stated that she'd run off with someone else and was living in Norfolk where she eventually died, a very old woman. What truly became of her will probably never be known.

Such is the story of the Green Children. Many have dismissed it as a mere fantasy, either dreamed up by monks or gullibly recounted as fact by them. But there may be some truth in the tale. There was, at the time, allegedly a book, copied down by one of Sir Richard's scribes and dictated by the green-skinned girl concerning the "ancient religions and practices of St. Martin's Land." This was supposedly read by Sir Richard's confessor—whose name is alternately given as Father Anthony or Father John—who found it so shocking that he hid it away and forbade anyone to read it again, declaring that "Christian eyes would never look upon the blasphemies that were writ therein." This book is still reputed to be somewhere in the vicinity of Bury St. Edmunds.

There are also certain references in some of the medieval literature to "Green Jack's Children." Although it is never properly specified what these "children" were, it might be that they were the remnants of some Pagan woodland fertility cult, which dated back to Celtic times. It might just be that these children were not from a subterranean world at all, but were really members of a cult—the term "green" being a misinterpretation. This oversight may then have been elaborated upon by subsequent authors who portrayed them as coming from some other sphere outside the Christian world. "St. Martin's Land," some have argued, is a corruption of "Merlin's Land," referring to ancient Celtic beliefs concerning the wizard of Arthurian fable.

There are also a couple of extremely plausible explanations. The first has been put forward by the Fortean writer Mike Dash, who says that the tale may have a more mundane interpretation. The children, he thinks, may have been two malnourished waifs from the Suffolk village of Fornham St. Martins—St. Martin's Land—who were caught up in the wars between King Stephen and the Empress Maud. Although today, the two locations are relatively close, in medieval England, they would have seemed like two different countries. It is extremely doubtful whether anyone in St. Mary's would have ever been to Fornham St. Martins, and the two areas might have spoken different dialects of English that might have initially appeared unintelligible to each other. However, the bells the children claimed to have heard were those of Bury Abbey, which was not terribly far away from Fornham, calling the monks there to prayer at certain times of the day. The children arrived at St. Mary's by way of a series of extensive Neolithic flint mines that stretched under Thetford Forest, and which might have given the impression of an underground kingdom. Their "greenness" might actually have been a disease known as "green chlorosis" caused by severe malnourishment.

In 1998, the writer Paul Harris set forward another explanation. This depends on the story of the discovery being slightly later in time and during the reign of Henry II (1154–1189), who succeeded Stephen. During both reigns, the east of England experienced an influx of Flemish immigrants, many of whom worked as fullers (dyers). During Henry's reign these "foreigners" were attacked, and in 1173 there was a great massacre of Flemish immigrants near Bury. Could it be that the boy and the girl had escaped this slaughter, and had fled into Thetford Forest to avoid being killed, there to live for a while as feral children? They were then discovered and taken to St. Mary's where they were treated as wonders. The "greenness" of their skin might well have come from constant exposure to fuller's dyes. It is certainly a plausible explanation, and one that may well fit in with the facts—many other accounts seem to suggest that they appeared during Henry's reign and not that of Stephen.

And yet, there are lingering mysteries that have never been explained. The fact that they would not eat meat such as beef—regarded as a "luxury food" and much sought after by many villagers—is one. The other is their clothing, which appears to have been "gown-like," and made of some material unknown to weavers around St. Mary's. Did they exist at all? Folklorists such as Kathryn Briggs have traced several elements in the tale common to several other stories, and have hinted that it may be no more than an invention— "a pleasing tale"—to entertain medieval listeners. St. Martin's Land has never existed.

In 1887, near the town of Banjos in Spain, two green-skinned children—a boy and a girl—were found cowering near the entrance to a large cave, which had been recently sealed by a landslide. They were dressed in long gown-like clothes of an unknown material and spoke in a strange fluting language. They were both described as being "Asian-looking" with almond-shaped eyes. They were brought back down to the town where they were taken in and looked after. What became of the boy is unknown, but the girl lived for about five years before dying in 1892. In that time she had learned a little Spanish (the boy does not appear to have learned it), and stated that she came from a "land that was far away," and that she and her brother had been lifted by a "mighty whirlwind" and deposited in Spain. The name of the land from which they came was called "San Martino" (St. Martin's Land). So who knows—perhaps somewhere far below, lies another country in which green-skinned people live and, from time to time, may even venture up into the sunlight to meet us.

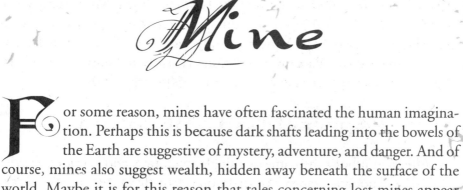

20

The Lost Dutchman Mine

For some reason, mines have often fascinated the human imagination. Perhaps this is because dark shafts leading into the bowels of the Earth are suggestive of mystery, adventure, and danger. And of course, mines also suggest wealth, hidden away beneath the surface of the world. Maybe it is for this reason that tales concerning lost mines appear frequently in the folklore of many cultures.

The most famous of all such places is, of course, King Solomon's Mines, said to be located somewhere on the African continent. Others disputed this location, and state that King Solomon's Mines lay somewhere near the splendid and fabulously wealthy port of Ophir, although no one is exactly sure where this was. The Mines were reputedly vast gold mines, and were linked with the name of the biblical king of Israel who was believed to have sent expeditions there to look for African wealth. From these mines, Solomon is supposed to have obtained a greater part of his legendary wealth. However, after the king's death, the location of the Mines was reputedly lost, although they were still known to a handful of native tribes living in their vicinity. The legend came to prominence once more with the publication in 1885 of Sir Henry Rider Haggard's famous novel *King Solomon's Mines*, which featured his rather swashbuckling hero, Alan Quartermain. The Indiana Jones of his day, Quartermain led an expedition through uncharted African territory to eventually find the entrance to the fabled workings. Haggard had undoubtedly heard the legend from his friend Sir Henry Bulwer, lieutenant-governor of Natal Province in South Africa, and his book raised interest in the possible existence of the Mines. This was the age of British exploration, and it was said that a number of expeditions were sent into both the deserts of North Africa and the forest of South Africa to look for the Mines, none of which were successful.

Although there were reputedly more fabulously wealthy mines, none have achieved the folkloric status of the Lost Dutchman Mine, somewhere in Arizona, which has enjoyed something of a legendary reputation to equal that of King Solomon. The Mine, reputedly based in the Superstition Mountain area to the east of Phoenix, is mentioned in story and song, and was even the subject of a pop record during the late 1950s/early 1960s.

Superstition Mountain

Although it bears the name of a single mountain, and is sometimes described as a "mountain range," Superstition is actually an area of rocky terrain full of cliffs, gullies, and blind canyons, with several "spires" and "peaks" amid the jumble. Large parts of this region remain unexplored, even today. It is not surprising that this strange and often eerie landscape has spawned legends and folktales about it.

The first people to see the region with its shadowy canyons and odd rock formations were most probably the Apache Indians who seem to have given it a wide berth—although some traditions say that they used it for a sacred burial ground. The first Europeans to see it were Spaniards (part of the expedition of Francisco Vasquez de Coronado as it headed north through Arizona to search for the Seven Cities of Gold in 1540). Coronado's guides told them that the area was rich in gold, but that it was also the domain of a powerful Thunder God who would take vengeance on those who entered his territory intent on stealing his wealth. It is said that Coronado dispatched several parties to investigate the region, but no one returned; the Indians could have been irrefutable evidence of the Thunder God's power. Although skeptical of their claims, Coronado did not investigate any further, and his expedition proceeded north. However, he named the region Monte Superstition, which is its name today.

Peralta's Fortune

For almost 300 years, the area remained isolated and inaccessible, and avoided by most people. Strange tales, mostly Indian legends, surrounded it, and white men seldom ventured into it. In 1845, however, a certain Don Miguel Peralta, a native and businessman from Sonora, Mexico, came exploring in the Superstition, drawn by the tales of rich veins of gold that were reputedly found there. In the shadow of a great rock formation shaped (according to Peralta) like a "sombrero," he found ancient workings that seemed suggestive of a shallow mine worked by the Apaches or even some earlier culture. Marking the spot in his mind, Peralta went to find those who would help him work the mine as a commercial concern. Upon return with men and materials, he began to mine in earnest, naming the place "The Sombrero Mine" after the rock that marked the spot in his mind. They had not been working long when they struck a rich vein of almost pure gold; soon Peralta was shipping many thousands of pesos' worth of the raw material back to Sonora. His good fortune was not to last, however.

In 1848, angered by continual incursions into their sacred territory, the Apaches formed a coalition of tribes to drive Peralta and his miners out. Peralta, however, had been tipped off about their attack and planned to move back to Sonora for a time before returning to Superstition. He began loading a train of burros (mules) with raw gold from the mine, ready for transport. In order for nobody else to find the mine in his absence, he took elaborate precautions to disguise the mine entrance, laying false trails up through the canyons. He delayed too long, for the Indians attacked with alarming ferocity before the mule train was out of the Superstition region. Peralta and all the miners were reputedly killed and the burros scattered. For years afterward the bones of dead mules with rotting saddlebags containing gold were found in various gullies and ravines all around the Superstition area. Although many tried to locate the Sombrero Mine, none were able to. Some adventurers claimed that the rock had not been hat-shaped at all, but an upright spire known as Weaver's Needle. This had allegedly been named after the famous mountain man, trapper, and Army scout, Paulino Weaver, who had partly explored some of the region. Others pointed to a similar spire-shaped rock known as "The Finger of God," but nobody was really sure. Peralta had concealed the Mines extremely well, and they remained hidden from quest-ing eyes. The last known instance of an individual finding a Peralta mule occurred in 1914. In this year, a rather mysterious gentleman named C.H. Silverlocke arrived in Phoenix carrying roughly $18,000 in raw gold. He claimed that there was more out in the desert and, gathering together some equipment, set out to increase his wealth. He never returned, and was deemed to be another victim of Superstition.

Dutch Discoveries

This brings us to the Dutchman who gave the mine its lasting name. The first thing to recognize about Jacob Walz (also given as Waltz or Weis) is that he wasn't Dutch, but German, born around 1810 in Wuttenburg, and having come to America as an immigrant in 1845. He first appears as a prospector and miner in North Carolina in the 1850s, working for other miners and panning for gold in some of the streams on the edge of the Smokies. He seems to have been a taciturn character, and something of a loner, which perhaps would later work to his advantage. He also seems to have led an itinerant sort of life, drifting from gold field to gold field and from one mine to another, never seeming to make his fortune but usually making enough to get by. He reportedly mined in the Sierra Nevada and also in California; wherever there was a reported gold strike, Jacob Walz seemed to turn up. In 1861, he became an American citizen at the Los Angeles County Courthouse in California and later that year appeared on the San Gabriel River gold field, working for a man named Ruben Blakeney. From there he struck out into the Bradshaw Mountain area of Arizona with a group of miners intent on making their fortune. Pickings were poor and around 1865 Walz was apparently working as a laborer on both the Big Rebel and General Grant Mines high in the Bradshaw Mountain area.

By 1868, he was still prospecting in Arizona, this time in the Rio Satillo Valley north of Superstition. He also seems to have been well known to local Apaches who had nicknamed him Snowbeard, because his beard had turned almost white. In fact, he appears to have been one of those crazy old prospectors who worked up in the hills, always on the very edge of a fortune, but never quite finding it. Once again, he seems to have made just enough money to get along. He is alleged to have worked in the Superstition area for about 20 years, sometimes prospecting for himself, sometimes working as a miner in the surrounding mines.

In 1870, he is alleged to have met another miner named Jacob Weiser while working at the Vulture Mine near the northern end of the Superstition. Weiser may have also been German, but there is a strong possibility that he came from Holland, and that he was the real Dutchman. The two set off into the Superstition to prospect together. There is a further story that Walz was dismissed from the crew of the Vulture Mine for secretly stealing gold that he had stored in the canyons of the region. Whether or not this was true is open to question—it would certainly fit in with his uneasy personality— but it might explain where the two men acquired the raw gold nuggets that they began to spend in the mining camps around Phoenix. Both men used various, and often conflicting, tales to explain their sudden wealth. For example, they said that they had befriended some Apache Indians who had taken them to a cave in the Superstition area where gold had been piled high against the wall. This had been the remnants of the treasure that Miguel Peralta had been transporting back to Sonora when the Apache war bands had struck. In other explanations, they said that they had rescued a Mexican from a band of Apaches, fighting off his attackers and escorting him to safety. The man turned out to be Don Miguel Peralta, a descendant of the original mine owner and, as a reward, he showed them a map that marked the location of his gold mine. What became of Peralta afterward is unclear. In yet another story that the two miners told, they came up on several men working a shallow mine in a canyon deep in the Superstition. Assuming them to be Apaches, the "Dutchmen" attacked and killed them, finding out too late that they were in fact Mexicans. The place where they had been working turned out to be the lost mine, and the saddlebags of the burros that they had been loading were crammed with gold. Whatever the truth of the story may be, the supply of gold that the two prospectors seemed to possess appeared endless.

Sometime after 1871, Jacob Weiser suddenly disappeared. Walz said that their camp had been attacked by Indians and Weiser had been killed; he (Walz) said he had buried the body out in a lonely canyon in accordance with the dead man's wishes. He alone now knew the location of the mysterious mine. And though he was frequently pressed and offered business deals, he refused to disclose where it was. All he would say was that it was somewhere in the Superstition.

Of course stories abounded around "The Dutchman." The most common tale stated that Walz had murdered his partner somewhere out in the lonely Superstition region, and had taken over the mine for himself. Of course, nothing could be proved. Others said that there was no mine at all—what the two men had found was a massive cache of the Peralta gold stored away in saddlebags taken from the burros, or else it was a haul that the two had removed from the Vulture Mine, and that eventually Walz had murdered his partner in order to get his hands on it. Again, this was simply speculation. However, Walz now took to disappearing into the Superstition for long periods, returning seemingly laden with gold nuggets.

Although he was by now quite an elderly man, Walz had developed a taste for hard liquor, gambling, and womanizing. He was something of a colorful character around Phoenix, and that color simply added to his legend. A central figure in many of the gambling cartels in the town, he never seemed to be short of cash; if he owed money, he would go out into the Superstition to return again with raw gold with which to pay his debts. His gambling and drinking continued for many years, but he was old and his hard living soon caught up with him.

In 1891, he took up with a Mexican widow named Julia Elena Thomas. There was some talk of marriage and Walz promised to show her "a grand wedding dowry" out in the Superstition. However, he claimed that the canyons out to the mine were impassable in winter, but he would take her there in the spring of 1892. She was not to see the mine, for The Dutchman died suddenly on October 25, 1891. His hell-raising life had finally overtaken him. And with him died the location of the gold mine—if it had ever existed.

Shortly after his death, his widow, who was still a young woman (29 years old), hired two German brothers—Rhinehart and Herman Petrusch—to travel into the Superstition following an old map that Walz was said to have drawn shortly before his death. After some time, however, they returned to Phoenix, empty-handed and disappointed. Walz's widow would later make her living selling false maps showing the location of the gold mine to anyone who would buy them.

With the Dutchman's death, speculation mounted as to where his mine lay, and many treasure-hunters mounted expeditions into the Superstition in order to find it; none did. However, a number of equally colorful characters grew up around the region, some of whom may have known where the mine might lie. The most famous of these was Elisha M. Reavis, widely known as the "Madman of the Superstition," who lived in the area between 1872 and 1896. He is said to have dwelt in a remote section of the region, and the local Apaches never bothered him because they were afraid of him. There was a tradition among a number of Indian tribes that those who were "touched by spirits" were supernatural beings and were to be avoided. Reavis certainly fit the bill—some accounts said that he ran through the canyons of Superstition, stark naked and howling like an animal; on other nights he would climb up to the highest points and shoot at the stars with a rifle. But on the rare occasions when he did come into Phoenix, he would buy goods with nuggets of raw gold. It didn't matter if the storekeepers charged him too much for his purchases, as he always said that there was "more gold" out in the Superstition.

Around April 1896, a man who had befriended him noticed that Reavis was overdue on a trip into town and went out into the Superstition to look for him. He found the "Madmans'" body in a remote canyon, half eaten by coyotes, and with his head cut completely off. There was some talk that Reavis had been murdered, but nothing could be proved—the body had been too long in the sun—and no trace of his wealth was ever discovered. Several individuals from Phoenix made their way out to see if they could find the source of the gold, but none ever returned.

There were those who said that the Dutchman Mine did not lie in the Superstition at all, but in the Salt River Valley nearby. The Salt River flows along the eastern edge of Superstition, and there are a number of small creeks and tidal backwaters near it, which are said to be the locations of gold-bearing rocks. Jacob Walz's widow is said to have given an interview to Pierpoint C. Bicknell, a freelance writer, upon her return from the Superstition area, and seemed to suggest that her late husband had hinted as much to her. But to the best of anyone's knowledge, she herself never looked along the Salt River for his mine. Certainly a couple of other rich mines were found in the vicinity of the River—the celebrated Black Queen and Mammoth Mines. The output of the Mammoth Mine alone amounted to more than $3 million in pure gold within a four year period. Was the Dutchman Mine an even richer lode?

Throughout the years many have tried to hunt down the elusive Lost Dutchman Mine and many have died in the process. And still the fabulous mine remains as elusive as ever.

21

The Hollow Hills

On the rugged North Antrim coast of Northern Ireland, beside a tiny harbor near the village of Ballintoy, the traveler is greeted with a unique sight. The towers of a rock city, complete with sea-carved steps and mighty archways, stretch out along the northern end of the bay, like some ancient and sleeping metropolis from another time. It is even possible to see spires and what look like windows in the stone, set in what appear to be the ends of buildings when passing along the cliffs above. And, of course, such a spectacular phenomenon has many folktales concerning it. It is said, for instance, to be an incredibly ancient city, turned to stone by the holy St. Patrick because of its incredible wickedness. Other stories say that it was a pre-Deluge city, which was somehow petrified by God because of the wickedness that dwelt within it. All along the coast, caves and inlets of the sea are supposed to conceal tunnels, which eventually led to hidden rooms and chambers within this forgotten city, and some of its inhabitants—monsters and monstrous beings—are said to live deep within the Earth beneath it, only emerging at night to haunt the petrified remains of their former homes. This can be known as the Hollow Hills.

Around the World

Of course, such a coastal phenomenon undoubtedly has more to do with the nature of the limestone (up until the early 20th century, limestone and burnt lime were exported from Ballintoy, and the remnants of old lime kilns can still be seen there), but it has had a powerful effect on local imaginations. Similar rock formations, odd hills, and mounds have often had the same effect in many other parts of the world.

In the southern Mexican area of Oaxica, for instance, in a region once occupied by the ancient Zapotecs, and near the ruins of their abandoned city of Monte Alban, lies a series of small hills which allegedly lead to an underground world; nearby stood the village of Liyobaa, which was known in former times as "the Village of the Underworld." A main cavern at the edge of the hills was nicknamed "The Cavern of Death," and no local Indian will enter it to this day. When, in the early 1600s, Jesuit missionaries first came to the area, they named the cavern and the hills "Hell," and instructed the cavern to be sealed off with earth and rubble. There seems little doubt that this entrance led to some underground temple or crypt, which had been used by the ancient kings of Theozapotlan for some sort of ritual purpose, probably involving human sacrifice. One of the missionaries, a Father Burgoa, reveals that there were at least four rooms well below ground level, all packed with "heathen artefacts and idols." He further hinted that these rooms were connected by passages, and that further passages led deep underground, perhaps to lower levels. The Jesuits were convinced that these led to the very gates of Hell itself. From the descriptions, however, it seems that these "rooms" were elaborate chambers, constructed many centuries before, where the worship of gods was carried out. Burgoa speaks of "altars" and chalices," all suggestive of some form of significant religious center, which may have extended far underground. It has been suggested that the lower levels may have held ceremonial burial vaults for the dead kings of the region, and this may have given the main cavern its sinister nickname. Nevertheless, the horror and suspicion with which the missionaries regarded such a deep, dark place must have been overwhelming.

They may also have been influenced by old South American legends concerning systems of tunnels and chambers running back and forth all across the continent. Such tunnels, according to Aztec legend, supposedly led to dim and lightless kingdoms far below, and in early times gods and people had moved freely along them between such realms and the surface. The lowest of these realms was known as Mictlan, which was the equivalent of the Aztec Hell. Warriors who had been killed outside of battle, and women who had died in childbirth, were sent to Mictlan—a long and difficult journey through the darkness of the Underworld, which lasted for four years. In this they were guided by the psychopomp (spirit guide) Xolotl who eventually led them to the underworld kingdom. Mictlan was regarded as an actual realm with mountains, rivers, cities, and towns, all lying in total darkness under a sunless sky.

An underground country appears in Incan mythology, too. It was from such an underworld that the first Inca, "Manco Capac," and his followers emerged into the sunlight and came to live on the surface of the world. Capac was considered to be the first king of Cuzco in Peru, ruling there for 40 years; but according to Inca tradition, he had also been the ruler of an underground realm far below, and had emerged from the cave of Pacaritambo (near the Urubamba Valley in the Andes), carrying a golden staff as a symbol of his high office. The first building that he founded was a large temple to the sun, because, it was said, his people had been dwelling in the underworld darkness for so long. In some legends he is sometimes confused with (and is portrayed as) Urcaguay—the great snake and guardian of underground treasures—who is also said to have emerged from a cavern, and whose worship, which often included human sacrifice, was usually at the mouths of deep ravines and caves. Indeed, in some ancient Inca myths, races of serpent men reputedly lived in an underground kingdom venturing to the surface only very occasionally, and then only to raid or take captives.

Another mystery connected to an underground realm can also be found in the southern tip of Peru, not far from the Chilean border and near a small pueblo village named Ila. This is a great rock monolith, standing alone on a hill (which is supposedly hollow), which bears all sorts of strange markings, some of which are vaguely reminiscent of the Judaculla Rock in North Carolina. This stone, which is composed of lava, was supposedly raised by a race that emerged from an underground kingdom and colonized the surface for a brief period before being driven back below ground again by the surface tribes. It is said that anyone who can decipher the writings on the rock will learn the entrance to a tunnel system that extends from one side of the South American continent to the other, and the location of a fabulously wealthy kingdom lying far underground. Madame Blavatsky, who visited the site in the late 1800s, appeared to concur with the legend and claimed that the monolith had been raised by a "superior race" of great intelligence and power. That race, she asserted, was still down in the darkness, awaiting contact.

Legends concerning tunnels to the upper surface from some country far below have sometimes transferred from South American legend into North American folklore. Usually, there are sinister overtones in such tales, and many concern people who have been spirited away by the denizens of such dark places. Perhaps this is because the Underworld has been viewed with awe and suspicion by the North American mind. The area directly beneath the surface of the Earth is often the domain of the dead. In New England, for example, the religious followers of Shadrack Ireland constructed artificial "hills" throughout the landscape during the early 1700s to house great stone-lined underground crypts where their dead could lie. Part of Ireland's belief was that the dead "Brethren of the New Light" (those who followed his teachings which he claimed came directly from God) should not be buried in the ground, but should lie in communal chambers until the Day of Judgement when they could walk out whole and uncorrupted to face the Lord. When Ireland's cult collapsed in the mid-1700s, it must have been rather disconcerting for those living in eastern New England to know that beneath their feet and in the hills close to their homes, ranks of dead people were lying in a series of interconnecting chambers, ready to rise up at any time. This may well have affected the folklore of the area.

Indian legends too may have played their part in the belief. Stories of dead Indians who returned from some other subterranean world were found in the lore of many tribes, and old Indian mounds scattered throughout North America may have re-emphasised this belief. Such mounds, it was said, were the actual entrances into these netherworlds. Thus, those living close to such places may have felt slightly ill at ease. And, of course, there is also the baffling mystery of the "balds" in places such as North Carolina.

Balds

"Balds," as they are known, are curious rounded hills upon the summits of which no vegetation, not even grass, will grow, leaving them completely "bald." Such phenomena sometimes appears in New England, in locations such as Massachusetts or Rhode Island, but they certainly seem to congregate in the Appalachian chain in the northwestern corner of North Carolina. Here on a number of "balds," no tree will grow, and although grass appears on the crowns of some of them, it is a thin, wiry, unhealthy growth that does not seem to last long. Others hold a shrub-like grass that spreads across the top like a fine covering. It is said that at least some of these "balds" denote the entrances to underground worlds, and that this prevents surface-world growths from sprouting or from taking hold there. It is said that these balds have existed since records began—there are tales of them among the Indians who will not approach some of them for fear of ancient powers lurking there— but none can truly explain them. There have been a number of explanations, such as strange soil composition to the activities of an insect known as the twig-gall wasp, but none of them truly hold up. On the top of some of the barren balds, long-range observers have thought they have seen faults, and landslips appear to have revealed small caves. Expeditions have been sent out to such caverns, only to find that they have disappeared. On Rambling Bald in the Lake Lure area of northwest, North Carolina, a large cavern appeared to exist—it was viewed through binoculars from some mountains nearby, but once again when searchers set out to find it, there was no trace on the mountain slopes. No trace of it was subsequently discovered, although several people claimed to have seen it.

It has been said that the balds are hollow inside, and may contain tunnels that lead down to subterranean kingdoms or may indeed contain a world within themselves. Their gently sloping roundness has led to suggestions that at least some of them may have been artificially created. The "caves," which seem to appear and vanish, are in fact access and exit points of these interior worlds, which are opened and closed from within. Who or what comes and goes through them is unknown. Occasionally, sounds will be heard echoing through the neighboring valleys, emanating from the balds. These sounds vary between dull roars—like falling rocks—or the steady motion of machinery, rising and falling in volume. A more fanciful explanation is that these are the sounds of underground engines operated by a subterranean race for some as yet unspecified purpose. Others have replied that these are simply the echoes of geological movements far underground, and that they are purely natural phenomena.

And yet, stories concerning these "hollow hills" still persist in the folklore of the region. Local farmers will tell tales of animals who are mysteriously spirited away while grazing on the lower slopes of these bald mountains, and from time to time there are stories of humans who have also vanished in the vicinity of the North Carolina heights.

The most famous of all such North Carolina fireside tales is that of the Reverend W.T. Hawkins, a 73-year-old retired Methodist minister who vanished one blustery evening in the 1930s in the Sapphire Hills on the South Carolina border. Tom Hawkins, who had the nickname "The Shepherd of the Hills" (presumably after the famous book written in 1907 by Harold Bell Wright, which centred on Ozark folklore), was a much loved and much respected figure throughout North Carolina. His disappearance became a talking point all through the hill country, and was linked to peculiar lights that were seen in the area at the time, and to rumors of a mysterious underground race.

Around 5:30 p.m. on a dull and windy evening in March 1930, there was consternation in the household of Joe Wright, the Reverend Hawkins's son-in-law with whom the old man lived. A family cow had been grazing up above the house on Timber Ridge, and now seemed to have disappeared. A creature of habit, she would usually come down the slope lowing to the door to be milked and put in for the night. This time it hadn't happened and Joe Wright was worried. However, it was a miserable evening and Joe was warming himself by the open fire. He didn't really want to go out again and look for her. Besides, there had been tales of strange lights—"Indian lights," as local people called them—up along the Ridge and up into the mountains and Joe was just a little scared. His father-in-law, Tom Hawkins, had no such reservations. Leaving his daughter with her pots and pans, and his son-in-law still warming himself, the old man pulled on a coat and went up onto Timber Ridge to look for the animal. On the way up, he passed a neighbor heading home and bade him a cheery "good night." He walked into the twilight and was never seen again; nor was the family cow. Somewhere up on the Ridge both of them disappeared forever.

As his supper grew cold on the kitchen table, Tom Hawkins's daughter began to worry. By now the gloomy twilight had given way to darkness and she grew more and more uneasy. Goblin tales that she had heard from some of her neighbors about queer lights moving along Timber Ridge began to creep into her mind. There was an old story about a girl who had allegedly vanished somewhere near the Ridge while berry picking there in the late 1800s. Some said that she had been carried away by beings of a subterranean race who were supposed to dwell in caverns deep below the Sapphire Hills, but who sometimes came up to the surface in order to hunt. There was supposedly some sort of underground city below the Hills, and from time to time odd noises would drift down to those below. These were just old Indian tales, and her father had frequently chided her for listening to them and had dismissed them as nonsense. At the time she'd agreed with him, but now she wasn't so sure. She looked at the table; Tom Hawkins hadn't returned.

Joe tried to reassure her—although the same sorts of stories were preying on his own mind. The old man had stopped off by the store, he said, and was gossiping with some of the neighbors. He had forgotten the time. She asked him to go down to see, and if the old minister was there, to bring him home. Joe walked down to the store. There, men often gathered in the evening to talk, swap stories, and whittle, but Tom Hawkins wasn't among them. Several of the men had seen him pass by on his way up to Timber Ridge—a couple had called out to him as he had passed—but no one had seen him come back down again. There had been lights running along the Ridge, one said, and that meant only one thing: "them that live below are huntin' again" and all should stay away. Joe Wright turned home again, his anxiety growing.

And as the hours crawled past and the meal still remained untouched on the table, that anxiety turned into alarm. The next day, when Hawkins still hadn't returned, Joe went around to his neighbors. His rational mind told him that the old man had probably fallen into a hollow or ravine and was probably lying seriously injured somewhere; yet another part of him remembered the old Indian tales of an underground race who had supposedly carried off a little girl to their own dark domain back in the 1800s. Not far away lay Whiteside Mountain with the sinister Devil's Courthouse on its slopes. This was supposed to be the entrance to a subterranean world from which creatures emerged every once in a while. Stories of mysterious beings from the depths were all too common in this region, and made him feel extremely uneasy.

News of the disappearance spread, and search parties were organized. The "Shepherd of the Hills" was such a popular figure that no effort was spared in bringing teams together, several with a number of experienced woodsmen who knew the Sapphire region well. But although Timber Ridge was combed again and again, not a trace of the missing clergyman was found, nor was there even a clue to the whereabouts of the cow for which he himself had been searching. It seemed, observed one of the searchers, "as if the ground had opened up and swallowed him." Given the folklore of the region, there may have been more truth in the comment than was intended.

Despite having the crack woodsmen in their group, the parties came down day after day with no word. Not even so much as a belt buckle had been found. A couple of the woodsmen admitted to finding "queer tracks" up along the Ridge, made by "not quite human feet" and drag marks through the foliage as if something bigger than a man (a cow?) had been taken along there. One of the woodsmen said that he'd seen similar tracks once before— up by the Devil's Courthouse on Whiteside Mountain. Maybe, one man observed, Hawkins had come on the underground hunters as they were carrying off his cow, and they'd taken him as well. It was a fantastic theory, but might it be true?

Some thought that Hawkins might have fallen into Lake Cashiers and the local authorities had the lake partly drained, but again nothing was found. Others said that the shepherd might have been whisked away in an automobile, but the roads up on the Timber Ridge were particularly bad, and few motor cars visited the area in which Hawkins lived. He could have been robbed and murdered, and his body removed from the area, but his daughter confirmed that he had nothing of any value on his person when he left. He'd simply pulled on a coat in order to go and fetch a cow. Had he run across moonshiners up in the hills who had killed him in order to protect their stills? But if that had happened, someone would have heard about it, and though the parson certainly disapproved of whiskey, he was known not to be an informer. There was also the theory that he had climbed up to investigate a nearly inaccessible cave, high up above the Ridge, and had somehow fallen and fatally injured himself. This theory was discounted as he had been going out in the twilight. However, it added to the idea that the aged minister had somehow been abducted by an underground race. Stories and hearthside tales began to flow back and forth across the region.

After two weeks, the search for the missing minister was abandoned. No one could determine what had happened to the shepherd of the hills and on dark nights, lights were said to be moving again up along Timber Ridge. Men were rapidly becoming afraid of going up there, especially as dusk was falling. A service was conducted in the old man's honor in the small Cashiers Valley church, in the churchyard of which his wife and mother both lay. The family gave up any hope of ever finding his body. But there was one last sinister twist to come.

One night, as the Wright family lay asleep, their home was suddenly and inexplicably enveloped in flames. The family escaped, but the house was completely destroyed; they were able to save very few valuables and were left virtually destitute, relying on the kindness of neighbors. Nobody knew how the fire started or why it had been started. However, one of the investigating police officers found odd tracks close to where the house had stood; tracks which a woodsman later identified as ones he had seen up on Timber Ridge after the old minister had disappeared. This led some to speculate that Hawkins had been murdered and that his murderer was now trying to kill Joe Wright and his family. Maybe somebody held a grudge against them all. And yet, at night, the moving lights up on Timber Ridge were seen once more, coming and going in the darkness. Could the two be connected? Others rubbished the idea and said that the fire had been started by a spark from the fire catching the tinder-dry shingles of the building. If there was any connection between the two events, it was never discovered.

Is there a lost land lying somewhere under the American continent? Certainly there seems to be a wealth of folkloric evidence from all over the continent that there is and, though the cynics may scoff, who knows what mysteries the distant hills may conceal?

Conclusion:

Whispers From Somewhere Else

The world is full of hints, rumors, and speculations. In early days, men and women looked out toward the horizon and wondered what lay beyond it. It was then that human guesswork and imagination took over, and that stories, tales, and suggestions began to circulate. Some even claimed to have been there, either in actuality or in dreams and/or visions; others merely guessed at what might lie out there. And what they described was only limited by their own imaginations. What lay out there were wondrous countries, inhabited by the gods or by mystical beings, where there were magical places such as a fountain that bestowed eternal youth or a palace that conferred absolute contentment upon those who dwelt there. Out there, too, lay centers that could bring peace and stability to the world—the influence of which could be felt all across the planet. It is possible, then, to argue that some of these places were actually an abstraction or symbol of peoples' hopes and dreams, and gave them something upon which to focus.

As time went on, and people actually did travel to distant lands and locations, they brought back to their own communities interpretations of what they had seen. And certainly some of the things that they had seen were vastly unlike anything they had ever experienced before. Once again, imagination began to play a significant role. They sometimes described the inhabitants, customs, and cultures of distant lands in exaggerated and wondrous terms, blending some of the things that they had seen with folktale and legend in order, perhaps, to make them even more spectacular to their listeners. Thus, anything that was remote or far away began to acquire a certain enchanted, mystical quality, in the common mind at least.

History also began to acquire some similar attributes. As life sometimes became harder and more complex, it was tempting to look back at some wonderful, less-complicated age where everything had been wonderful and much more simplistic. This might have been a perfect native state (as in the Garden of Eden) or some relatively advanced civilization in which life was much easier (such as Atlantis). These places always seemed to exist somewhere in the past—even today there is a tendency to look back to the "good old days" of an idyllic yesteryear—which made them as unattainable as some of the far-off lands about which travelers told. It was in fact the sheer inaccessibility of such places that allowed imagination and speculation to run riot. Whether it was some unreachable island lying in uncharted waters or some almost forgotten realm now lost to history, the impulse was the same—to imagine and to speculate.

This is not to say, of course, that such locations certainly did not exist. Indeed, as we have seen, some of the legendary places may well be rooted in actual historical and geographical fact, but it is human imagination and speculation that have given them both their color and mystique. In this respect, they have been partially created by the human mind, and to some extent by human yearnings.

Exploration, too, opened up new vistas for the human imagination to investigate. As previously unknown continents began to yield their secrets, they sometimes posed more questions than they answered. Had great and vanished civilizations once flourished there? Had now extinct cultures held a knowledge that was now lost to the world? Had others actually been there before, leaving at least some traces of their presence behind? During the early 19th century, explorers such as Mungo Park brought back stories from the

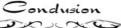

then "dark continent" of Africa concerning stone cities deep in the dense jungles while at the beginning of the 20th century, the occultist and explorer Alexandra David-Neel returned from the Himalayas with tales of lost mystical kingdoms ruled by monks somewhere among the towering peaks. Whether or not such kingdoms existed (and some of them certainly did), they all added to the idea of mystery and romance that surrounded the concept of such an isolated place.

Because of the almost limitless scope of the imagination surrounding distant and "lost" locations, it has only been possible to give the briefest outline of such a topic in this book. Indeed, any one of these locations could warrant a book on its own. Some of them may simply have been concepts, a struggling to visualize somewhere beyond a largely static society; others may have been interpretations of places or events far away, but all have stirred and stimulated individuals. Even if such places do not actually exist outside the human mind, they are an important part of our culture and of who we are in relation to the wider world. They are, in fact, the summation and the crystallization of all our own (and our society's) hopes and fears in a "tangible" and concrete form. And while they may never appear on any map or chart, they are unquestionably there in our minds and hearts; maybe that is their true location.

Bibliography

Blashford-Snell, John, and Richard Snailham. *East to the Amazon*. London: John Murray Publishers, 2002.

Blavatsky, H.P. *Isis Unveiled*. Wheaton, Ill.: Quest Books, 1997.

———. *The Secret Doctrine*. Pasadena, Calif.: Theosophical University Press, 1984.

Cayce, Edgar. *Edgar Cayce on Atlantis (*Edgar Cayce Series*)*. New York, N.Y.: Grand Central Publishing, 2000.

Chaney, G. *Images of the East*. New York, N.Y.: Centaur Press, 1951.

Childress, David H. *Lost Continents: The Hollow Earth: I Remember Lemuria*. Kempton, Ill.: Adventures Unlimited Press, 1999.

———. *Technology of the Gods*. Kemton, Ill.: Adventures Unlimited Press, 2001.

Curran, Bob. *Encyclopaedia of Celtic Mythology*. Belfast, UK: Appletree Press, 1999.

Dowling, Kenneth. *The Waters Under the Earth*. London: Redemption Publishing, 1971.

Favata, Martin, and Josez Fernandez, eds. *The Account: Alvar Nunez de Vaca's Relacion*. Houston, Tex.: Arte Publico Press, 2001.

Fenwick, Col. James. *Vanished Peoples of the Antediluvian World*. London: Noble, 1889.

Fisher-Hansen, Tobias, ed. *Recent Danish Research in Classical Archaeology*. Copenhagen: Museum Tusculanum, 1991.

Fitting, Peter. *Subterranean Worlds: A Critical Anthology*. Middletown, Conn.: Wesleyan University Press, 2004.

Fortune, William. *A Dictionary of Classical Romance*. New York, N.Y.: Spottiswoode Books, 1901.

Gantz, Jeffrey, ed. *Early Irish Myth and Saga*. New York, N.Y.: Penguin, 1981.

Goodrick-Clarke, Nicholas. *Black Sun: Ayrian Cults, Esoteric Nazism and the Politics of Identity*. New York, N.Y.: New York University Press, 2003.

Goodwin, Jocelyn. *Arktos: Polar Myth in Science, Symbolism and Nazi Survival*. Kempton, Ill.: Adventures Unlimited Press, 1996.

Greenberg, Gary. *Myths of the Bible*. Naperville, Ill.: Sourcebooks, 2000.

Hannestad, Neils, and John Lund, eds. *Late Antiquity: Art in Context*. Copenhagen: Museum Tusculanum, 2001.

Herman, Marc. *Searching for El Dorado*. New York, N.Y.: Vintage Books, 2003.

Jones, Kevin. *Cornwall's Legends—Being a Collection of old Tales told in Cornwall*. Norwich, UK: Oakmagic Publications, 1997.

Joseph, Frank. *Atlantis Encyclopedia*. Franklin Lakes, N.J.: New Page Books, 2005.

Kraft-Minkel, Walter. *Subterranean Worlds*. Port Townsend, Wash.: Loompanics Unlimited, 1989.

Krasskova, Galina. *Exploring the Northern Tradition—A Guide to the Gods, Lore and Celebrations from Norse, German and Anglo Saxon Traditions*. Franklin Lakes, N.J.: New Page Books, 2005.

Levy, Joel. *The Atlas of Atlantis, Lemuria and Other Lost Civilisations*. London: Godsfield Press, 2007.

MacLellan, Alec. *The Hollow Earth Enigma*. London: Souvenir Press, 1999.

Mailer, Norman. *Unholy Alliance: A History of Nazi Involvement with the Occult*. London: Continuum, 2000.

Mansfield, K., and L. Farrina. *A Quest for El Dorado*. Jacksonville, Ore.: Stormbird Press, 1977.

Miller, Elaine Hobson. *Myth, Mysteries and Legends of Alabama*. Birmingham, Ala.: Seacoast Publishing, 1995.

Morris, Paul, and Deborah Sawyer, eds. *A Walk in the Garden: Iconographic and Literary Images of Eden*. London: Continuum, 1992.

Muhawi, Ibrahim. *Speak Bird, Speak Again: Palestinian-Arab Folktales*. Berkeley, Calif.: University of California Press, 1989.

Parrish, Mayfield. *The Arabian Nights*. New York, N.Y.: Simon and Shuster, 1993.

Pennick, Nigel. *The Eldrich World*. Leics, UK: Lear Publications, 2006.

———. *Lost Cities and Sunken Lands*. Coppell, Tex.: Coppell Ban Books, 1997.

Plato. *Timenus and Critas*. New York, N.Y.: Penguin Classics, 2000.

Reinstedt, Randal A. *Tales, Treasures and Pirates of Old Monterey*. London: Ghost Town Publications, 1976.

Scott, Thomas. *Travels in Tibet*. London: Dent and Son Press, 1927.

Serwer-Benstein, Blanche. *In the Tradition of Moses and Mohammed: Jewish and Arab Folktales*. Landham, Md.: Jason Aronson, 1994.

Shepard, Aaron, and B. Jowett. *The Atlantis Dialogue: Plato's Original Story of the Lost City, Continent, Empire, Civilisation*. London: Shepherd Publications, 2001.

Singer, John D. *Ireland's Mysterious Lands and Sunken Cities*. Philadelphia, Pa.: Xlibris Corporation, 2001.

Standish, David. *Hollow Earth: The Long and Curious History of Imagining Strange Lands, Fantastical Creatures, Advanced Civilisations and Marvellous Machines Below the Earth's Surface*. Cambridge, Mass.: Da Capo, 2007.

Sugrue, Thomas. *The Story of Edgar Cayce: There is a River*. Virginia Beach, Va.: ARE Press, 1997.

Thomas, Hugh. *Rivers of Gold: The Rise of the Spanish Empire*. Gwent, UK: Orion Press, 2004.

Todeschi, Kevin. *Edgar Cayce on the Akadic Records—the Book of Life*. Virginia Beach, Va.: ARE Press, 1998.

Wilson, Colin. *The Atlantis Blueprint*. New York, N.Y.: Time/Warner, 2000.

Index

About the Author

Dr. Bob Curran was born and raised in a remote area of County Down, Northern Ireland. He has held a variety of jobs including gravedigger, lorry driver, professional musician, journalist, teacher, and lecturer. His rural background has given him an interest in folklore and mythology, and he has written extensively on these subjects in both books and journals. His books include *Vampires, Encyclopedia of the Undead, An Encyclopedia of Celtic Mythology, Bloody Irish, Walking With the Green Man*, and many others. Dr. Curran is also a historian and lecturers extensively on culture and history. In this capacity, he sits on a number of cultural advisory bodies in Ireland, both North and South, and has produced several academic papers on various topics of cultural interest. He currently lives in the North of Ireland with his wife and young family.

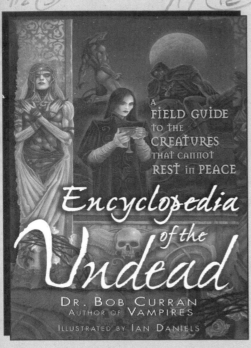
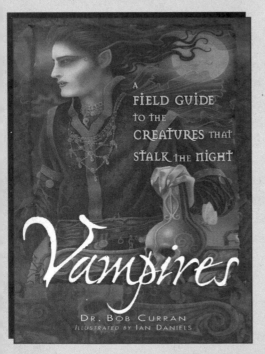